Banks, Borrowers,
and the Establishment

BANKS, BORROWERS, AND THE ESTABLISHMENT

A Revisionist Account
of the International
Debt Crisis

KARIN LISSAKERS

BasicBooks
A Division of HarperCollins*Publishers*

For Mamma and Pappa,
who gave me a New World

All quotations not otherwise attributed are from interviews
conducted by the author.

Library of Congress Cataloging-in-Publication Data
Lissakers, Karin.
 Banks, borrowers, and the establishment: a revisionist
account of the international debt crisis/ Karin Lissakers.
  p. cm.
 Includes bibliographical references and index.
 ISBN 0-465-00605-1 (cloth)
 ISBN 0-465-00606-X (paper)
 1. Debts, External. I. Title.
 HJ8046.L57 1991
336.3′435—dc20   91-70406
                                                            CIP

Designed by Ellen Levine

93 94 95 96 CG/RRD 9 8 7 6 5 4 3 2 1

Contents

Preface

When the first oil-price shock jolted the world economy in late 1973, I was on the staff of the Subcommittee on Multinational Corporations of the U.S. Senate Foreign Relations Committee. The subcommittee was charged to examine the impact of multinational corporations on U.S. foreign policy. For the next several years, much of the subcommittee's work concentrated on the two industries most dramatically affected by the shock—oil and banking. Members of Congress were concerned about the political implications of the U.S. economy's twin dependencies on the Middle East. The Foreign Relations Committee authorizes foreign aid appropriations and U.S. contributions to the IMF, the World Bank, and the other multilateral lending agencies. The Committee worried about the rapid growth of bank lending to developing countries. The subcommittee's chairman, the late Senator Frank Church of Idaho, and ranking Republicans, the late Senators Clifford Case of New Jersey and Jacob Javits of New York, were early critics of the Ford and Carter administrations' laissez-faire approach to petrodollar recycling. They warned again and again that the American taxpayer would ultimately have to pay the tab for the banks' lax lending. Their warnings went unheeded, and matters took their course.

My own participation was as principal staff investigator on the banking aspect of the oil shock. I wrote a 1977 staff report, "International Debt, the Banks, and U.S. Foreign Policy." When I started, there was little written about the Eurocurrency market where most of the sovereign lending went on, and nothing at all about petrodollar recycling. (I later married one of the few writers who at the time did give a coherent explanation of the banking phenomenon.) I learned, by necessity, the value of firsthand interviews with the people involved.

My fascination with large commercial banks and the interplay of their international activities and public policy has never left me. I followed the saga of sovereign lending through the boom and the bust, writing about it as a senior associate at the Carnegie Endowment for International Peace, testifying before Congress after leaving government, debating the problem with bankers, and most recently, teaching it to graduate students at Columbia University.

Much has been written about the international debt crisis and its causes and solutions over the past two decades—journalistic descriptions, academic treatises, economic analyses. Each contributed pieces of the puzzle, but some also perpetuated a certain mythology that I think misrepresents reality. No study, I feel, has presented the full complexity of interplay of the banks, the borrowers, and the international political establishment that guards the international financial system. I decided to try to put all the pieces together. In chapters 3 and 4 in particular, I let the participants in the lending boom speak for themselves. Chapter 5 adds a crucial piece to the puzzle—taxes—that other accounts missed.

I went back to some of the contacts I had made at the banks back in the 1970s and proceeded from there. I interviewed private bankers, central bankers, and other government officials in New York, Washington, D.C., Chicago, Miami, San Francisco, Pittsburgh, Detroit, London, Frankfurt, Madrid, Paris, Stockholm, Brasilia, Rio de Janeiro, São Paulo, Buenos Aires, and Mexico City.

I am very grateful to all who assisted me in my research, and to the many, identified or not, who took the time to talk to me, to take me through the intricacies of financial transactions and political maneuvers. (Interviewees are identified by the titles they carried when interviewed.) Many interviewees subjected themselves to multiple visits. Many bankers agreed to talk even knowing that I was quite likely to criticize what they were doing. I would particularly like to thank Fred Allen of JP Morgan and Kevin Corrigan of Chase Manhattan Bank for coming to my assistance repeatedly in arranging interviews. Riordan Roett did double duty, helping with contacts in banks and Latin American governments.

Jerome Levinson's extensive contacts and personal introductions to people all over Latin America were invaluable; his counsel—and criticism—on the manuscript equally so. Fernão Bracher and Ambassador Marcilio Marques Moreira, who later became his nation's Minister of the economy, gave expert guidance on Brazil's debt problem. Arturo O'Connell helped me repeatedly with Argentina. I owe thanks to Simon Bonnier for helping with Latin American business contacts. And over the years, Bob Bench has patiently answered my oft-times ignorant questions about banking regulations and accounting principles.

I want to thank my publisher, Martin Kessler, for believing that while the fashionableness of this subject has faded, its importance has not. My special thanks to Judith Miller and to Debbie Ishlon who bucked me up when I complained that writing a first book was like digging to China: one knew vaguely where one wanted to go, but didn't really believe one would ever get there.

Most of all I am grateful to my husband, Martin Mayer, for his advice, and counsel and patience. He put up with my fits of depression and ill temper when I got bogged down, or lost confidence, and never, never reminded me that he turned out six books in the time it took me to write one. Lastly, a big hug to Freddie and Henry for cheering Mommy on.

1

Banks and Sovereigns

We stop this recital with misgivings, for our prophetic soul tells us what will happen in the future. Adjustments will be made. Debts will be scaled down and nations will start anew. The investor will receive sufficiently satisfactory explanations as to how it is to his advantage to accept new promises in place of old ones which were repeatedly broken. All will at last be forgotten. New foreign loans will once again be offered, and bought as eagerly as ever. New methods will be employed by originators and distributors of loans. Prospectuses will be made more roseate and impressive than ever. They will give more unreliable information. And the process known for more than two thousand years will be continued. Defaults will not be eliminated. Investors will once again be found gazing sadly and drearily upon foreign promises to pay.

Max Winkler, *Foreign Bonds: An Autopsy* (1933)

CROSS-BORDER LENDING: RETREAT OR RECOVERY?

Third World debt is no longer fashionable. The debt crisis has moved off the front pages of the world financial press. More significantly, banks in the industrial countries have virtually stopped lending outside their home region. The conventional wisdom is that they never should have been involved in the first place—that the credit relationship between commercial banks and poorer countries that grew and flourished in the 1960s and 1970s was a mistake for both sides. "Over the long term, borrowing by less developed nations from commercial banks should be seen as an aberration," said investment banker Richard Debs as he presented a study by the prestigious Group of Thirty eminent economists and former central bankers. The report recommended that these countries henceforth look to multinational government-supported agencies like the World Bank for external financing.[1] This view is widely held in both government and banking circles.

This book argues, however, that the break in relations between banks and these borrowers will not be permanent. The economic needs of developing countries, including Eastern Europe, and the competitive drive of the large commercial banks will lead to a resumption of significant lending, probably before the end of this century. The forms will be different from those used in the 1970s—should be different—but business will revive. Eastern Europe is already knocking on the door, and the same blend of political and commercial interests that prevailed in the 1970s will cause governments in the West to encourage banks to respond favorably. Eventually, important Third World countries will be let in the door, too.

The current disillusionment with sovereign-risk lending is understandable. More than two-thirds of the $650 billion that Third World countries and Eastern Europe owed to commercial banks at the peak of indebtedness have been subject to rescheduling, payment interruption, or significant interest arrears since 1982. These countries owe hundreds of billions of dollars to official lenders, and many of these debts, too, are unserviced. What at the beginning was billed by both debtors and creditors as a "temporary liquidity problem" turned instead into a long and grinding insolvency that has devastated debtor-country economies, damaged world trade, and threatened the existence of some of the world's largest banks.

Developing countries had sought to finance rapid growth with foreign bank credit in part to escape political intrusions by official aid givers or economic domination by multinational corporations; in the end, they sacrificed both growth and economic autonomy for more than a decade. Banks that sought to escape overregulated and overbanked home markets by expanding rapidly abroad damaged—in some cases fatally—their future capacity to compete in a truly global market. And the success of "petrodollar recycling"—banks' acceptance of oil exporters' deposits and on-lending to needy countries—created an illusion that the financial disequilibria caused by two massive oil-price increases would have no lasting economic costs. The governments that ducked responsibility for managing those shocks in the 1970s now have to pick up a bigger tab in the 1990s.

The process of closing the books on this costly chapter has finally begun under the U.S. Treasury's Brady Plan (named for Treasury Secretary Nicholas F. Brady) for a negotiated reduction of developing countries' foreign bank debts. But the reductions achieved so far have been inadequate. Countries continue to struggle with debts they cannot fully service, and the unsettled obligations effectively block renewed access to foreign credit, discourage domestic investment, and consume the fiscal resources and intellectual capacities of debtor governments. The billions of questionable loans still on the banks' books require massive loan-loss provisions that depress stock values, drain bank capital, and weaken the institutions' ability to undertake new ventures.

FINANCE AND INTEGRATION

The protracted debt crisis has left many countries out of step with a rapidly changing world economy: the phenomenon of the "globalization" of economic activity has so far encom-

passed only a small, exclusive club of rich and highly indus-
trialized countries. Real globalization must mean the eventual
integration of less developed countries and Eastern Europe
into the mainstream economic and financial life of the strong
industrial nations. President Gorbachev has recognized this
as a necessity for the Soviet Union, and new leaders in Mexico
and Brazil and many other developing countries have reached
the same conclusion. The alternative is continued marginali-
zation of national economies and of whole populations, life
on the international dole, and the creation of a permanent
underclass of nations.

Domestic reforms, economic and political, are crucial to
the integration process. But massive investment will also be
needed to bring economic recovery, modernization, and
growth to the economies now being bypassed. Even with debt
relief, large countries like Brazil, Mexico, or Venezuela cannot finance their development solely from domestic savings
and cannot meet their external financing needs exclusively
with official development aid. Yearly interest payments on
Brazil's foreign debt alone (even if interest rates never go
above 10 percent) would soak up nearly half the World Bank's
entire annual worldwide loan budget. Estimates for the capital needs of Eastern Europe and the Soviet Union range in
the hundreds of billions of dollars over the next ten years.
Even wealthy Germany's federal budget is being severely
strained by the expense of absorbing the eastern provinces.
The new European Bank for Reconstruction and Development (EBRD) will have about $12 billion in capital (after five
years), and the World Bank expects to lend $8 billion to $9
billion over three years to supplement bilateral official flows
to Eastern Europe. Multiples of these sums will be required
to finance an historic economic and political transformation.

It is also questionable that official institutions are the most
appropriate channel for foreign financing if private enterprise is to be the engine of growth in economies that used

to be centrally planned and in countries with heavy public-sector participation in the economy. Although there is currently an effort to change the institutional philosophy, multilateral agencies like the World Bank have always preferred to funnel money to the public sector. They indeed must share some responsibility for the bloated state sectors in countries that depended most heavily on their development advice and money. For reasons explored in this book, the commercial banks followed the same pattern in their dealings with developing countries, but private-sector financing is the heart of their business elsewhere.

Equity investment is seen as an alternative form of capital transfer and in many ways preferable to debt. But in the real world, debt and equity tend to flow together (indeed, what appears as foreign direct investment is often in fact debt). A country that is deemed an unacceptable risk by banks is unlikely to attract large sums from foreign investors. Moreover, even in the best of times the total flow of direct investment to developing countries has averaged only $10 billion to $15 billion per year, compared to debt flows from private lenders of $50 billion to $80 billion per year in the late 1970s. The latter was clearly unsustainable, but a more normal rate of debt accumulation would be expected to exceed investment flows in most years.

There are bonds, of course—the most traditional instrument for long-term financing. Investment bankers are crowding into Eastern Europe, but what they bring to the party is unclear. Their hope is to garner fees for advice, not to lend. Investment or merchant banks rarely invest large sums themselves, and the investors they advise—pension funds, insurance companies, money-market funds, and the like—are unlikely to have large appetites for Polish or Hungarian securities until those countries are much farther along the road toward economic Westernization.

Ultimately, the integration of marginal economies will require active participation by the large multinational banks that have dominated international lending for much of this century—banks like Citibank and JP Morgan, Deutsche Bank and Dresdner, Barclays and Lloyds, Royal Bank of Canada, Swiss Bank, Crédit Lyonnais, and (more recently) Bank of Tokyo, Sumitomo, Industrial Bank of Japan, and the other Japanese behemoths. For all their colossal errors in international lending and the resulting balance-sheet woes, the banks are still the best-qualified, best-equipped institutions to serve as intermediaries for the funds these countries will need. The barriers to their renewed participation, however, are both psychological and real.

THE VIEW FROM THE BANKS

"Sure we're paying close attention to Eastern Europe—to make sure we don't lend them any money," said the international head of a large Canadian bank.

"Maybe three generations from now, banks will start lending to these countries again. But never in my lifetime!" said a very senior (but young) officer of one of the three biggest international lenders. Latin America and Africa are dismissed with a wave of the hand.

Banks have entered what Charles P. Kindleberger, in his classic analysis of financial crises, *Manias, Panics, and Crashes*, called panic or "revulsion." Not only are they not making new loans, but they are selling off their portfolios at distress prices. Cross-border lending continues to expand strongly, but almost exclusively within the Organization for Economic Cooperation and Development (OECD) group of countries. Cross-border bank claims within the industrial countries increased by $416 billion in 1988 and by another $590 billion in 1989.[2] Loans to countries outside the reporting area increased only $7.5 billion in 1988 and declined by $20 billion between June 1989 and June 1990.[3] The flight from exotic markets is particularly strong for U.S. banks, which have reduced their outstandings to *all* foreign regions outside Canada, Europe, and Japan.

Since 1982 rising young stars at the big banks—"Those MBAs with their Guccis and their $30 million lending limits," as a veteran Latin American officer for First Chicago once described them—no longer elbow each other for a spot in the international loan division. International lending departments have been turned into "asset enhancement divisions" tasked with somehow transforming bad foreign loans into saleable assets, and loan officers have become work-out specialists. Elaborate home-office "country-risk analysis" apparatuses have been unceremoniously dismantled. There is a shoot-the-messenger mentality: no one wants to hear the bad news about Third World loans any more. Bankers Trust went so far as to auction off its entire international economics department to the highest bidder. Economists who were not bid for by another department were let go. "A slave auction!" protested a nervous economist at a rival West Coast institution, adding glumly, "Don't think management didn't notice." Banks have closed marginal foreign branches and representative offices, and not just in Latin America. Wells Fargo, the eleventh-largest bank in the United States, shocked the City of London when it announced in 1985 that it was closing its branch there. "Banks don't close offices in London: they open them!" exclaimed a British journalist who covers the financial district.

The financial troubles of sovereign borrowers are only one reason for the retreat. Chuck Coltman, head of Philadelphia National Bank's international division, expounded what he called the "accordion theory" of banking: "international asset generation always moves in the opposite direction of domestic asset generation." In the early 1970s banks were flush with deposits from the Organization of Petroleum Exporting Countries (OPEC), but the industrial countries' response to the oil-price increase produced an economic downturn that depressed loan demand in banks' home markets. The big multinational banks looked to developing countries and to the Eastern bloc, made respectable by détente, to take up the slack of faltering loan demand from large corporate clients at home. Medium and small regional banks in Michigan, Ohio, and Pennsylvania, with little previous international experience, followed their lead as the industrial heartland of America suffered a deep post–oil-shock recession.

In the 1980s the tide of world finance flowed in a different direction and through different channels than it had in the 1970s. Banks were no longer awash in the liquidity that fueled the lending binge of the 1970s. Japan replaced Saudi Arabia as the world's largest capital exporter, and Japanese investors had investment preferences different from those of the oil sheiks. The United States became the largest capital importer, and the industrial countries as a group were net takers of funds rather than net suppliers to the rest of the world.

Finally, the structure of world financial markets underwent rapid and dramatic change. "Global bang" is what the *Financial Times* called the avalanche sweeping away geographic, institutional, and regulatory boundaries within the financial services industry. The technology of financial services has undergone an electronic revolution, and governments for reasons of necessity have scrapped, rewritten, or ignored the rules that have controlled and compartmentalized the industry since the Depression of the 1930s. In most countries, banks, savings associations, insurance companies, and investment houses can now do what used to be each other's business. The lines of demarcation that distinguished the international Eurocurrency markets from national, domestic financial markets have also become blurred or are disappearing altogether. This revolution means that the regulatory differential favoring international over domestic lending is disappearing: banks are increasingly being allowed to do at

home and in the domestic markets of other industrial countries the kind of business that they previously were permitted
to do only in the special context of cross-border lending, if
at all. New capital requirements on banks and tax changes in
the United States have further reduced the appeal of old-
fashioned cross-border lending.

But economic trends are not forever. OPEC's surpluses did
not rise to the moon, and neither will Japan's. The United States
will someday develop the political will to confront its fiscal and
economic weaknesses and stop gobbling up foreign savings. Cy-
clical downturns in the industrial economies will cause banks
to look once again beyond their home turf for business. Even
the wave of financial deregulation will eventually push them in
that direction. With financial firms increasingly free to reach
into each other's territory and line of business, the competition
for prime customers and market share grows more fierce and
profit margins narrow in an already overbanked OECD market.
Many investment houses and banks that plunged eagerly into
Tokyo and expanded in London following deregulation a few
years ago have begun to retrench in the face of soaring costs
and meager earnings or outright losses.

Under these circumstances, São Paulo, Mexico City, and
Monterrey, Seoul and Manila, Moscow and Budapest—whatever
their current problems—will begin to exert renewed pull on
banks for the most basic of reasons: exotic markets may be
among the few places where large multinational banks still
enjoy a significant competitive advantage over regional banks,
investment houses, and other financial intermediaries.

WHY THE SYSTEM FAILED

Are banks and foreign borrowers then condemned to repeat
"the process known for more than two thousand years" so
that lenders will "once again be found gazing sadly and drea-

rily upon foreign promises to pay"? The answer depends largely on what the players have learned from their recent disastrous experience. Explanations for what went wrong abound, but they are full of contradictions.

Greed and stupidity have been identified as principal causes of the upheavals that periodically strike the world of finance, including the sovereign-debt calamity. As this book points out, lending to developing countries in the 1970s was far more profitable than has been generally recognized, and many of today's leading bankers were swept to the top of their profession on the stream of earnings generated by these loans. Certainly there was stupidity, or at least naiveté. In a hilarious account of the era in *Selling Money*, a young former banker from Ohio describes his experience as an international lending officer for the Cleveland Trust Company: "Before my twenty-sixth birthday, after less than two years in the bank, I had been to twenty-five countries and was one of four bankers managing a $150-million international loan portfolio. . . . In Hong Kong, I was met at the airport by a chocolate-brown Rolls-Royce, in the Philippines by a red Jaguar, in Saudi Arabia by a stretch Mercedes."[4] On the debtor side, few borrowers, whatever the level of indebtedness, had the self-restraint to turn down a proferred loan. In many cases, the flood of borrowed money fed corruption, visible in the obscene accumulation of wealth by the deposed Marcoses of the Philippines and by still-presiding Zairian president Mobutu and in the lavish Swiss retirement of former Mexican president López Portillo (nicknamed *López Porpillo* by his constituents, *pillo* being Mexican slang for "robber").

But for every Zaire there was a Brazil with its dynamic entrepreneurial class, a plan for financing its expansion, and highly trained technocrats to carry it out; for every Cleveland Trust with a single lending officer prowling the airports, there was a Morgan, a Citibank, a Deutsche Bank, or a Lloyds with committees of distinguished experts. The scores of smaller banks became involved in sovereign-risk lending as bit players—buying a piece of the action being offered by the big multinational banks—on the not unreasonable assumption that the banks putting together the Eurodollar loan syndications knew what they were doing and had their governments support.

The lead banks, after all, had decades of experience in international lending. The first foreign bond issued in the United States was done by Morgan in 1899 for the government of Mexico.[5] National City Bank of New York (later Citibank) opened its first South American branch in 1914. Dresdner Bank has been in Latin America for over 100 years. Bank of Nova Scotia was a large presence in the Caribbean in the middle of the last century. The British and French multinational banks had grown up servicing their empires. A few Japanese banks like Sumitomo had foreign branches before World War II. Japanese banks joined the Euromarket lending frenzy late, as followers rather than leaders, but they loomed large once they came in.

The big banks had institutional if not personal experience of earlier international debt crises. National City Bank had seen its Russian branches expropriated and its loans repudiated by the Bolsheviks in 1919. A senior officer of Morgan negotiated a settlement of Mexico's prerevolutionary debts that gave foreign bondholders a few cents on the dollar. Chase was the agent for the settlement payments. Large U.S., British, and continental banks lost money, and their clients lost money, on the widespread Latin American defaults of the 1930s.

In the 1970s the big banks assembled country-risk teams,[6] equipped with sophisticated computer programs to weigh the risks and rewards of cross-border lending. The banks put thousands of people in the field in the borrowing countries, who knew the local economies into which they were lending and knew the political scene. By the early 1980s Citibank had 6,000 people in Latin America doing mostly local banking, plus

2,000 in London working on cross-border lending. Deutsche Bank employed 750 people just in Argentina. The head of Bank of America's operation in Mexico was a Mexican national said to wield considerable influence in the country's ruling circles.

Finally, the banks were operating under the supervisory umbrella of the sober-minded and powerful officials of the U.S. Federal Reserve System, the Bank of England, the Bundesbank, the Japanese Ministry of Finance, the International Monetary Fund (IMF), and an extensive regulatory apparatus designed to prevent financial markets from repeating the excesses of the 1920s. Matters went badly off track despite all this.

"Responsible authorities" like the U.S. Treasury and the International Monetary Fund point to wrongheaded policies and economic mismanagement in the borrowing countries as the principal cause of the 1980s debt crisis. Excessive government spending, overvalued exchange rates, subsidies, price controls, protectionism, "pharaonic" projects, corruption, and political instability are among the sins recited. But policy errors in the borrowing countries should not have caught either lenders or their regulators by surprise. On the contrary, many of these countries borrowed abroad primarily to sustain weak domestic policies.

Rather than responding like a "rational" market and either curtailing credit or raising the price to such borrowers, the banking markets behaved perversely, rewarding weak borrowers with increased credit at lower prices. Market participants measured "efficiency" by the volume and speed of credit dissemination. Discretion was not a priority. Two central features of sovereign-risk lending in the 1970s that enhanced this kind of "efficiency"—multibank syndications and floating interest rates—encouraged creditors to underestimate greatly the risks, and borrowers to misjudge the real cost of foreign bank loans. The willingness of the market to lend, not the borrower's ability to pay, became the accepted measure of creditworthiness.

Bankers contend that there would be no crisis if flight capital—the money the citizens of the borrowing countries sent abroad for investment and safekeeping—were available for debt payments. But these same bankers are active promoters of flight capital through their private banking departments and special affiliates in Miami, Panama, Montevideo, and similar money havens whose main function has been to help the money leave Latin America and other regions where they lent.

Some lenders have charged that their own governments pushed them into "petrodollar recycling"—which wasn't even profitable. As late as 1989 the U.S. banks presented data to the Comptroller of the Currency indicating that hair-thin interest margins—the difference between what banks pay for deposits and what they charge for loans—made sovereign lending unprofitable. The clear implication is that now the loans have turned sour, the banks deserve a government bailout. But anyone who heard or read the contemptuous utterances about government by the greatest recycler of them all, Walter Wriston, has reason to doubt that Citibank let Washington tell it how much to lend Brazil during his reign as chairman—especially if there was no money to be made.

The truth is more complex. Governments did encourage banks to lend, sometimes through exhortation but more often inadvertently, through the tax code. The method of taxation in the borrowing countries combined with the treatment of those taxes under U.S. tax law—and significantly, similar tax provisions in the United Kingdom, Japan, and Canada and other countries where the lending banks are based—produced a hidden layer of profit for the banks from their Third World loans. The hidden tax subsidy had the effect of artificially holding down the cost of borrowing for developing countries while inflating bank profits. The result was a further distortion of the market's perception of risk and reward.

Bankers and debtors offer the ultimate defense that economic forces entirely outside their control created the debt problem. High oil prices followed by soaring interest rates and protectionism in the industrial countries are to blame for the collapse of an otherwise sound credit market. But four of the biggest borrowers—Mexico, Venezuela, Nigeria, and Peru—are oil exporters and a fifth, Argentina, is oil self-sufficient. Oil prices were certainly a crucial factor in the debt disaster, but there was little correlation between a country's level of borrowing and its oil-import dependency.

Henry C. Wallich, who was the Federal Reserve Board of Governors' leading expert on international financial matters, wrote in 1984, "It is true, of course, that the oil-price increases and the rise in real interest rates could hardly have been foreseen as such. But it is not plausible that international risk can validly be evaluated on the assumption of permanent fair weather, continuing prosperity, political stability, and perpetual negative real interest rates. Over the life of a medium-term loan, lenders must recognize the possibility of major shocks. That is the difference between short-term lending and medium-term lending. Evidently, the market was not well prepared to make that kind of risk assessment. Indeed, one is almost bound to conclude that the organization of international lending contained strong biases against proper risk assessment."[7]

As we shall see, the banks' risk-management structure was a Potemkin Village designed more to impress the outsider than to perform a real function, and the regulators' judgment of what they were seeing was colored by their government's own policy agenda. On the other side, borrowers were given no reason to believe the market wouldn't go on financing them forever and therefore saw little reason for self-restraint.

What in retrospect is most remarkable about the international lending binge of the 1970s and early 1980s is that so many capable, knowledgeable, and experienced private bankers, central bankers, finance ministers, and bank regulators considered it a proper and prudent way to run the world.

WHY LOOK BACK?

When Professor Winkler was writing his autopsy of sovereign lending in 1933, countries were in default on more than $20 billion (approximately $120 billion in 1980 dollars) owed to foreigners, mostly private lenders, and interest arrears exceeded $12 billion. Eighty-two percent of Latin America's dollar bonds were in default, as were 40 percent of U.S. loans to Europe.[8] Banks like JP Morgan and Citibank (then National City Bank of New York) had acted as underwriters of these foreign bonds but also had extended substantial loans of their own. Many of the bank loans also went unpaid. This earlier debt debacle was followed by a hiatus in private foreign lending of more than twenty years during which few countries had access to commercial financing outside their own borders.

Perhaps the biggest mistake banks made in the 1960s was to resume lending to countries that had reneged on their debts in the 1930s without studying their prior experience. In the wholesale retreat from the international scene in the 1930s and 1940s, banks wiped out their institutional memory. When they turned back to these markets a generation later, they started with a clean slate as if they had never been there before. The same was true of the borrowers. In Latin America, a whole continent turned inward in the 1930s, while the Cold War shut off Eastern Europe from all but perfunctory financial links to the West. By the time these countries decided to return to the foreign markets, they too had forgotten the lessons of the 1920s.

Banks and debtors are now in renewed retreat, and no one is inclined to look back. Banks have abandoned the borrowers but not the practices they adopted in lending to Third World countries. As a London banker cautioned in the mid-1980s, "If you liked the Latin American debt crisis, you'll love securitization!" Recent fashions in banking—bridge financing of leveraged buy-outs, interest-rate and foreign-currency swaps, packaging mortgages into saleable obligations—bear many of the worst traits of sovereign lending: the quest for large volume, wholesale, big bang transactions; the belief that the increasingly complex and exotic products engineered in Wall Street's financial laboratories can guarantee quick profits without risk to the intermediary; the skimming of up-front fees and selling off of riskier assets to smaller, less sophisticated institutions; the hope that joining a new game aggressively will save the big banks from extinction.

The protracted credit squeeze has compelled some debtor countries to set a new economic course. If the reforms that have begun in parts of Latin America and Eastern Europe take hold, they will offer some protection against a repetition of the 1970s. But at the same time, the extreme economic reversals these countries suffered in the 1980s and recent economic and political upheavals in Eastern Europe have magnified social tensions. If the international credit situation should ease, governments will be tempted to try to paper over these tensions with money, just as they did in the 1970s. A new generation of leaders has come to power, and when financial markets once again begin to beckon, they may not see the risks.

In Washington there is no institutional memory except perhaps in Congress. The Treasury Department, the State Department, and to some extent even the Federal Reserve, turned over completely during the 1980s as the Reagan administration carried its ideological purge deep into their ranks. Not even civil servants were safe if they had exercised any policy responsibility at all in previous Democratic administrations. In institutions like the IMF and the World Bank, the long siege of the debt crisis has taken its toll as some resident experts have simply burned out.

This book, then, is an effort to provide a permanent history of the last international debt crisis of the twentieth century. It draws extensively on the work of others. For the most part, however, the account is based on interviews with scores of bankers, government officials in the developing countries, and regulators and other responsible individuals in the major creditor countries, some going back to the earliest days of the debt crisis when memories of events that led up to it were still fresh in the minds of the participants. It is their story.

2

The Shock

According to [Hyman] Minsky, events leading up to a crisis start with a "displacement," some exogenous shock to the macroeconomic system. The nature of this displacement varies from one speculative boom to another. . . . But whatever the source of the displacement, if it is sufficiently large and pervasive, it will alter the economic outlook by changing profit opportunities in at least one important sector of the economy.
—Charles P. Kindleberger, *Manias, Panics, and Crashes* (1978)

PETRODOLLARS AND CONFIDENTIALITY

On the morning of 11 September 1975 an extraordinary gathering took place in the ornate chambers of the United States Senate Foreign Relations Committee in the Capitol's north wing. On one side of the committee's massive oval table sat Senator Frank Church, Democrat of Idaho and chair of the Subcommittee on Multinational Corporations, flanked by the subcommittee's ranking and junior Republicans, Clifford Case of New Jersey and Charles Percy of Illinois, and a handful of staff. Arrayed on the other side were senior representatives from five of the nation's largest commercial banks: Lewis

Preston, then vice president of Morgan Guaranty Trust; Al Costanzo, vice chairman, and Hans Angermueller, counsel, for First National City Bank of New York; William S. Ogden, chief financial officer (CFO) for Chase Manhattan Bank; Leland Prussia, CFO for Bank of America; and Gaylord Freeman, chairman of the board of First National Bank of Chicago. Also present were two governors of the Federal Reserve Board, Henry Wallich and Philip E. Coldwell; the president of the Federal Reserve Bank of New York, Paul Volcker; Treasury Under Secretary for Monetary Affairs, Edwin Yeo; and Assistant Secretary of State for Economic Affairs, Thomas Enders. The subcommittee was in "executive session," closed to press and the public.[1]

The banks had asked for the closed-door meeting to discuss the subcommittee's request that thirty-nine of the nation's leading banks tell the subcommittee how much money they had loaned to and taken on deposit from a select list of foreign countries, country by country. The banks represented at the meeting had refused the subcommittee's request.

The subcommittee was charged with examining the effects of multinational corporations on U.S. foreign policy and began an inquiry into the international operations of U.S. banks soon after the first oil-price shock of 1973 to 1974. U.S. banks clearly were playing an important role in recycling the surplus petrodollars being earned by a handful of oil-rich and population-poor Persian Gulf states—accepting deposits from the oil exporters with surplus capital and on-lending the funds to countries that were capital-short. The senators wanted to know the extent of this involvement and were astonished to find that neither the U.S. Treasury nor the Federal Reserve had the answer: no one in the U.S. government kept numbers on the total foreign exposure of U.S. banks. Although each bank periodically had to open its books to an examiner from one of the regulatory agencies, the only systematic data gathered by the government on banks' foreign operations concerned the foreign loans and deposits made by the banks' U.S. home offices. Since most of the petrodollar recycling was being done in the Eurodollar market through the banks' foreign branches and subsidiaries—which were not covered by the data—a large part of the picture was missing.

The subcommittee decided to ask the banks directly. Twenty-two of the smaller banks in the survey complied with the subcommittee's questionnaire, some grumbling about having to fill out yet another government form. But with the big banks—the banks with the biggest presence abroad—the subcommittee ran into a stone wall. Morgan Guaranty's chairman, Ellmore Patterson, explained in a letter to Senator Church that the information requested "would involve a breach of our obligation to keep confidential the affairs of particular clients, and all of it could adversely affect our ability to compete with other banks here and abroad." He respectfully declined to provide the data.[2] Chase Manhattan Bank also argued confidentiality and competitive interests in refusing to supply the information, adding that regarding information on some of the Chase's overseas offices in so-called bank secrecy havens, "under the laws of certain of the countries in which such subsidiaries and affiliates are organized and conduct their business, submission of such information would either be unlawful or would subject the affiliates and subsidiaries to liability for damages."[3] Nevertheless, the officer assured the subcommittee that "by definition, our Bank or its holding company is in control of such subsidiaries and affiliates."

Hans Angermueller, general counsel of First National City Bank, offered yet another reason for noncompliance: the data requested from the banks would be misleading. His letter pointed out that First National City and other major international money-center banks issue large-denomination certificates of deposit (CDs) that are freely transferable and payable to the bearer and that "substantial amounts of what might be

termed petro-currencies flow back from oil exporting countries through purchase, either directly or through other
financial intermediaries, of such large denomination multi-
currency certificates of deposit. Accordingly, the information
called for ... may not be an accurate criterion for ascertain-
ing deposit concentrations in your Subcommittee's analysis
of the role of U.S. banks in the petrodollar recycling process
or the impact of petrodollar flows on the international financial system." In other words, much of the oil money on deposit in the banks would not be identifiable as such.

Marine Midland did not bother with an explanation and
sent a one-sentence reply: "With reference to your letter of
April 7, 1975, we do not feel it appropriate for us to comply
with your request for this confidential information." As the
associate counsel of the subcommittee later told the members,
"We got these 'thank you but no thank you's' from a few and
an extremely impolite 'you can go straight to....' "[4]

When the chairman indicated that the subcommittee was
prepared to subpoena the information, the banks—with the
active support of the Gerald R. Ford administration—
mounted an intense lobbying effort to halt the inquiry. David
Rockefeller, chairman of Chase Manhattan Bank and brother
of the then vice president, flew to Washington on his private
jet for a hastily arranged breakfast with Senator Case and
later lunched with Senator Church at the State Department;
Arthur Burns, chairman of the Board of Governors of the
Federal Reserve, telephoned the subcommittee chairman to
try to talk him out of pursuing the information; the Treasury
Department arranged for Senator Percy to meet with the finance minister of Kuwait. According to Percy, the minister
told him Kuwait was "looking for some place to put $6 billion
this year, $7 billion last year," and warned that disclosure of
his country's deposits with U.S. banks would cause Kuwait to
withdraw its money from U.S. banks.[5] The subcommittee, it
seemed, had hit a raw nerve.

Although the questionnaire covered both bank assets (loans) and liabilities (deposits), it quickly became clear that the banks did not object to the request for information on foreign loans. Governor Coldwell told the subcommittee, "We understand from the banks that they were not that greatly concerned about the asset side of this package and that whatever the [Federal Reserve] and subcommittee agree to were perfectly acceptable."[6] The issue was deposits—specifically deposits from the Organization of Petroleum Exporting Countries (OPEC); more specifically still, Middle Eastern OPEC deposits. That was the deposit data the subcommittee wanted most and the banks were least willing to disclose.

The United States had recently been the target of OPEC's "oil weapon," and although the Arab oil embargo did not diminish U.S. support for Israel, memories of the previous year's long gasoline lines were still fresh. Some senators worried that the oil producers were now adding a "money weapon" to their arsenal and that the flood of petrodollars into U.S. banks created another pressure point. The Arabs might use their large financial holdings to disrupt the banking system and influence U.S. foreign policy.

The banks, however, did not regard the flood of petrodollars as a threat but as a golden opportunity. Approximately 50 percent of OPEC's 1974 financial surplus was deposited with banks in the industrial countries. These deposits, net of OPEC's own borrowing, were enough to finance all the net lending by banks in the major industrial countries to borrowers outside their own area.[7] In the four years following, approximately 30 percent of the surpluses went directly into the banks, and in 1979, after the second oil-price shock, 56 percent of OPEC's surplus earnings were deposited with banks.[8] As of year end 1980, when OPEC's income peaked, the oil states had $160 billion in deposits with Western commercial banks—as well as $70 billion in loans from them. OPEC's $90 billion net creditor position vis-à-vis the banks corresponds roughly to the $102 billion net debtor position of non-OPEC developing countries vis-à-vis these banks by 1981.[9]

Bankers generally deny that the infusion of petrodollars into the banking market in the early 1970s had any effect on their lending policies. James Green, retired former head of the international division of Manufacturers Hanover Bank in New York and later president of American Express International Bank, said of that time, "The business was completely asset-driven. I don't ever remember hearing a banker say, 'My God, they're making us lend when we don't want to.' Petrodollars meant banks had no funding problems, but didn't pressure us to lend right away. If we had more liquidity than we needed, we just bid for funds at the low end of the market" (that is, offered the depositor such a low rate of interest that it would take its money to another bank).

Gross lending by banks in the Eurocurrency market to nonresidents jumped 63 percent in the first six months of 1974 when the initial surge of oil money hit the banks and continued to grow through the end of the decade. But Green makes an important point. During the 1960s, the growth of American banks in particular had been constrained by periodic funding squeezes, when a combination of domestic monetary policy and domestic interest-rate controls limited their ability to attract deposits. The massive infusion after 1973 of OPEC dollars into the so-called Eurocurrency market (where no monetary and few bank prudential controls applied) relieved banks of their funding worries. Henceforth, banking would be "asset-driven": the rate of growth in the industry would depend on the speed with which lending opportunities could be identified.

Bankers spared no effort to be solicitous of OPEC depositors, including satisfying their desire for anonymity. The bankers claimed that if the information sought by the subcommittee were to become public, relations with Arab depositors would be hurt and the competitive position of U.S.

banking would be seriously damaged. First National City Bank counsel Angermueller told the subcommittee,

> The U.S. banking industry in the competitive environment throughout the world seems to be losing some degree of ground.
> Twenty years ago probably three-quarters of the largest banks in the world were U.S. banks. Today I believe only four of the largest 20 banks are U.S. banks. In other words, the competition is getting stronger and more aggressive. . . .
> The fact that our disclosure may become known to our customers, this knowledge would, we feel, place us at a serious disadvantage with our foreign competitors, particularly in the sensitive area of confidentiality.
> Simply put, we run the risk that our loan assets and our foreign deposits may flow from us to our foreign competitors.[10]

First Chicago chairman Gaylord Freeman echoed the argument:

> I was hoping to move on and make my point that the information would be of interest, it might be useful, but is it necessary, and then the question becomes what is the price that you pay for getting that information?
> . . . For instance, I think each of the OPEC countries has an approved list of banks that he will deposit with and won't deposit with others.[11]

Senator Percy, supporting the banks, gave voice to their suspicion that the subcommittee inquiry was pandering to American Jews: "If Saudi Arabia and Kuwait withdrew their bank deposits, the biggest single loser would be the city of New York [then in a fiscal crisis], and I would say the American Jewish community probably, centered in New York, would be the larger loser of that. . . . I think we are dealing with dynamite right now and I think this is the cause of concern for Arthur Burns, for David Rockefeller, for a lot of them."[12]

In truth, the banks were probably more concerned about protecting their own confidentiality than OPEC's. A bank-by-bank, country-by-country breakdown of OPEC deposits would have revealed an embarrassing concentration of short-term deposits from a few OPEC depositors in a very few banks, and that might have raised questions about the stability of the funding base of certain banks. Leland S. Prussia, then cashier of the Bank of America and later its vice chairman, told the Senate Multinational Corporations (MNC) Subcommittee that "there are 14,000 banks in the United States but there is only a handful of them really dealing in this kind of market. Probably if you took the 20 largest banks in the country you would get 90 percent perhaps of the total deposits."[13] Ogden of Chase suggested the concentration of deposits was even greater: "In Saudi Arabia, you are talking about one or two or three depositors. You are talking about 10 banks or probably 20 and probably the first 5 represent way more than half of it."[14] In 1980, shortly after the second major oil-price increase, fully one-third of the deposit base of First Chicago's London branch (which did most of the bank's medium-term international lending) came from a single Persian Gulf account. The MNC Subcommittee staff concluded on the basis of its interviews with bankers that Citibank, Chase, and Morgan together probably had about 75 percent of all OPEC funds on deposit with U.S. banks in 1975.[15]

The U.S. Treasury Department was at least as anxious as the banks to curry favor with the oil states and just as protective of information on OPEC's investments. Treasury Secretary William Simon entered into an agreement with Saudi Arabia and Kuwait in 1975 not to disclose the size of their U.S. holdings in any published U.S. government report. Treasury even refused to share its own data on these investments with the Department of Commerce, which complained bitterly but to no avail, and chastised the Central Intelligence Agency (CIA) for making too much information on OPEC investments available to Congress. Early in the Iran hostage crisis in 1979 Treasury went so far as to withhold data on Iranian bank deposits from the Iran Consultation Group—high-level senior officials from the Departments of State, Defense, and Energy, the CIA, and the National Security Council staff who wanted to know how vulnerable U.S. banks might be to an Iranian withdrawal of funds or loan default.[16]

Treasury, like the banks, was fearful of scaring away the oil money. Under Secretary Ed Yeo warned the MNC Subcommittee that its fact finding might sabotage efforts to convince OPEC to finance part of the U.S. government's budget deficit:

> I would like to put it in the context of the Treasury's announcement yesterday of its financial plans to raise between $43 billion and $47 billion in the second half of the calendar year and the first half of calendar 1976.
>
> I think that we know that there are some potential depositors that are sensitive to disclosure of their deposits, I think that I can report to you that there is a competition of sorts, a national competition, for funds.
>
> In my conversations with the Finance Ministers from other countries, they like us are concerned with how are they going to finance their deficits and they are starting to emulate some of the things that we have done in this country in an effort to attract some of the funds that are at issue and before this subcommittee.[17]

A compromise was eventually worked out with the MNC Subcommittee whereby the banks agreed to report both loan and deposit data to the Board of Governors of the Federal Reserve, which would aggregate the data so as not to identify individual Middle Eastern depositors or individual banks before turning the information over to the subcommittee. The deposit data revealed that so much OPEC money was concentrated in the top three or four banks that the Fed refused to supply three-bank aggregations as agreed and instead presented six-bank aggregations.[18]

The results of the Fed survey showed that as of December 1975 the identifiable combined liabilities of twenty-one large banks was $14.5 billion to the Middle Eastern and North African oil producers and $3.7 billion to other members of OPEC. Seventy-eight percent of the Middle Eastern–North African deposits were in the six largest banks, half of these in maturities of thirty days or less. On the other side of the balance sheet, the combined claims on Argentina, Brazil, and Mexico were $12.35 billion. In an era of trillion-dollar debt, these numbers seem almost trivial. But they mark a profound shift in the post–World War II pattern of international financial relations.

THE OIL-PRICE SHOCK

In his classic history of financial crises, *Manias, Panics and Crashes*, Massachusetts Institute of Technology economist Charles P. Kindleberger suggests that speculative financial cycles have a common beginning. Extrapolating from the works of monetary theorist Hyman Minsky, Professor Kindleberger writes that the first stage of financial disasters—the phase he calls "speculative excess" or "mania"—usually starts with a "displacement," defined as "some outside event that changes horizons, expectations, profit opportunities, behavior":

> The nature of this displacement varies from one speculative boom to another. It may be the outbreak or end of a war, a bumper harvest or crop failure, the wide-spread adoption of an invention with pervasive effects—canals, railroads, the automobile—some political event or surprising financial success,

or a debt conversion that precipitously lowers interest rates. But whatever the source of the displacement, if it is sufficiently large and pervasive, it will alter the economic outlook by changing profit opportunities in at least one important sector of the economy.[19]

In late 1973 and early 1974 the world experienced the kind of economic displacement described in the Minsky-Kindleberger model. Between October 1973 and January 1974 the official world price of crude oil (Saudi light marker crude) was pushed up from $3.01 per barrel to $11.65 per barrel. This quadrupling of the price of the world's most important commodity over a period of only a few months was an event that changed "horizons, expectations, profit opportunities, behavior" in at least two important sectors of the economy— energy and banking.

Significantly for both the banks and the world economy, the oil-price shock led to an apparently permanent doubling in the demand for international financial intermediation. The Bank of England has estimated that the total of current ac-count surpluses and deficits worldwide (excluding the Com-munist countries) increased from approximately 1 to 1.5 percent of world output per year during the period 1950 to 1973 to 2 to 3 percent of world output after 1973. That is to say, after all countries have netted out the value of goods and services exchanged (shown on the "current account" of the balance of payments), the remaining gap between countries in surplus and countries in deficit that has to be financed has been twice as large since 1973 as it was in the twenty-three years preceding the oil-price hike.[20] Internationally active commercial banks were particularly well placed to step into this gap.

The finance ministers and central bankers of the major in-dustrial countries met in Rome in the spring of 1974 to dis-cuss the implications of the oil shock. According to a former assistant to the venerable Otmar Emminger, chief of the German Bundesbank, officials at that meeting decided that the balance-of-payments disruption caused by the oil-price rise was temporary and no long-term economic adjustment would be required. When the World Bank and the International Monetary Fund held their annual meeting that fall, the financial surpluses of oil exporters were mounting, but an explicit decision was made not to try to channel those funds into the official multilateral lending institutions for on-lending. Denis Healey, new Chancellor of the Exchequer of the United Kingdom, later recalled, "I tried very hard, my early months as Chancellor, to persuade my colleagues to organize some sort of international official scheme for recycling the OPEC surpluses. But the Americans, particularly, were very hostile to this idea. Basically, they didn't believe in government mucking around in what they thought should be the role of the private sector. They would leave it all to the bankers who were licking their lips at the thought of what they would get out of it."[21]

The view that the oil-price hike would be short-lived stemmed in part from the fact that the rise appeared at first to be the result of political rather than economic factors. In October 1973 the Arab oil-producing states responded to the Yom Kippur War, an outbreak of fighting between Israel and its Arab neighbors, by cutting back production and embargoing the shipment of oil to the United States and the Netherlands, which were seen by the Arabs to be backing Israel. This wielding of the oil weapon caused near panic in the oil-importing countries, particularly the United States, where the perceived energy shortfall created chaos in an automobile-dependent society and caused mile-long queues of angry motorists at gasoline stations across the nation.

Although the Yom Kippur War, Middle Eastern production cuts, and OPEC's price hikes were inextricably linked in the public perception, the stage had been set for OPEC's price push well before the outbreak of the Yom Kippur War. During the more than twenty years that the oil industry was dominated by the so-called Seven Sisters cartel[22] (five U.S. and two U.K. and U.K.-Dutch oil companies that among them controlled 70 percent of the noncommunist world's oil production), the per-barrel price of oil had fluctuated between $1 and $2. Meanwhile, the world grew steadily more dependent on oil. The one critical weak spot in the seven-company cartel's grip on Middle Eastern oil production, however, was Libya.

Libya's King Idris had avoided the Seven Sisters by granting sizeable production concessions to "independent" oil companies like Occidental Petroleum and Bunker Hunt Oil. These independents, which had few other sources of crude under their direct control, rewarded the king by rapidly stepping up Libyan production—from 182,000 barrels per day in 1962 to 3.3 million barrels per day in 1970. In the process, the independents undermined the cartel's carefully crafted production control arrangements that were designed to keep cheap and plentiful Middle Eastern oil from flooding the world market. When Idris was overthrown by Colonel Muammar el-Quaddafi in a 1969 coup, the independents violated the cartel's coordinated pricing strategy by conceding to the revolutionary leader's demands for an immediate $0.40 per barrel increase in the price of Libyan crude.

Quaddafi, who wanted to produce less oil and charge more per barrel, subsequently turned on the independents, nationalizing some concessions and putting production ceilings on others. But the die was cast: the governments of the other oil-producing states now followed the colonel's example and began to demand immediate price increases for their oil as well as a bigger share of the total take.[23] By the early 1970s power over the world price and supply of oil had quietly shifted from the seven-company cartel to the rulers of the oil-producing states and *their* cartel, the Organization of Petroleum Exporting Countries (OPEC). The oil-price stability of the preceding two decades was at an end.

The rise in oil prices was not just the result of Arab political awakening, of course, but reflected an underlying shift in the oil supply-demand balance in the producers' favor because of a steady rise in world demand and the decline of continental U.S. oil production. And OPEC's pricing moves were supported, as Martin Mayer wrote in *The Money Bazaars*, by

> the decision by all the industrial world's finance ministers and central bankers to bull their way out of the recession of 1969–71 by slamming the gas pedal to the floor. The explosion of money creation following Nixon's removal of the gold constraint produced an immense rise in *all* commodity prices in 1972–73 and the beginnings of the inflation that would wrack the democratic societies for a decade. When the oil producers began leapfrogging their prices, the money was there. Given the centrality of energy as an input in industrial societies, and the inflexibility of the plans both governments and corporations had made to expand energy use in the 1970's, the quintupling of energy prices between the summer 1973 and spring 1974 met virtually no resistance from consumers.[24]

In 1973 the share of crude oil in total world commercial energy consumption peaked at 56 percent; OPEC's share of world oil supply peaked in 1976 at 65 percent of the market; and OPEC's total oil production hit a high in 1977 with 31.2 million barrels per day.[25] These were the benchmarks of OPEC's power.

In 1974 the oil exporters' earnings exceeded their expenditures on imports by around $68 billion.[26] As recession in the industrial countries temporarily cut into oil demand and as their own appetite for imported goods and services increased, however, these "current-account" surpluses began to shrink. By 1978 OPEC's import expenditures had virtually caught up with earnings, and the surplus for the group was around $2 billion. (The aggregation disguises the fact that some members, like Iraq and Iran, with large populations, spent more than they earned almost from the beginning while others, like Kuwait and Saudi Arabia, enjoyed substantial surpluses throughout.) Moreover, 90 percent of OPEC's oil income was in dollars, and by late 1979 a two-year burst of inflation in the United States had debased the real value of the 1973 to 1974 price increases. Once again Middle Eastern politics intervened to aid the oil exporters. This time it was the turmoil in Iran after the Ayatollah Khomeini's overthrow of the shah, which revived concerns about the availability of oil. In the months following the takeover official oil prices surged as high as $34 dollars a barrel, with spot prices even higher, and OPEC enjoyed three more years of substantial surpluses before losing control of the market. Taking inflation into account, this second major oil-price shock was about of the same magnitude as the first: altogether, each oil shock represented an income transfer from oil consumers to OPEC equal to approximately 2 percent of world GNP.[27]

By 1982 OPEC again had lost its grip on prices as conservation and the development of alternative sources of energy and new oil fields outside OPEC's control were enough to offset Saudi Arabia's "swing capacity" of approximately 5 to 6 million barrels per day—the amount of oil Saudi Arabia has shown itself willing and able to add or withhold from world oil supplies to support a given price. Deep divisions between income maximizers like Iraq and market-share maximizers like Saudi Arabia also weakened OPEC's supply-price strategy: oil prices plummeted, and Middle Eastern oil producers slipped into deficit. But then the whole cycle began again, with rising consumption and slowing production growth outside OPEC allowing OPEC to slowly push up prices. Saudi Arabia took the biggest share of increased market demand and saw its bank deposits rise by $20 billion from 1987 to mid-1990. Saddam Hussein's basic quarrel with Kuwait and Saudi Arabia in 1990 was his belief that OPEC was once again in a position to push up prices far more without losing control of the market, and their unwillingness to adjust their production downward to make room for more Iraqi oil and to achieve his price goal.

THE AFTERMATH: PANIC AND HUBRIS

OPEC's first oil-price shock induced in the rest of the world a combination of panic and hubris—panic about how bigger oil bills could be paid and how the depressing effects on economic activity could be cushioned; hubris about the money-making possibilities presented by the sudden concentration of wealth in the oil-exporting countries. OPEC's ability to accumulate wealth at the expense of the rest of the world seemed unlimited. The quadrupling of the price of oil—sextupling if one goes back to 1971—combined with a 32 percent increase in OPEC exports by volume between 1970 and 1973 created a dramatic shift in financial flows. As former Senate Foreign Relations Committee staff analyst Steven Emerson put it in *The American House of Saud*, the petroleum crisis became a petrodollar crisis:

> The second-stage effects of the so-called 1973 "oil price revolution" were just beginning to be felt throughout the world. The real "revolution" had very little to do with oil. It concerned money—hundreds of billions of dollars.... Some Arab states were earning 12.7 million dollars an hour.... By the end of 1978, OPEC had earned a staggering $603.5 billion, a sum that constituted about two-thirds of the 1978 value of the total Eurocurrency market.[28]

Between the surplus income of members who earned more than they spent, and the foreign borrowings of those who didn't, the OPEC countries had a cumulative investable cash surplus of approximately $475 billion for the period 1974 to 1981.[29]

One finds it difficult now, and more than a little embarrassing, to recall the atmosphere of those first years of soaring oil prices: the obsequious currying of favor with sheiks and the shah, the mad scramble to profit from the petrodollar bonanza by selling the newly oil-rich something, anything—Cadillacs, tanks, icebergs, certificates of deposit, thirty-year treasury bonds. Central bankers and finance ministers vied with commercial banks, auto dealers, and armament peddlers to capture some part of the oil billions. OPEC's billions—the billions to be spent and the billions to be invested abroad—mesmerized the rest of the world.

Businesspeople flocked to the Persian Gulf, where much of the oil wealth was concentrated. In 1974 Saudi Arabia, Iran, Kuwait, and the United Arab Emirates (UAE) accounted for 60 percent of OPEC's total oil revenues. Saudi Arabia alone produced almost one of every three barrels of OPEC oil. Its revenues had jumped from around $3 billion in 1972 to nearly $30 billion in 1974. Saudia, the national airline, saw its passenger and air-freight traffic rise 200 percent almost overnight. The U.S. National Association of Manufacturers set up a special task force to study ways to "recycle" petrodollars; North Dakota's state legislature passed a resolution promoting trade with Saudi Arabia and sent a mission.[30] Not to be outdone, the U.S. government set up a joint economic commission with Saudi Arabia in 1974; the only other countries with which this has been done are the Soviet Union and the People's Republic of China. The Treasury Department established a special Office of Saudi Arabian Affairs. Among its responsibilities was overseeing the 1,500 officials from various U.S. bureaucracies ranging from the Farm Credit Administration to the Arizona Highway Patrol who were sent to assist the Saudis develop departments such as their own highway squad. No other country had a special office at the Treasury Department.[31]

The rich industrial countries were, unsurprisingly, in general more successful than either the smaller developed countries or the non-OPEC developing countries in selling to OPEC and attracting OPEC's surplus cash. Germany, the United States, Japan, France, and the United Kingdom quickly offset higher oil costs—partly through riding out a recession, which reduced demand for oil and other imports, but also by stepping up exports to the oil producers, whose appetite for foreign goods, particularly arms, exceeded all expectations. U.S. arms sales to the Middle East had totaled $2.8 billion for the twenty-one years from 1950 to 1971; between 1972 and 1981 it sold $50 billion in arms to the region, not counting sales to Israel. The shah of Iran bought $14 billion of U.S. military hardware before being toppled from his peacock throne, and Saudi Arabia, with an armed force of only 47,000 men, managed to spend $17 billion on U.S. arms and another $17 billion on military construction projects supervised by the United States.[32]

Weaker industrial countries like Greece and Portugal and developing countries not blessed with huge oil deposits—or as in the case of Mexico, not yet able to fully exploit them—fared less well. Non-OPEC developing countries at first greeted the oil exporters' price coup as a victory for the entire Third World, despite its catastrophic effects on their own economies. William Cline of the Institute for International Economics estimated that oil-price increases added $259 billion to the import bills of non-OPEC developing countries in the ten years from 1973 to 1982, over and above what their imports would have cost if oil prices had simply kept pace with U.S. inflation.[33] But with visions of emulating OPEC's success with other raw-material cartels and buoyed by a temporary surge in non-oil commodity prices, these countries were determined to maintain high levels of growth and imports in the face of widening trade deficits.

Although GNP growth in the industrial countries fell sharply from 6.1 percent in 1973 to 0.7 percent in 1974 and was negative in 1975, growth in the developing countries fell only slightly—from 6.7 percent in 1973 to 4.2 percent in 1975. These countries made little apparent effort to cut back non-oil imports to compensate for higher oil prices and smaller demand for their exports in the industrial countries. The brief surge in non-oil commodity prices and some increase in exports to OPEC were not sufficient to prevent a sharp overall deterioration in the balance of trade for many developing countries. (Some did effectively reduce oil-related deficits by penetrating the Middle Eastern market. South Korea contracted out so many of its skilled construction workers to the Persian Gulf that its own ambitious domestic housing and industrial building program had to be delayed.)[34]

These countries would get little direct help from OPEC in financing their economies. Declarations of Third World solidarity notwithstanding, OPEC preferred to keep its money in the First World. The rich industrial countries' success in selling to OPEC was matched by their success in attracting OPEC's spare cash. In 1974 almost three-quarters of the OPEC identifiable surpluses ended up in the United States and Britain, mostly in government securities and bank deposits. The IMF estimated that of OPEC's total $475 billion investable surplus through 1981, $400 billion or 85 percent was placed in the industrial countries. Only $60 billion or 15 percent flowed to developing countries, including contributions to the World Bank and IMF.[35] Much of the concessional financing went to a small group of oil-deficient but politically important states in the Middle East and North Africa. About 50 percent of OPEC's bilateral aid went to three countries— Egypt (until the 1979 peace agreement with Israel, which caused other Arab states to break relations with Egypt), Syria, and Jordan. (Nevertheless, Persian Gulf countries like Saudi Arabia and Kuwait have given a far larger proportion of their

GNP in foreign aid in some years than any industrial country has ever given.)[36]

Thus an historic pattern was broken. From the end of World War II to 1973 countries in current-account deficit were financed directly by countries with large surpluses, primarily through direct long-term investment by multinational corporations and with foreign aid—official multilateral and bilateral transfers of loans and grants, usually on concessionary terms.[37] After 1973, as OPEC channeled its surplus income to the countries least in need of capital inflows, some form of intermediation was needed to finance the oil- and non–oil-related deficits of other countries. That role was eagerly seized by the commercial banks.

THE IMPACT OF OPEC SURPLUSES ON THE BANKS

Impressive as they are, the gross numbers on OPEC's financial surpluses do not by themselves explain the full significance of the petrodollar phenomenon for the big banks. The situation after the first oil-price shock was in many ways unique.

Three countries—Saudi Arabia, Kuwait, and the United Arab Emirates—accounted for more than 80 percent of OPEC's accumulation of foreign assets.[38] Saudi Arabia enjoyed by far the biggest surplus, building up net foreign assets of at least $160 billion from 1974 to 1982. Kuwait's cumulative surplus was an estimated $80 billion, and the UAE's $35 billion as of 1982. Libya had foreign holdings of about $22 billion, and Iran had substantial foreign holdings until the shah was ousted by the Ayatollah Khomeini.

Japan has had current-account surpluses even larger than those Saudi Arabia enjoyed when its oil income was at its peak, and foreign bankers flocked to Tokyo in the 1980s and 1990s as they flocked to the Persian Gulf in the 1970s. But there are important differences between the two situations.

The balance-of-payments surplus of an industrial economy like Japan's represents the sum of millions of transactions mostly by private individuals and commercial entities: the disposition of these earnings is determined by an equally large number of individual decisions and actions. A foreign bank hoping to garner some of these foreign earnings for its own account will have to establish relations with literally thousands of corporations, pension funds, and private investors, and it will have to compete with powerful and sophisticated Japanese financial institutions as well equipped as any U.S., U.K., or Swiss bank to place the country's surplus foreign earnings. It is a costly and time-consuming process, and the returns so far have been modest. As it turns out, Japanese investors have shown a strong preference for real estate and corporate and government securities over money-market instruments offered by banks. This preference by the new leading exporter of capital is one reason the focus of international financial intermediation shifted from bank credit to the securities market in the 1980s.

The oil-rich Persian Gulf countries in the 1970s presented far easier targets for foreign banks. Virtually the entire surplus income of a country like Saudi Arabia or Kuwait results from essentially one transaction—the sale by the government to a group of foreign companies of the right to lift and market the country's oil. Consequently, the disposition of the oil income is concentrated in the hands of a few key officials: the government sells the oil concessions, and the government disposes of the proceeds. Brookings scholar Richard P. Mattione estimated that the Saudi Arabian Monetary Authority (SAMA), a combination central bank and investment manager, controlled 84 percent of Saudi Arabia's accumulated foreign assets as of mid-1983, with other government entities controlling another 2 percent.[39] The Kuwaiti government—meaning the extended al Sabah family—controlled $64 billion of that country's total foreign assets of approximately $85 billion. Most of the UAE's earnings are managed by the rulers of the seven sheikdoms that make up the federation. A foreign bank seeking to tap the petrodollar flow thus had only to establish business relations with a few agencies and with a relatively small number of officials.

In the case of Iran, all oil payments went initially into government accounts at Chase Manhattan Bank. Royalty payments were credited to the Chase account of the National Iranian Oil Company (NIOC), which paid its foreign bills and expenses before transferring the remainder to the central bank. "Income tax" payments from foreign oil companies passed through the government of Iran's account at Chase to the central bank's account. The central bank in turn immediately credited the government's account at Bank Melli with the equivalent sum in ryahls. The central bank was in charge of managing all of the country's foreign exchange. Once the central bank had decided how to invest the holdings, Chase would be instructed how much to transfer where.[40]

Most of the Saudi income was taxes and royalties paid to the government by the oil production entity Aramco, which in the 1970s was still a Delaware corporation wholly owned by Exxon, Mobil, Standard Oil of California, and Texaco. (The Saudis gradually took over ownership of Aramco, completing the takeover in 1980, but the same companies still buy most of Aramco's production.) The oil companies initially made their payments quarterly and later paid monthly to smooth the flow. On the fifteenth of each month billions of dollars would be transferred from the oil companies' bank accounts to the accounts of SAMA. Its dozen or so bureaucrats—aided by a team of seven advisers rented from Merrill Lynch and the British investment firm Baring Brothers—had the daunting task of placing these petro-billions profitably and, above all, safely. David Mulford, later U.S. under secretary of Treasury and the man in charge of U.S. debt policy in the Bush administration, spent ten years in Saudi Arabia as a financial adviser to SAMA.[41]

Abdul Aziz Alquarishi, the former head of the Saudi civil

service with no experience in banking, became head of SAMA in 1974. By 1981 he was investing $2 billion a week. The *Wall Street Journal* wrote, "Actually nobody outside the Saudi inner circle knows exactly how large the total is. But it is generally agreed that Mr. Alquarishi controls a larger fund of assets than any other banker—public or private—in the world."[42]

Unlike the Saudis—who preferred bank deposits, government securities, and other liquid holdings that could be quickly converted to cash—the Kuwaitis favored long-term commitments to stocks or real estate and direct investment. Lacking the vast oil reserves of its neighbors Saudi Arabia and Iraq, Kuwait put its money in foreign investments that were likely to yield a substantial income in the future when its oil income dried up. Even so, it provided business for the banks. Citibank managed a number of equity and other investment portfolios for Kuwait, reportedly worth $7 billion in November 1980[43]—roughly one-third of all the funds in Citibank's investment management unit at the time.[44] Bankers who dealt with both Saudi Arabia and Kuwait commented on the two countries' different expectations in the early 1970s. In Kuwait at that time, they said, the attitude about the country's future was that when the oil runs out, "the last one out the door turns out the lights." The Kuwaitis' reaction when their country was taken from them by Saddam Hussein's troops in 1990 indicated attitudes may have changed.

In 1974 Saudi Arabia launched an ambitious five-year $142 billion development plan to turn the primitive desert kingdom into a modern industrial state.[45] And in the meantime, Saudi Arabia would keep its money in the bank. The U.S. Treasury estimated that in 1974 two-thirds of Saudi Arabia's foreign assets were bank deposits. At the end of 1976, 47 percent of those deposits were in U.S. banks.[46] A Middle Eastern publication reported that only two Saudi banks were on SAMA's list and both of those were partly owned by the government.[47]

The Middle Eastern oil producers favored large foreign banks, particularly the British and American banks with close ties to the Seven Sisters, the major oil companies that until now had been the principal representatives of Western economic interests in the Middle East. In Saudi Arabia Aramco almost constituted a state within a state. Chase Manhattan and Citibank came out of the same Rockefeller empire as Exxon (Standard Oil of New Jersey), Mobil (once Socony Mobil, Standard Oil of New York), and Socal (Standard of California). A former chairman of Chase, John J. McCloy, often represented the Seven Sisters' interests in Washington; Exxon's chairman sat on Citibank's board; a senior officer of JP Morgan served on the board of Aramco.

American banks also benefited from the fact that the oil shock restored the dollar's dominance in international finance just at the time it seemed to be losing its attractiveness to foreigners and when other strong currencies might have assumed a greater international role. President Nixon had closed the gold window in 1971 after a period of rapid monetary expansion, and a growing U.S. trade deficit had created a crisis of confidence in the dollar. Ending the convertibility of the dollar into gold in effect allowed the dollar to float against other currencies and ended the Bretton Woods regime of fixed exchange rates.

But the demand for dollars created by the oil-price increases and OPEC's insistence on being paid in U.S. currency ensured that the dollar would be the preeminent medium for international borrowing and lending for the rest of the decade: 80 percent of the oil payments were in U.S. dollars, and the rest mostly in British pounds sterling. When sterling got into trouble in 1976 the Saudis stopped taking pounds, however, and since then nearly all oil transactions have been paid in dollars. SAMA tried to diversify the currency composition of its assets, but a dearth of liquid instruments denominated in other strong currencies thwarted these efforts.

Mohammed Yeganeh was governor of the central bank of Iran from 1973 to 1976. During his tenure the central bank had a list of twenty foreign banks with which it would place deposits. Ten were large American banks, based in New York, Chicago, and California; there were no regional banks on the list. The others were leading European and Japanese banks. Yeganeh said the banks chosen "had to have the highest credit rating, and a long relationship with the country"—that is, to have been helpful in the past in raising money for Iran. (Iran was a major borrower as well as depositor with the international banks.) "We tried to avoid the newcomers. There were many, many banks coming, but we kept to our old customers." The choice of banks was also influenced by a desire to diversify holdings away from the dollar—in part to reflect the country's trade pattern, said Yeganeh, and in part for political reasons. "We worried under certain circumstances they [the assets] might be frozen." Loans to the IMF and the World Bank were regarded as both politically and financially safe investments. Yeganeh, of course, had far less money overall to invest than the Saudis so diversification was easier.

Once the list of banks and the desired mix of currencies and maturities was agreed, Yeganeh's chief money-market manager and two or three deputies were free to shop among the twenty commercial banks for the best terms. However, there was a ceiling on how much Iran would place with any single bank, based on the size of a bank's capital and assets. Thus Bank of America and Citibank, as the largest banks, were likely to end up with more Iranian deposits than Chase, despite Chase's favored position thanks to its chairman David Rockefeller's close relationship with the shah. "I tried to keep [domestic] politics out of our investment decisions." Yeganeh said he never once had the impression that any bank was trying to discourage a deposit by bidding too low an interest rate for it. On the contrary, he said, they always seemed anxious for more.

Yeganeh noted sardonically that the Ayatollah Khomeini's revolutionary government abandoned his cautious portfolio approach to managing Iran's foreign assets: "Although the fundamentalists are not supposed to accept interest, their major criterion became the highest rate of return. For me, that was the lowest priority. Safety came first."

According to Yeganeh, after the revolution Iranian foreign reserves held in other currencies were converted into dollars, and deposits with European and other banks were transferred to American banks because they offered the best rates. The oil-collection accounts were moved from Chase to Bank of America, which was not tainted by close ties to the shah. Says Yeganeh, "They were not paying attention to what was happening with relations [with the United States]. Then they woke up and found that 80 to 90 percent of the country's assets were frozen!"

The concentration of a significant share of the world's savings in the hands of a few Middle Eastern investors who preferred to channel a large part of their investments through a small number of American and European banks fueled the growth of a highly liquid international interbank market. The few banks on the oil exporters' approved list could not always find an immediate corporate or other borrower for the money and loaned their excess funds to other banks, short term, for a small interest charge. One-third to one-half of all transactions in the Eurocurrency market[48] consists of such short-term "loans" by banks to each other. Smaller, less internationally experienced banks became indirect beneficiaries of the liquidity injected into the market by OPEC. And many of these same banks became eager or easily persuaded first-time participants in large loans to Latin America, Eastern Europe, and other exotic places.

Funding patterns at the large banks changed profoundly. Certificates of deposit (CDs) had been invented by Walter Wriston of First National City Bank of New York in 1961 to give banks an instrument that could compete with treasury bills for the surplus cash of large corporations. The Federal Deposit Insurance Act prohibited banks from paying interest on domestic deposits left with them for less than thirty days. Unlike an old-fashioned bank deposit, a CD could be sold like a security and was thus a plausible investment for companies that did not wish to lock their money away for a longer term. The oil states became major purchasers of bank CDs. "Bought money" quickly became more important for most large banks than the collection of deposits from individuals and corporate customers through a vast network of retail banking branches. Chase Manhattan historian John Wilson writes,

A quarter-century earlier Chase had relied almost exclusively on demand deposits to finance loans and investments. Funding costs were relatively stable, as were interest rates on loans, most of which were extended on a fixed-rate basis. But by 1975 Chase was dependent on borrowed money for 80 percent of its funds, and interest rates had become increasingly volatile. Interest paid for funds represented almost two-thirds of all costs. How money was borrowed—when, in what markets, and at what maturities—had become a matter of vital concern. On the asset side, how loans were priced—floating rates, fixed rates, tied to the prime rate or Eurocurrency rates—as well as the mixture of loans and investments, was of no less significance.[49]

After 1973 most of the "bought money" was foreign. The reliance on foreign funds outlasted OPEC's surpluses. In 1990 more than half the liabilities of the nine largest U.S. banks were overseas deposits. Morgan got 70 percent of its funding overseas.

The growing dependence on volatile, short-term deposits led banks to apply variable interest rates, adjustable every three or six months, to the medium-term loans these deposits were funding. Any shift in the cost of funds to the bank could then be passed on almost immediately to the borrower, protecting the bank (but not the borrower) against an interest-rate squeeze that could result from the maturity mismatch of deposits and loans.

Finally, the oil shock propelled commercial banks into a new role as the principal financial intermediaries among sovereign states. Banks not only held the oil states' financial reserves, they wholeheartedly embraced a business they had completely abandoned in 1931 and began to rediscover only during the 1960s. Awash in oil money, with credit demand depressed in the home market, commercial banks resumed large-scale lending to developing countries and their governments. For U.S. banks international borrowing and lending was transformed from a limited adjunct of domestic business to an activity that dominated the balance sheet. While their domestic business languished, international activities exploded, accounting for 95 percent of the earnings growth of the nation's ten largest banks during the first half of the decade and probably more than half of their total earnings in the late 1970s. Many of the biggest borrowers were neither oil importers nor suffering large trade imbalances but simply countries that decided to use easy foreign credit to meet domestic financing needs.

Neither the banks nor their governments and regulators worried about the stability of a credit market structured so that, as an OECD report put it, "large volumes of long-term financial needs are being met through medium-term credit instruments funded by short-term deposits."[50] The oil shock fostered a climate in which government policy makers in the industrial countries were disinclined to try to dampen the speculative excesses of borrowers and lenders. On the contrary, the success of petrodollar recycling was hailed as if the real costs of OPEC's price increases had somehow been made to vanish and the massive flows of credit from OPEC to the banks and from the banks to the borrowers did not represent future claims on real goods and services. The world economy has paid dearly for that delusion.

3

Political Risk

From the early 1970s Mexico began relying more and more on bank credit. The money was there, the market was there. We had great needs, so we took it.

> —Francisco Suarez Davila, deputy minister of finance of Mexico

A MODEST BEGINNING

Retired banker James Green recalled that overseas operations were a modest affair when he joined the Central Hanover Bank from the U.S. Foreign Service in 1955: "We didn't have an international banking division at that time, just a 'foreign department' consisting of a few people sitting around opening letters of credit and doing a little foreign exchange. We were willing to take almost no risks abroad at all. There was no ambition to expand the overseas exposure. . . . We had no business really; we were novices. The board would call a meeting if Pemex was one day late in an acceptance payment!" Most of the bank's foreign exposure was to Canada; altogether, the foreign department accounted for maybe 7 percent of total earnings.

Hanover Bank,[1] then the seventh- or eighth-largest bank in New York, was not unique. In Green's estimation there were no international banks in the United States in the 1950s except maybe First National City Bank of New York, if *international* means a bank having a knowledge of and willingness to assume risks outside the United States. The function of Hanover's foreign department was to take care of the needs of domestic clients abroad plus a few foreign companies. "We had an unimportant bank in London going back before World War II, which we thought about closing. It was mostly an 'accommodation office'—a service to rich Park Avenue matrons on their visits to England."

The foreign department—at that time the name alone suggested something not quite respectable—was held in low regard by the rest of the bank. "I remember some of the Princeton brahmins in the bank who knew little of what we were doing and didn't care. It was said one could always tell when one was in the foreign department because everyone smelled of garlic and wore mustaches." The head of Hanover's department was a Russian; the man in charge of foreign business at Chase Manhattan Bank was German.

First National City Bank may have had more international ambitions in the 1950s than Hanover Bank, but George Moore, the former chairman of City Bank, admits in his memoirs that he referred to the international end of his bank as "Siberia" before moving from the domestic division to head the overseas division in 1956.[2] City Bank, like other large banks, had retreated from foreign markets after 1930. "In 1930 City Bank had 83 foreign branches with 29 percent of its total loans, and the overseas division accounted for 30 percent of the total profits; by 1955, we were down to 61 branches with 14 percent of the loans, contributing 16 percent of the profits."[3] When Moore, still on the domestic side of the bank, asked his young protégé Walter Wriston to move from the domestic division, where he was running shipping and transportation, to the desk supervising the London office, which was losing money, "I had a terrible time selling the idea to Wriston, and could do it, finally, only by offering him a repurchase agreement: when and if he grew unhappy in the overseas division, I would take him back, no questions asked."[4] When Moore moved up to become president of the bank in 1959, Wriston was put in charge of the overseas division, taking over just as a new era of expansion in international banking was beginning.

Hanover Bank began in the 1950s, according to Jim Green, "in the most tentative, controlled way" to grant lines of credit to foreign entities, but "only to institutions deemed to be doubtless for the risk. We began to refinance sight letters to 90 days, then, very adventurously, we went to 180 days, but at first no clean advances. Little by little, there were clean advances to 180 days, allegedly linked to some trade, but not really. Then one-year advances. Then someone wanted to make term loans." The borrowers at this stage were mostly trade-oriented foreign entities—state oil companies, food importers, and the like. Then, says Green, "Competition began working its magic. In the first stage, a few New York banks were doing it, then all, then banks in Chicago and San Francisco. Rates were chipped away so we became more adventurous and extended maturities to compete. We offered to discount the loan portfolios of foreign local banks. At first, we did all the traveling. Then some bright guy in Peru or Bolivia said, 'I will visit them in New York'—and was astonished to go home with a $20 million or $30 million credit line—more in local currency than he could hope to generate in a generation. He had found the cookie jar, the munificence of which exceeded his wildest dreams!"

An official of the Mexican central bank explained his country's response to the banks' rising interest: "I think the government felt that there were many pressing needs—social needs, education, health. For once, we had a real opportunity to make a big dent in these problems. For a while we did. The level of investment was the highest in our history. We had real opportunities to break a number of ancestral problems and make a real advance.

"When some people would point out dangers [of borrowing], the president would say, 'Don't be afraid. How can you refuse that village? Perhaps we will borrow a little more.'

"There seemed to be no limit on our supply of credit, no concern about our ability to service it. We had high growth, a decade of political stability, and huge oil reserves. It seemed that nothing could go wrong."

REDEFINING POLITICAL RISK

When bankers speak of political risk in foreign lending, they mean the risk that revolution or war or some other upheaval will make a foreign borrower unwilling or unable to pay its debts. Modern bankers have assumed that these political risks are minimal: although political upheavals and violent changes of government do occur from time to time, countries at war need their bankers more than ever, and postrevolutionary regimes sooner or later find it in their interest to restore relations with foreign creditors. Bankers point to the fact that default—the failure to pay on time—happens frequently, but outright repudiation of sovereign debts has rarely occurred in this century. The two most notable exceptions—the Soviet Union and the People's Republic of China—have found it necessary to come to terms with their creditors and settle their debts, if only with nominal payments.

A close examination of the history of sovereign loans, however, suggests the current definition of political risk is too narrow. The greatest political risk in sovereign lending is not war or revolution but the outcome of placing unlimited credit in the hands of politicians whose natural inclination, the world over, is to promise the moon to every constituent and to postpone making difficult decisions as long as possible. In the 1970s, thanks to the largesse of foreign bankers, political leaders from Warsaw to Santiago were able to enjoy a decade of domestic wish fulfillment in the face of generally unfavorable external economic conditions.

Bankers now say that their great error in the 1970s was to do balance-of-payments financing—lending money to help countries meet their foreign expenditures after the oil shocks. But in many cases foreign borrowing, at least at first, had little to do with a need for foreign exchange per se. Higher oil bills and adverse conditions for world trade only partly account for the rise in foreign debt. When a team of Federal Reserve Board economists compared cumulative changes in external indebtedness, external assets, and trade and current account balances of eight major debtor countries for the period 1973 to 1982, they found that trade deficits were a minor factor in the debt build-up. In fact, "the cumulated trade deficits of Brazil, Chile, Mexico and Peru were less than one-fifth as large as their build-up of external debts. Argentina and Venezuela ran substantial cumulative trade surpluses."[5]

During most of the 1970s foreign banks financed development strategies designed to legitimize weak governments by maintaining high rates of growth and modernize economies without challenging entrenched power structures. In Poland Western bank loans financed Gierek's attempted shortcut to industrial modernization, which he hoped to carry out without fundamental economic and political reforms. In Latin America rapid economic expansion and an explosive rise in consumption financed with foreign credit enabled weak dictatorships and pseudo-democracies to deflate political opposition.

This does not mean all of the borrowed money was wasted. On the contrary, the strong export performance of many debtor countries and their rising share of manufactures in recent years attest to a high level of investment in the previous decade that yielded real returns. But there is little evidence that bankers distinguished between good investments and bad or knew or cared which investments their money was financing. Argentina, where rising debt was accompanied by economic stagnation and capital flight, paid less for loans in the Euromarket than did Brazil, where rising debt was associated with a decade of spectacular growth and investment.[6]

Increased foreign borrowing after the 1964 military coup allowed ambitious Brazilians to embark on massive capital investment, financing without difficulty in the Euromarkets the simultaneous undertakings of the two largest hydroelectric dam projects in the world, five state-of-the-art steel complexes, an eight-plant nuclear power program, aluminum plants, housing for nine million families, roads and railways, and the development of an indigenous arms and aircraft capability. As the Argentine economy stalled in the mid-1970s its upper class lived extravagantly at home and abroad, and the ruling generals and admirals spent billions to equip their forces for modern warfare. (The original target of the Argentine military build-up was the rival junta in neighboring Chile; it made the mistake of taking on the British navy instead.) In Mexico, as President Luis Echeverria's radical tax-reform proposal failed, he turned to foreign banks to pay for the social programs that had become a political necessity for the ruling Permanent Revolutionary Party after the violent student uprising of 1968. Foreign credit allowed his successor, Lopez Portillo, to spend like the ruler of an oil state while most of the country's ample petroleum resources were still in the ground.

Because bankers were willing to make available almost unlimited funds with few questions asked, all of this could be done without the restraints that limited resources and policy mistakes normally impose. Failures could simply be papered over with more loans, and unpopular decisions put off until the money ran out.

Eduardo Wiesner, for many years the director of the IMF's Latin America division, has called the debt crisis "a fiscal manifestation of a political struggle":

> No other set of factors explains more of the debt crisis than the fiscal deficits incurred by most of the major countries in the hemisphere. . . . The figures for the period 1979–82 cannot be more eloquent. In only four years the three largest countries of the region—Argentina, Brazil, and Mexico—more than doubled the size of their non-financial public sector deficits, which rose from the already high levels of around 6 percent of GDP to well over 15 percent. Behind these growing fiscal deficits were strong political pressures for higher public spending. As long as external financing permitted total absorption to exceed domestic income, it was possible to accommodate those demands. But as the world recession worsened and as it became evident that the additional financing from abroad was not being accompanied by a corresponding increase in exports or in domestic capital formation, capital inflows dropped substantially and the fiscal imbalance became an exchange rate and a debt crisis. In brief, the debt crisis can be traced back to a fiscal disequilibrium and ultimately to an unresolved political struggle between competing groups which wanted to have a larger share of income.[7]

In many debtor countries, foreign credit was the glue that held together fragile political coalitions of urban workers, a growing middle class of mostly public-sector employees, and the military. "Every time Brazil had a new government, the new finance minister, first thing, would go to New York and to Washington to borrow for 'infrastructure,' " said Lars Janér, a Brazilian paper importer. Foreign money enabled governments to survive without resolving fundamental political and economic inequities in their countries. In many cases, rapid economic growth financed with foreign credit was the trade-off for limited political freedom or outright repression.

And foreign loans helped pay for government subsidies that were to compensate the economically disenfranchised who did not benefit directly from the expansion. Holding down the price of beans and rice, bread, gasoline, and public transport by subsidizing producers was politically more expedient than trying to correct glaring inequities in income distribution through land and wage reforms, education reform, and progressive taxation. Thus starting in the late 1960s, maximizing the inflow of credit from abroad was a political as well as an economic priority for borrowing countries.

THE SEARCH FOR FINANCIAL INDEPENDENCE

"The beginning of the story is 1967–68," said Aldroado Moura da Silva, a Brazilian economist who has written extensively about his country's debt problem. "The lack of foreign exchange and of capital had been a big restraint on our growth and development. We were dependent on the IBRD [International Bank for Reconstruction and Development] and other official institutions. The Mexicans began in 1965 to borrow from foreign banks. It was seen here as successful. So we prepared to enter the market. . . . We tried to get access to foreign banks and get Brazilian banks out into the market."

Development experts and policy makers in the industrial countries today accept as almost holy scripture that although it may be acceptable for industrial countries to borrow from the private markets, developing countries should rely primarily on official development agencies and foreign equity investors to meet their supplemental capital needs. This notion was fashionable in the 1950s and 1960s too. But when capital-hungry sovereigns and commercial banks began to rediscover each other after a thirty-year hiatus, many developing countries had already worn out their welcome at official lending institutions, and multinational corporations had pretty much worn out *their* welcome in the less developed countries (LDCs).

Industrial countries began pumping grants and officially backed loans into developing countries in the 1940s to ensure an adequate supply of strategic materials for the war effort and sometimes to keep wavering governments on their side during the hostilities.[8] The programs continued modestly after the war—the largest financing flowed from the United States to rebuild Europe—to develop markets for production from industrial countries that was expected to be in oversupply, to maintain old colonial ties, to advance new imperial ambitions, and to wage the Cold War. By the late 1960s developing countries were already deeply in debt to official lenders.

Private lenders were almost completely out of the picture. "The crisis of the thirties," wrote financial expert Paul Einzig, "led to a widespread abandonment of the liberal policies towards foreign lending that had developed during the stable conditions of the 19th Century. The outbreak of the second World War brought issuing activity for private purposes virtually to a standstill. All foreign lending came to assume the form of inter-Government transactions."[9] Capital controls in effect until the mid-1950s in every major country except the United States made private international financial transactions generally difficult. The 1934 Johnson Debt Default Act forbade any U.S. person (including a bank) from lending to any country in default on its debts to the United States. Britain had a similar law. The Glass-Steagall Act, enacted the same year, barred U.S. deposit banks from underwriting or selling corporate or foreign government securities in the United States. Finally, World War II drew national savings into government hands. A history of Citibank notes, "Wartime banking at National City and other banks was largely a matter of helping the Treasury sell bills and bonds needed to finance the war." By war's end, two-thirds of National City's total domestic earning assets were U.S. government bonds.[10] Those assets were liquidated to meet strong postwar private credit demand at home.

According to a blue-ribbon commission on development headed by Canada's Lester Pearson, the public sector of developing countries owed $47 billion to foreign lenders as of 30 June 1968, three-quarters of it to foreign governments and official multilateral institutions.[11] Many of these loans were in default. As Jerome Levinson and Juan de Onis pointed out in their study of the Alliance for Progress launched by John F. Kennedy in 1961, "When the Alliance began, many Latin American countries were deeply in debt and virtually unable to meet their debt payments. A substantial amount of early Alliance lending went to refinance the existing debts." More than half the money Latin America was receiving from all external sources was absorbed by debt servicing.[12]

Anthony Solomon, now of the S. G. Warburg Group, recalled taking charge of dispensing increased U.S. aid to Latin America under the Alliance effort when he was deputy assistant secretary of state for Latin America in 1964–65: "I told the Latins to seek debt reschedulings with their official creditors. They didn't like it, but I could see that otherwise they would end up using our aid money to pay their other foreign creditors. We negotiated the restructuring in the Paris Club with of course the U.S. pushing for better terms than the Europeans were at first inclined to give." (The "Paris Club" is where lending governments get together to renegotiate terms with a debtor government.)

Brazil rescheduled its official loans in 1961 and again in 1964, Argentina in 1962 and in 1965, and Peru in 1968. Chile, Ghana, India, Indonesia, and Turkey also rescheduled official loans during the 1960s.[13]

Even if these countries had been deemed creditworthy, the total availability of financing from government programs and foreign direct investment (FDI) was small relative to their expanding financing needs. The entire World Bank lending program was less than $1 billion per year when Robert McNamara took over as president of the institution in 1968.[14] Total annual bilateral aid from Western industrial countries was about $5 billion, and Latin America's share was small— only $1.26 billion net annually in the period 1964 to 1967.[15]

Lastly, official aid came with strings. Bilateral aid often served the commercial interests of creditors at least as much as it served the development needs of the recipient, and multilateral lending followed the fashion of the day. In the 1960s roads and dams were all the rage. Between 1961 and 1965, 77 percent of all World Bank lending was for transportation and electric power; in contrast, 6 percent was for agriculture, and 1 percent for social services. Countries seeking funding for a different set of development priorities risked being left out. In 1968, the Bank's operating slogan under its new president shifted to "meeting basic human needs," with the emphasis on alleviating rural poverty. This held little attraction for governments whose political survival rested heavily on keeping local industrial elites, urban workers, and the military happy and who were convinced the key to development lay in building heavy industry and developing modern technology.

Direct investment from multinational corporations (MNCs) was also seen to have serious drawbacks. By 1970 foreign firms, mostly U.S.-owned, accounted for 28 percent of total manufacturing in Mexico, and half of the country's 300 largest manufacturing firms were affiliates of foreign multinationals. In Brazil foreign-owned firms were even more dominant and in 1972 accounted for half of total manufacturing sales.[16] The benefits of this foreign penetration were hotly debated, with opposition from both left and right. In Latin America this opposition had historical as well as contemporary roots.

During the 1930s depressed commodity prices and the collapse of the foreign bond market forced Latin America to slash imports and the larger countries to develop domestic industry for import substitution. The state became an active promoter of this shift. Continued isolation during World War II reinforced the policies of domestic substitution and protection and of direct government participation in the industrialization process. According to Levinson and de Onis, "The industrialists emerged from the wartime years as a strong interest group that lobbied aggressively in government circles and used political spokesmen and the press to promote the doctrines of economic nationalism in opposition to the free-trade position of the old commercial interests. The military (which had acquired a penchant for state-owned industries), organized labor, aspiring technocrats and economists emerging from the universities, and the political left in general took the side of the industrialists."[17]

In the 1960s the dependency theory of economic development took hold. Among its tenets, as summed up by Albert Fishlow, were that export-led growth does not improve the lot of most people because low wages in developing countries hold down the price of exports—which benefits the purchaser and not the seller. Second, direct investment "provides an opportunity for multinational firms to pursue their global strategy at the expense of national concerns." Third, dependent capitalist growth may produce rapid industrial production but will fail to meet the needs of people who lack employment and effective demand.[18]

Hostility was fed by sometimes subtle, sometimes blatant attempts at political manipulation by some foreign companies, the most notorious example being International Telephone and Telegraph's conspiracy with other multinationals and with the Central Intelligence Agency to block the election of Salvador Allende as president of Chile in 1971.

Moreover, statistics seem to bear out the critics' assertion that multinational corporations were taking out substantially more money from many countries than they were putting in (not unreasonable from the companies' point of view and not without justification if the local economy also benefitted significantly from foreign investment). American multinationals, for example, brought back to the United States $9.2 billion more in income from Latin America in the 1960 to 1972 period than they invested there, even when reinvested earnings, royalties, management fees, and other corporate financial transactions are taken into consideration.[19]

A broad study by the U.S. Tariff Commission that encompassed not only investment and remittance flows but also the balance-of-trade impact of U.S. multinational corporations on countries accounting for about 70 percent of U.S. investment in manufacturing abroad concluded, "MNCs, in their dealings with their parent country, exerted a large and growing negative or adverse influence on host country balance of payments."[20] Finally, even these estimates of foreign direct investment may overstate the capital contribution of MNCs. Perhaps as much as 75 percent of all foreign direct investment in manufacturing in Latin America has been financed with debt, not equity, raised in either the local capital market or, more likely, in the Euromarkets.[21]

Nationalism, socialism, and economic self-interest of local industrialists joined forces in a movement to restrict foreign multinationals. Mexico's president Luis Echeverría adopted a series of laws culminating in the 1973 Law to Promote Mexican Investment and Regulate Foreign Investment, which gradually excluded foreign firms altogether from electrical utilities, railroads, and communications. Telecommunications, urban, air and maritime transport, forestry, and natural gas distribution were restricted to 100 percent Mexican-owned firms. (Many industrial countries, including the United States, have similar restrictions on foreign ownership in key sectors.) Subsoil mineral rights were reserved for the state, and new firms in steel, cement, glass, fertilizer, cellulose, and aluminum production and other areas had to be 51 percent Mexican-owned. Automobile parts manufacturers had to be

60 percent Mexican-owned. Brazil not only limited foreign ownership and reserved certain sectors to the state, but it required foreign manufacturers to secure a rising proportion of their inputs in Brazil. The automotive sector, for example, was completely dominated by foreign firms that had entered before the enactment of ownership restrictions—Ford, Fiat, Volkswagen, Mercedes-Benz, Saab (the latter trucks and buses). But until the liberalization brought about by the Collor government in 1990, the domestic content of Brazil's manufacturing had to be 98 percent by value and 95 percent by weight. The same pattern of limiting foreign multinationals was followed throughout the Third World.

To governments already deeply in debt to foreign official entities and, as they saw it, confronting in multinational corporations a formidable threat to national sovereignty, foreign banks seemed a preferable source of capital on almost all counts. Bank loans raised no troubling issues of foreign ownership; bank loans were quick-disbursing and available in seemingly unlimited quantities; and they almost always came without political strings or policy conditions and could be deployed to suit the borrower rather than the lender.

The changing pattern of external flows to Latin America after 1965 was marked. Official sources supplied 59.8 percent of the average annual external resource inflow in 1961 to 1965, dropping to 40.4 percent in 1966 to 1970, then to 25.3 percent in 1971 to 1975, and supplied only 12.1 percent of the total inflow in 1976 to 1978. The share of private foreign direct investment also declined sharply, from a peak 33.7 percent of total foreign inflows in the second half of the 1960s to 15.9 percent in the second half of the 1970s. Meanwhile the share of foreign bank and bond finance rose steadily, from 7.2 percent in the early 1960s to 46 percent in the early 1970s, and 64.6 percent of all foreign financing in the late 1970s.[22]

The U.S. government and other official lenders regarded

this progression as "natural" and indeed kept constant pressure on countries like Brazil and Argentina to "graduate" altogether out of official concessionary loan programs.

THE CAMPAIGN TO BORROW

The Mexican financing strategy Brazil decided to emulate consisted of a series of laws and government policies to stimulate both private- and public-sector use of foreign commercial credit. Fiscal policies encouraged companies to finance with debt by making dividends subject to heavy taxation while interest payments were fully tax deductible. Then to expand the availability of credit in the economy, the Mexican government authorized domestic banks to fund peso loans in foreign currencies. Mexican banks borrowed, mostly dollars, from foreign commercial banks, converted the foreign exchange into pesos with the central bank, and on-lent the proceeds to domestic borrowers, including Mexican state enterprises. The banks—known entities and acceptable "names" in the foreign credit markets acting as intermediaries—could thus give local companies access to foreign credit that the companies could not attract on their own. The ultimate borrower bore the exchange-rate risk of these "pass-through" loans. Although the loan would be repaid to the local lender in pesos, the amount to be repaid would be determined by the dollar-peso exchange rate prevailing when the loan came due. As long as the country maintained a stable exchange rate, as Mexico had for many years, this risk was not of great concern to the borrower.

The transaction, of course, also rested on the assumption that the central bank would have adequate foreign-exchange reserves when the time came for the Mexican bank to reconvert the loan to dollars to repay the foreign provider of funds. But a steady inflow of new credit assuaged any concerns in this regard. As the Brazilians noted, the Mexican law was a great success. By 1981, *42 percent* of the assets of Mexican banks were domestic loans funded with foreign borrowings. Furthermore, these funds acquired abroad were augmented by "Mex-dollars"—local deposits that were denominated in U.S. dollars and that any Mexican resident was entitled to have. By 1981, 25 percent of all Mexican domestic bank deposits were also dollar denominated.[23]

In 1967 Brazil followed Mexico's lead. It amended the central banking act to allow Brazilian banks to borrow foreign currency abroad at medium or long term and on-lend the equivalent in cruzeiros to domestic borrowers, short term, for up to one year. The resolution promised banks a priority claim on foreign exchange in a crunch. These so-called Resolution 63 loans "became the main activity of Brazilian banks in the 1970's," according to Carlos Lemgruber of Banco Boavista, and "the law worked very well." (Lemgruber served as one of a succession of central bank chiefs in José Sarney's revolving-door administration.)

Foreign banks were not only eager lenders; some were also local on-lenders. According to Peter Woicke of Morgan Guaranty in São Paulo, a foreign bank with a license to do local-currency lending "could make a killing on Resolution 63 lending." The parent bank made a Eurodollar loan to the local branch in Brazil at the usual spread—say, 2¼ over LIBOR (London interbank offered rate)[24]—then the branch on-lent to the nonbank borrower at an additional two-, three-, or four-percentage-point spread. The effective return to a bank from this double dipping could be more than 7 percent (not counting tax benefits). The local representative of a competing U.S. bank estimated that 80 percent of Citibank's exposure in Brazil was dollar-funded loans extended locally by its Brazil branch. Citibank is one of only a handful of foreign banks with full local banking privileges in Brazil. Banks without branching privileges, like Manufacturers Hanover, could make Resolution 63 loans through their leasing affiliates. (This two-stage lending put some banks in an awkward position in the 1980s when many of the local loans went bad. One British banker whose exposure to Brazil was mostly through Resolution 63 explained that his bank put up new money in the rescheduling "partly to refinance debt of state companies and partly to finance overdue loans to ourselves.")

Another statute, Law 4131, permitted Brazilian companies to borrow directly from foreign banks for domestic investment purposes. This direct foreign borrowing was done primarily by large corporations and by state enterprises like Petrobrás and Eletrobrás with independent standing in the international financial markets. Law 4131 also was used by state banks like the National Bank for Economic and Social Development (BNDES) and the Banco do Brazil, which intermediated foreign funds and on-lent the domestic-currency equivalent at subsidized rates to sectors and industries the government wanted to support. And state and local governments used Law 4131 borrowings in part to escape the fiscal restraints imposed by the central government and limited local tax bases.

From 1969 on the commercial credit markets supplied an increasing share of total flows. At year end 1969, 43 percent of Brazil's foreign debt was owed to official agencies and 36 percent to banks. By 1973, *before* the first oil-price shock began to reverberate throughout the world economy, the private-market share had climbed to 62 percent, and only 23 percent of the country's external debt was owed to foreign governmental entities.[25]

During the "miracle years" of 1968 to 1973, under the guidance of Finance Minister Antonio Delfim Neto, Brazil's economy grew at more than 11 percent per year. "Security and development" were the bywords of the military regime, a motto taken from the Brazilian war college. "Growth was a way of legitimizing the power structure which was already under criticism," said Torquato Jardim of the Instituto de

Estudos Políticos in Brazília. "It gave the middle class the illusion that everything was OK because they could buy a lot." Income distribution, however, worsened in this period.

Remarkably, Brazil's merchandise trade account stayed roughly in balance as both imports and exports grew rapidly. Imports more than tripled, but the ratio of foreign-exchange reserves to imports actually rose—from 14 percent in 1968 to 104 percent in 1973. Foreign credit was clearly fueling domestic expansion. The "excess" reserves were "high-powered money"—like an inflow of gold—that permitted an exponential increase in domestic lending. So much money was coming in from 1971 to 1973 that at times the central bank required borrowers to redeposit 40 percent of their loan proceeds with the central bank in order to control the multiplier in the domestic money supply as borrowed dollars were converted into cruzeiros.

Nevertheless, the government did nothing to discourage borrowing. According to Joau Certa, who was with the central bank in those years, "The important thing was to have money coming in. There was no fixed policy to assign priority to certain sectors. Sectors were all competing for money. It was a rather chaotic process." As economist Monica Baer concluded in an exhaustive study of the internationalization of Brazilian finance, "Throughout this period ... policy supported the process of growing foreign indebtedness, in as much as the inflow of foreign capital and the consequent buildup in reserves were understood as [proof of] the successful performance of the development strategy that had been adopted."[26]

In 1973 the Banco Central do Brazil issued a manifesto titled "The External Sector and National Economic Development"—a lengthy defense of the rapid increase in Brazil's external debt. Heavy foreign borrowing, the central bank argued, hastened economic development, raised the level of domestic savings above where it would be with less borrowing, and in fact made the country less rather than more vulnerable to foreign shocks even from the foreign debt market. A Harvard Business School professor and OECD debt consultant later commented, "The 54-page pamphlet provides abundant data profiling export growth and external debt management, including projections over a 25-year period. . . . It may well be less important for its specific arguments than for what it says to lenders about the country's economic managers: they know what they want, they know what they are doing, and they are in control."[27]

As the numbers attest, no developing country had greater success in winning the credit market's confidence. In the period 1970 to 1978 Brazil absorbed roughly 15 percent of all Euromarket loans destined for developing countries and by 1978 accounted for 8 percent of total reported Euromarket lending. Among developing countries only Mexico loomed as large in the commercial credit market.[28] Even in 1983 Citibank's chief spokesman on Third World lending insisted, "The Brazilians have an absolutely fabulous record of managing their international financial situation. We have a great deal of confidence in them. We don't feel unduly exposed."[29]

The first OPEC oil-price shock did not cause Brazil to alter its development strategy. It merely increased Brazil's need for foreign credit, which now had to finance both continued rapid industrialization and an oil-import bill that went from $654 million in 1973 to $2.7 billion by 1975. "We said, from an economic point of view, it is correct for Brazil to borrow rather than adjust," said Carlos Lemgruber. "The interest rate [on foreign loans] was negative, and there was a positive real return on money here." He admitted that "Brazil forgot about the risk of floating-rate interest. There was an implicit assumption that the cost of funds was fixed."

Marcílio Marques Moreira, a banker who became Brazil's ambassador to the United States and an important player in the perennial debt negotiations, then economy minister in the Collor government, called the decision to "borrow through the crisis" "one of the milestones of Brazil's formidable development process. It was a bold attempt—which, basically, proved successful—to simultaneously meet two crises head on: the epidemic crisis of the oil shock with its dire consequences—world recession and sharp deterioration of terms of trade—and the endemic crisis of underdevelopment—unbalanced growth led by durable consumer goods, by a fragile and limited industrial plant, weakness in the production of basic input and capital goods, dependence on energy from abroad, and a general lack of productivity and competitiveness."[30]

The Brazilian central bank required foreign loans to have a minimum maturity of seven years. But beginning in 1976 borrowers were allowed to deposit proceeds of Resolution 63 or Law 4131 borrowings with the central bank, which would pay the going cruzeiro interest rate and carry the exchange risk. Fernao Bracher, São Paulo banker and also for a time Brazil's debt-restructuring negotiator, called this reverse maturity transformation "one of the most intelligent inventions" because it reconciled the government's macroeconomic goal of securing long-term financing with the commercial needs of borrowers who might only want a one- or two-year loan. The provision was a stimulus to continual foreign borrowing, guaranteeing a steady inflow of foreign exchange. But it also decoupled the level of foreign borrowing from domestic economic trends—from private-sector credit demand and rates of investment. Although GNP growth dropped to a modest (by Brazilian standards) 5 to 6 percent in 1977 to 1979 from the previous heady 9 to 10 percent growth, Brazil's foreign debt continued to expand at a rate of 23 percent per year.[31]

FOREIGN LOANS AND DEVELOPMENT

The massive credit inflow from abroad had a profound effect on the pattern of economic development in borrowing countries. Mexico's deputy minister Suarez Davila defended Mexico's debt policy by pointing out "Since 1970 we probably doubled or tripled our industrial plant, and this was in large part due to the borrowing." The same can be said of other debtors. Brazil transformed itself from a country earning 70 percent of its export revenue from one commodity, coffee, into a major producer and exporter of a multiplicity of industrial goods including steel, pulp, aluminum, petrochemicals, cement, glass, armaments and aircraft, and of processed foodstuffs like orange juice and soybean meal. Rio de Janeiro and São Paulo have new subway systems, railroads have been built to take ore from huge mines deep in the interior to new ports on the coast, and major cities are linked by a modern telecommunications network. Not everyone spent the money well. In Buenos Aires, the average office secretary might have as many as a dozen rotary-dial telephones on the desk in lieu of a digital exchange. When large Argentine businesses in desperation began stringing their own phone wires from office building to office building, the public phone company took revenge on this usurpation of its power and sent vigilantes to cut down the wires. President Carlos Menem's decision in 1990 to target the phone company as one of the first state enterprises to be privatized understandably enjoyed wide public support.

But even defenders of Brazil's more productive financing strategy like Marques Moreira have admitted, "We made some mistakes. We thought demand would grow at 7 percent forever and all investment was planned on that assumption." And he agreed many of the projects were and are fantastically expensive—"conspicuous investment," he called it. The massive capital inflow enabled the government to make domestic credit available at interest rates below the rate of inflation to benefit both private and state firms. The World Bank estimated that in 1979, credit subsidies were equal to about 10 percent of GDP. Cheap credit, in turn, stimulated inflation which hit 100 percent in 1980.

The energy sector is a case in point. Between 1974 and 1986 Brazil invested $48 billion in electric power and raised installed hydroelectric-power-generating capacity from 18 gigawatts (one gigawatt equals 1 billion watts) to 45 gigawatts. The daily power generation of Brazil's largest project, Itaipu Dam, equals the power generated by 600,000 barrels of oil.[32] But Itaipu cost more than $14 billion to build, and associated interest costs may be as much as $2 billion per year. Furthermore, the dam was built on a river bordering Paraguay, which insisted that half the generators run on the fifty cycles used there rather than the sixty cycles employed in Brazil. Paraguay has no use for this electricity, and Brazil, which does, spends another $1 billion per year converting power from Paraguay's half of the dam for use in Brazilian homes and factories. "Maybe it cost three times more than it should," said a foreign banker about Itaipu. "But at least it's there, not like Argentina."

Brazil successfully raised its domestic oil production from 15 percent to 65 percent of liquid-fuel consumption. But most of this oil comes from deep underwater wells that produce some of the highest-cost oil in the world. Ninety percent of new cars on the road are manufactured domestically and run on a gasoline fuel mixed with alcohol produced from Brazilian sugar cane. The gasohol mix is priced lower than regular gasoline to encourage use. The subsidy expense to the government has been roundly criticized by the World Bank, particularly when oil prices fell below $20 per barrel. Worse, perhaps, subsidized cane production, which requires quality land, is replacing primary food crops in Brazil's most fertile agriculture areas. Finally, the eight-plant nuclear power program undertaken with Germany's assistance has yet to produce any energy.

Instead of passing on the high cost of this massive investment to energy consumers, the Brazilian government allowed the real price of electricity to fall steeply. The real average price of electricity for industrial use in 1986 was at least 15 percent lower than in 1974 and for home use had fallen by more than half. Consequently, the rate of return on investments in this sector fell from 11.4 percent in 1976 to only 4.2 percent by 1985. A sector that in 1975 had been able to cover 60 percent of its total financial requirements from revenues could cover only 30 percent of expenses from its own earnings a decade later. The gap was covered by foreign borrowing. The electrical sector owes more than $22 billion abroad, about one-fifth of Brazil's total foreign debt.[33]

Brazil's energy sector is by no means unique in Latin America or other heavily indebted countries. The easy availability of foreign loans, year after year, obviated the need to maintain a rational relationship between costs and rates of return on major investments. State enterprises could be assigned missions other than simply producing X or Y at the lowest cost. They became instruments of broad social and economic policy, often vehicles for subsidizing certain groups or sectors. This, as much as corruption and bureaucratization, is at the root of the "inefficiencies" of many state enterprises.

DEBT AND GROWTH OF THE STATE

The other structural consequence of heavy borrowing may be less obvious but is equally profound. That was the enlarged role of the state in the economy.

The authors of an independently commissioned 1975 U.S. Senate Foreign Relations Committee study of the response to multinational corporations in Mexico and Brazil concluded:

Ownership of privately held production is being fundamentally altered in Mexico and Brazil. The rapid MNC penetration has resulted in a marked decline in the share of the national market held by private host country entrepreneurs.... As a partial reaction to this situation, governments have emerged as the primary countervailing force to the MNCs. Both the Mexican and Brazilian governments have increasingly relied on state-owned enterprise.... Government-run enterprise has come to represent the national parry to the foreign thrust.[34]

In many developing countries, governments were either ideologically disinclined or too weak to challenge the indigenous, entrenched economic powers—family-dominated industrial-bank *grupos* in Mexico, landed aristocracy, protected coffee barons in Brazil, meat and grain barons in Argentina, sugar interests in the Philippines. So the state became a surrogate for private enterprise that could drive modernization without challenging these entrenched interests—indeed, would continue to protect them—and without turning the country completely over to foreign interests. The state enterprises, along with the military, also performed a vital social function of providing a channel through which the lower classes could rise to middle-class status. (Hence even reform-minded new democratic governments, whose core power base is the middle class, have found it difficult to reduce the public-sector payroll.) Finally, the state and its multiple enterprises provided indirect subsidies to the large, unenfranchised classes by providing basic goods and services at below-market prices.

The Brazilian government in the 1970s was a "typical military administration—give one general one sector to run," as an American working for Fuji Bank in São Paulo put it. There were 12,000 reserve officers in government and private-sector jobs. These so-called amphibians—military officers turned civilian but still tied to the military—controlled the most im-

portant state enterprises and projects, including Petrobrás, Eletrobrás, Informatics (computers and telecommunications), and
the Itaipu Dam project. At the same time, Brazil's active military
was happy with the massive investment in industrial capacity and
technology that enabled the country to produce sophisticated
guns, tanks, and aircraft—in factories also controlled by the military. As one Brazilian businessman commented, "Fortunately,
our generals prefer to export arms rather than import them."

In Argentina the military's holding company, Fabricaciones
Militares, played a key role in the Argentine economy. "No
one really knows what businesses they are in," said a private
Argentine banker. "Steel, chemicals, mining, munitions, even
a whore house, everything. The military have a monopoly on
mineral extraction. Hence we have no mineral extraction."
The military also decided that petrochemicals were a "national security" item and barred private investment in that
sector. And unlike the Brazilian military, Argentina's forces
liked to import. Perhaps $8 billion of Argentina's $40 billion
debt was used to purchase Exocet missiles, six frigates at $600
million each, and other sophisticated arms. An estimated 85
percent of German bank lending to Argentina was tied to the
purchase of arms, including three submarines. Asked about the
submarine loans, a German banker in Frankfurt giggled ner-
vously and said, "So you know about that! It's a sensitive issue."

In Mexico the ruling Institutional Revolutionary Party (PRI)
stalwarts, rather than the military, controlled the state enterprises (which grew in number from 39 in 1970 to 677 in
1982).[35] In either case, the power structure meant that no mere
economic technocrat who thought the borrowing excessive
could say no. With the creation of a separate Ministry for
Programs and Planning in Mexico in 1976, the spenders ruled
the roost. The new ministry set spending plans and approved
all budgets, while responsibility for raising revenue continued to reside in the Ministry of Finance. Not surprisingly, the
minister of programs and planning became the second most

powerful political figure after the president. Carlos Salinas headed the planning ministry before becoming president, as had Miguel de la Madrid before him. In theory, Mexico's Congress approved all spending and borrowing, but the executive had authority to exceed the budget projections without legislative approval. (In 1984 the General Law of Public Debt was amended to require that Congress be informed within forty-five days of the end of each quarter of changes in the level of public debt.)

This explosion of state enterprises, many of them unprofitable (in an accounting sense, if not to the participants), could not have been financed with the meager and inept taxation prevalent in developing countries. A more efficient tax-collecting effort would have threatened the existing power structure. The state's growth was instead financed, without political pain, through foreign commercial bank loans. As Stanford University political scientist Jeff Frieden wrote, "In the pursuit of local control over local investment, the state has taken over; yet, paradoxically, this state involvement in the economy has been based on borrowing from foreign banks."[36]

In Argentina foreign debt was the last stage of an economic model of import substitution and "state-assisted capitalism" that was already worn out when the borrowing began, said Juan Sourrouille, minister of finance in the mid-1980s. "The economy was not generating a strong expansion and economic surpluses to finance the government. So the government took loans."

Luis Rubio, director of the Center for Development Research in Mexico City, wrote that in Mexico,

The government's refusal to liberalize and its simultaneous appeasement of the political tensions that surfaced in 1968 led to even greater government participation in the economy. . . . The government of Luis Echeverria Alvarez (1970–76) opted for increased government spending to attain the twin objectives of augmenting the size of the market while satisfying the needs of those groups that believed they had not benefited from economic growth. Increased government spending, financed by inflation and foreign indebtedness, would eventually lead to the disaster of 1982.[37]

"Historical reasons plus the relatively small size of domestic economies thus favored those who advocated that the state have a major role in industrialization," argues Wall Street banker and former minister Pedro-Pablo Kuczynski. "It was not, however, until international bank lending started to soar in the 1970s that governments obtained the resources to dramatically expand state enterprise."[38]

The state role in borrowing and investing fed on itself: central governments borrowed because they wanted to make investments but also because in their various guises they were the most acceptable "names" in foreign capital markets. "The argument that private companies are better than a government never held here at Morgan," said Alfred Vinton, the bank's general manager in London. "You don't lend to companies unless you know their commerce, the industry, intimately. Thus we had little private-sector exposure in Mexico." Banks wanted sovereign debt—not unknown, unrated private companies—and this gave the state the resources to dominate the economy. Nacional Financiera (NAFINSA) was the Mexican government's investment bank and principal instrument for channeling resources to sectors it wished to support. By 1976 NAFINSA was Mexico's second-largest debtor, holding one-third of Mexican public external debt and surpassed only by Pemex.[39] In Brazil, NAFINSA's counterpart, BNDES, was one of the top three borrowers, along with Eletrobrás and Petrobrás, according to Isac Zagury, BNDES's director of international affairs.

"Since all these banks were knocking at our door and the money was cheap, 'higher authorities' decided going into debt wasn't that bad," said Jaime Pellicier, assistant to the now legendary Angel Gurria, director of Mexico's Office of Public Credit and eventually the country's chief debt negotiator. The level of government spending became a function of how much foreign credit was available. "We tried to match the level of spending with the level of savings—external and internal," said Pellicier. By 1978, 43 percent of the Mexican government's budget deficit was being financed by foreign borrowing, and 86.6 percent of the financing for *parastatals* (state-owned enterprises) came from abroad![40] "The Mexican central government," said one Mexican academic, "acted like a holding company for state enterprises." And the holding company received most of its financing from foreign banks.

From 1970 to 1980 Latin America's private-sector foreign debt grew fourfold, but sovereign foreign debt grew eightfold.[41] The public sector's share of total investment rose steadily. The average public-sector share of gross domestic investment in twelve Latin American countries climbed from 32 percent in 1970 to 50 percent in 1982.[42] Chile was the exception in this group. There the leading businesspeople of the post-Allende period—known popularly as the "piranhas"—used foreign loans to finance the purchase of state enterprises privatized by Pinochet's cadre of "Chicago school" economic advisors. This did not save the government from the debt crisis, however. When a 1979 maxi-devaluation threatened to put these investors into bankruptcy, foreign banks bullied the Chilean government into assuming their unguaranteed foreign debts.

Governments became the biggest users of instruments intended to encourage foreign financing of the private sector. Marques Moreira notes the end-users of Resolution 63 loans by Brazilian banks were at first mostly private companies, but then state companies began taking a bigger and bigger share. "So foreign private banks lent to private Brazilian banks who lent to public companies." U.S. bank reports to the U.S. Treasury Department on their foreign lending for 1982 showed a Brazilian exposure of roughly one-third private nonbank sector, one-third banks, and one-third public sector. But the public sector was probably the ultimate borrower in most of these transactions. A World Bank study shows that 75 percent of all foreign currency loans contracted by foreign lenders under Brazil's Resolution 63 and Law 4131 had been absorbed by the public sector and by state enterprises.[43]

In 1976 Mexico had signed an IMF stabilization agreement that limited public-sector borrowing abroad. To sidestep the limit the government pushed private Mexican banks to borrow abroad on its behalf. The loans could then be shown as internal government debt, although the government's repayment obligation was in U.S. dollars. "The federal government borrowed from private banks, encouraged them to keep borrowing abroad," said Jaime Pellicier. "It was a very informal process. The credit office did it over the phone—'Please pass $20 million to such and such agency'—when it was short. Documentation might follow three days later."

At a dinner party in New York during the Falklands War, a member of Citibank's board of outside directors vehemently denied that banks had anything to worry about in Argentina. "Al Costanzo [head of the bank's international division] has assured the board that all our loans are guaranteed by the government." "Which government?" came the response from fellow diners. "Why, . . . ours, I assume," said the director, suddenly looking pale.

MANAGING THE BORROWING BINGE

Sovereign borrowers attempted to exercise a modicum of order and centralized control over the public sector's dealings with the international credit markets. The Brazilian central bank set guidelines for the maturities and spreads at which various state entities could borrow and established a *queue*—the order in which entities would enter the market. The latter was less to prevent overborrowing than to avoid overloading the market at any given time and risk driving up the cost of borrowing for the country. As a rule, only one state enterprise could be in the syndicated market at a time. "Club loans" could, however, be done outside the queue. Club loans, as Robert Barbour of American Express of São Paolo explained, are "when you [the lead bank] don't send out telexes. You just call some banks and say, 'Do you want in on this deal?'"

According to Pellicier of Mexico's Office of Public Credit, "We arranged the queue according to the state of the market, sending in a 'sexy lady' like Pemex or the Banco de Obra (construction finance) first to assure a positive response. If we were really unsure, we would send a small entity for a small credit, $50 million or so to test conditions, then a big state enterprise to follow. Sometimes we would try to push an obscure entity to get it known in the market. We would rearrange the queue according to the market response.

"The smallest government entities would not be sent into the market. Larger agencies would borrow on their behalf. Pemex sometimes would be sent in to borrow for a state enterprise that couldn't go to the market but had room in its budget for more funds. The public banks were constantly borrowing, sometimes beyond their own immediate needs."

Lending banks, says Pellicier, rarely asked what the money was for: "The sexiest lady was the central government itself, which would go in when necessary. But that was usually because it had a special project—for example, to get matching funds for the World Bank."[44]

In Argentina, said Maximo Flugelman of the national development bank, a state enterprise waiting in the queue "got the green light from the central bank. 'Your window to the market is October 1 to 12.'" The borrower would then inform major banks in New York, London, and Tokyo about this borrowing window through their local representatives and ask them to form as many groups of offering banks as they saw fit. Potential lead managers would be asked to provide a term sheet of offers. "It was a case of getting the best possible deal from whomever was willing to lend."

In Brazil once the central bank approved the proposed borrowing, state enterprises were free to select a lead bank or "give the mandate" and to negotiate bank fees and commissions and tax arrangements. The large state enterprises or projects that were constantly in need of financing developed close relations with individual banks: Petrobrás with Chase and Bank of America, Siderbras (steel) with Manufacturers Hanover, and so on. Citibank had a lock on Minas Gerais and together with Morgan managed much of the financing for Itaipu. According to Barbour, the "inside bank" would win the mandate to lead a syndication 90 percent of the time.

Zagury says BNDES borrowed from about 100 foreign banks, with Chase and Commerzbank usually acting as lead agents: "The amount borrowed was decided by the total needs of BNDES plus the central bank's need for foreign exchange. We tell the banks, 'This is for general funding purposes,' but they know what projects we are financing. Sometimes a country had a special interest in a specific project—for example, Japan in the Carajas mining project. Then we would get Japanese bank loans."

THE "VIRTUOUS CIRCLE" BROKEN

A classic theory of economic development holds that an underdeveloped economy should import capital and use the surplus savings of developed countries to finance internal investment. Investments financed with foreign money eventually generate sufficient income to repay foreign investors with interest, raise local living standards, and finance further development.

Marques Moreira sees 1979 as a turning point, when both the purpose and management of foreign borrowing changed, when the "virtuous circle"—the positive relationship between capital inflows and development that classic economic development theory posits—broke down. World Bank data show a positive correlation between investment rates and foreign borrowing for Latin America until 1978. Foreign savings supplemented rising domestic savings and the rate of investment increased. After 1978, however, foreign savings increasingly substituted for declining domestic savings, and total investment as a percentage of GNP fell.[45]

Statistical analyses of the balance of payments of debtor countries by the Federal Reserve Board staff also support Marques Moreira's thesis. They show that from 1973 to 1978 trade deficits plus the build-up of reserve assets had accounted for 40 percent of the foreign debt Brazil accumulated. But between 1979 and 1982 a decline in reserves more than covers the country's trade deficit. *All* of the foreign exchange brought into the country through Brazil's post-1978 borrowing was used to cover debt servicing and a small implied capital outflow. The figures for Mexico are roughly the same: 38 percent of its pre-1979 borrowing is accounted for by trade deficits and reserve accumulation; post-1978 virtually all of the borrowing finances debt servicing and—in Mexico's case—substantial capital flight.[46]

Foreign borrowing may, of course, serve several purposes simultaneously, and balance-of-payments data present an incomplete picture. The Mexican government, for example, borrowed dollars to finance payments on its foreign debt and to cover large domestic operating budget deficits. That is some of the borrowed dollars served as reserves against which the central bank could create pesos which the government used to pay its domestic bills. Meanwhile, Mexican citizens who had decided to move domestic savings out of the country (capital flight) could cash in *their* pesos and buy the dollars brought into the country by the government's borrowing, to send abroad. Balance-of-payment data misses this intermediate step and only shows a foreign capital inflow offsetting a debt-servicing and capital flight outflow. The cycle is discussed more fully in chapter 6.

In 1979 external economic conditions turned against heavily indebted developing countries. Oil prices spiked sharply, then fell; nonoil commodity prices weakened; world interest rates soared in response to tight money policy in the United States; and the industrial economies went into recession. These adverse conditions first caused debt-servicing costs to soar and then led public confidence to plunge in the heavily indebted countries. The trade effects were offset by falling imports. Latin America's merchandise trade deficit in 1981 was less than $3 billion, about the same as it was in 1978. But the gap in services payments widened from − $15 billion in 1978 to − $41 billion in 1981. Thus interest payments (and in the case of Argentina and Venezuela, foreign travel) accounted for almost all of the deterioration in current accounts.[47] The drop in public confidence in these countries manifested itself in the form of accelerating capital flight which became endemic for countries like Mexico and Argentina. (Capital flight shows up not on the current account but on the capital account. It is usually defined as "errors and omissions"—that is, any otherwise unexplainable difference between the accumulation of debt and the deficit on payments for goods and services.)

The initial response of most debtor governments was to try to bull their way through as they had during the 1974 oil-price shock, to maintain rapid growth and levels of imports, and to cover foreign-exchange needs by borrowing still more. Argentina and Brazil went into deep recession in 1981, but their borrowing needs continued to escalate. The markets were still receptive, in part because the new flood of OPEC deposits in 1979 to 1980 (and deregulation in Japan, which allowed its banks to do more foreign lending) had expanded the universe of banks eager to do "petrodollar recycling."

The tenor of debt management changed. The purpose of the queue was no longer to keep order, hold down borrowing costs, and control the maturity profile. Its function now was to send out as many state entities as the market would accept and to borrow as much as possible regardless of terms or the individual borrower's budgetary needs. Spreading loans among many government entities, explained Marques Moreira, also made it easier for already heavily exposed foreign banks to circumvent the legal limits their regulators put on the amount that could be lent to a single borrower.[48]

Mario Brodersohn, speaking as president of Argentina's Banco de Desarollo, the state development bank (he later became chief debt negotiator), said, "There was a massive capital outflow at the end of 1980 which the government tried to cover by borrowing more, by encouraging state companies to borrow.... We were requested to have our creditor banks disburse more than we needed. We deposited [the money] with the central bank and then later drew what we actually needed for our projects."

In 1980 there were monthly Euromarket syndications for Brazilian state entities. According to Brazilian economist Paulo Nogueira Batista, Jr.,

After 1979 state enterprises were forced to borrow even though they had no investment. They just handed over the proceeds to the central bank. They were out borrowing on the basis of false projects the government knew would not be done. Or they were only half real.

We also accepted sort of countertrade deals with French, British, European banks that involved imports we didn't need.

That is, Brazil would ask for $2.5 billion in loans and those countries would make us take $1 billion in imports from them as condition for the loans.

It is my impression the big banks knew why it was happening, that it was a short-term solution to avoid a crisis until the world economy recovered.

It was a time to "send out the sexy ladies" or the "big animals," as the state enterprises most favored by the banks were sometimes called. Brazil's Petrobrás, said Robert Barbour of American Express International, took trade credits from banks and said it was to pay for oil. "But it already had suppliers' credits for those oil imports. It funneled the money to the central bank which used it to fund its short-term cash deficit." Mexico's Pemex, according to New York Federal Reserve estimates, borrowed at least three times more than it needed for its own investments. In 1981 a $2.5 billion, 180-day acceptance facility managed by Bank of America was raised to $4 billion. (The facility was oversubscribed.)[49] YPF, Argentina's state oil company, increased its debt by 33 percent from 1980 to 1981 without a corresponding increase in investment and with its oil production actually declining.

At the same time the government raised domestic interest rates to force the private companies to go abroad for credit. Brazil began requiring private companies to secure 360-day foreign financing for their imports, even though foreign suppliers normally gave only 180-day credits. "This means we have to take out a 180-day loan to cover the rest of the period, though we've paid the exporter, and deposit the proceeds with the central bank," said SAAB Brazil's Håkan Frisk. SAAB's money, of course, but not its debt, showed up in Brazil's official reserve data.

Central banks provided exchange-rate guarantees to steer banks and companies fearful of a devaluation away from the foreign credit markets. Such guarantees gave a borrower taking on dollar debt the right to buy back dollars needed for debt servicing from the central bank at the rate prevailing when the loan was taken. Argentine economist Arturo O'Connell estimates that by 1984, and several maxidevaluations later, making good on these guarantees was costing the Argentine government approximately 1 percent of GNP per year.

In 1979, before the oil-price rise, Chile had enacted its own "Resolution 63" and authorized Chilean banks to borrow abroad to finance domestic loans. Until then, Chilean banks had been under strict limits on the medium-term foreign obligations they could assume. But the Pinochet government's anti-inflation program depended heavily on reducing tariffs and increasing imports that had to be financed. The foreign exchange brought in by the banks under Law 1196 provided the necessary reserves and created a brief boom in the Chilean economy, which grew 8 to 10 percent. The private sector did most of Chile's foreign borrowing, using some of the proceeds to buy up privatized state companies. Alejandro Foxley, finance minister in the Alwyn government, stated in 1990 that the Pinochet regime's sales of public enterprises were "not transparent" and often were made to people with "inside information" who reaped huge capital gains.[50] Pinochet called a presidential referendum to extend his term in 1980 in the middle of the boom. "This is no doubt why he got a majority," says a foreign banker who was there at the time. "Pinochet is not a fool."

Under the new regulation borrowers were assured foreign exchange from the Chilean central bank when the loan matured. "With high domestic interest rates and a fixed exchange rate, arbitrage obviously became very attractive," said Riccardo Angles, who ran Citibank's Santiago operation. It made economic sense to use foreign-currency loans to make domestic-currency purchases. "There were even personal 1196 loans. People used foreign bank loans to buy a house, for example," said Angles. "We didn't do that kind of lending, but other banks did. And when the exchange rate changed, they couldn't pay." As in Mexico, the inevitable crisis forced even this right-wing, market-oriented government to intervene directly in the private banking system. Pinochet's tough new finance minister, Rolf Luders, at first suggested that only depositors, and not the foreign banks that had lent to failed Chilean banks, would be paid. Private companies and individuals who had borrowed directly from the banks also would be allowed to default. Luders was dissuaded when the foreign banks threatened to block any restructuring of the nation's debt.

As payment pressures on the borrowing countries mounted, attempts to control the maturity profile of external debt went out the window. Increasingly wary bankers thought they could protect themselves by shortening the maturities in their loans. By 1982 half of Mexico's foreign bank debt had a maturity of less than one year.[51] And the U.S. Federal Reserve was dismayed to find that Brazilian banks were using their access to overnight Federal funds and other short-term interbank borrowings abroad to finance Brazil's growing payments deficit. By 1982 "Banco do Brazil, not Citibank, was Brazil's biggest foreign creditor," said Nogueira Batista. Brazilian banks had short-term interbank credits of more than $9 billion being continuously rolled over until banks stopped lending in 1982. In December 1982 the inability of Brazilian banks to cover their open positions at the end of the day almost caused the international dollar-payment system (Clearing House International Payment System, or CHIPS) to fail.[52] Nogueira Batista estimated that if trade credits are included, Brazil might have been relying on as much as $25 billion in short-term credit to finance long-term deficits.

Mexico's Pellicier summed up the final pre-crisis frenzy: "In 1981 there was a real surge. We needed a lot of new funds to support the exchange rate and cover the capital-flight outflow. By the end of the year people were queuing to buy dollars, to put them abroad. It was a political decision not to impose exchange controls. We [the office of public credit] couldn't do anything. It was our job to keep borrowing."

A FATAL POLL

Paul Volcker likes to tell the story of how certain finance ministry officials warned Mexican president Lopez Portillo at the beginning of 1981 that the government would have to modify its plans and slow expansion because foreign banks would not be willing to supply the credit that would be needed to pay for all the development programs. Some months later when foreign banks showed no signs of cutting back the flow of credit, Lopez Portillo fired the technocrats for being excessively gloomy.

Mr. Volcker may not have known that in late 1980 the Mexican government had polled the community of foreign banks about their lending intentions for the coming year—perhaps to help settle the internal debate. The foreign banking representatives, fearing that the government was about to put a lid on borrowing and would use the polling results as a basis on which to ration mandates, greatly inflated their lending projections. One midsize New York bank projected a fivefold increase in its lending to Mexico from year end 1980 to year end 1981, just to assure itself of enough headroom for the lending it actually wanted to do. The local representative said, "Every bank did the same, showed the maximum possible lending. Everyone showed the same companies on the list of potential borrowers so there was a lot of double counting. But it was credible given the country's inflationary boom." The central bank's poll consequently gave a misleading picture of the foreign lenders' plans and provided a strong justification for prolonging the government's and the country's spending binge. Mexico borrowed almost $20 billion from foreign commercial banks in 1981—twice as much as in the previous year.

Altogether, between mid-1978 and mid-1982, Mexico tripled its obligations to foreign banks, Brazil doubled its bank debt, and Argentina's and Chile's foreign bank debts increased nearly fivefold.[53] But on August 13, 1982, in the words of one old U.S. Treasury hand, the Mexican finance minister Jesus Silva Herzog "showed up on our doorstep and turned his pockets inside out" and brought the lending frenzy to an abrupt halt. Mexico and Brazil owed foreign banks around $70 billion each; Argentina and Venezuela owed at least $30 billion each; Chile and the Philippines owed more than $10 billion; and Nigeria, $7 billion. Poland, which had experienced payment difficulties several years earlier, owed more than $14 billion. Altogether, developing countries and Eastern Europe owed foreign commercial banks nearly $500 billion.[54] Most of the debt was, or would soon become, sovereign debt.

4

Winning the Mandate

Banks compete on credit risk, not the cost of manufactured widgets. Costs are the same for all of us. Markets determine the cost of our products, so when banks compete, it's by taking greater credit risk. That is how you take market share away from the other fellow.
—CEO of a British clearing bank, London, 1987

Perhaps the new era of international lending was doomed from the first syndicated loan. It was too easy, and the borrower's appetites were insatiable. Each year's syndicated loan income had to be duplicated and increased by double digit percentages in the next annual budget. As more banks joined the competition, the margins steadily decreased and thereby multiplied the volume necessary to meet the budgeted earnings increases and targets for generous incentive compensation bonuses.
—John G. Medlin, Jr., president and CEO of
First Wachovia Corporation, 27 April 1987

THE BATTLESHIP STRATEGY

Bill Ford is a former president of the Federal Reserve Bank of Atlanta who later served a stint in the savings and loan industry. Ford has ample experience with financial disasters·

in-the-making, having served as chief economist of Wells Fargo Bank during that California bank's foray into international lending. Banks in those days, says Ford, were "monetary drug-pushers." He rates his own bank's participation in a $300 million Eurosyndication for Pemex to build a new headquarters in Mexico City as one example of economically unjustifiable lending. "I had a feeling of seeing things go awry but having little power to influence."

As chief economist, Ford was responsible for assessing country risk. Like most banks, Wells had a formula for rating countries according to numerical weightings of risk factors— including the borrower's outstanding debt, trade balance, gross domestic product, current account, political stability, and so on. Banks conducted the exercise partly to satisfy shareholders and investors that cross-border lending risks could be precisely calculated and partly to satisfy bank regulators whose examination of the "safety and soundness" of a bank includes an assessment of its internal controls and risk-management techniques.

Ford eventually convinced his bank to throw out the complex country-risk computer calculations: the data input was always suspect, and economists never did agree on how much debt a country could safely take on. The debt-servicing ratio was a common measure of creditworthiness. A borrower whose annual debt-servicing costs did not exceed 20 percent or so of exports was said to be a good risk. This ratio was of doubtful validity as a predictive tool when the debt carried a variable interest rate, however. As debtors discovered in 1979 the numerator (interest costs) can change dramatically almost overnight. And a sharp change in the price of a country's exports, such as oil, will change the denominator just as swiftly. The late Henry Wallich, the most distinguished economist to serve on the Federal Reserve board of governors in recent years, argued that the country-risk assessments by banks overemphasized export growth. "Debt," he argued, "is financed out of a country's whole income—its GNP and not just exports." The goal of good debt management should be to stabilize the ratio of debt to total productive capacity. Borrowing should grow in parallel with growth in the economy, he said, adding that in the late 1970s borrowing was moving at a pace that was not sustainable.

Ford proposed an alternative method for setting the limits on how much Wells Fargo should lend to any country. A U.S. Navy submariner during the Korean War, he dubbed it the "battleship strategy." The operative principle was to compare Wells's exposure in a given country, measured as a percentage of bank capital, with that of its larger competitors. If, for example, Bank of America's exposure to Brazil was equal to 90 or 100 percent of capital and Citibank's exposure was 110 percent, Morgan's 100 percent, and so on, Wells should hold its exposure to around 60 percent so that "when the torpedos start coming, the big battleships take the first hits." Wells, Ford reasoned, "which is just a tug boat in this business, should hug the shore." Ford's boss, a Peruvian who headed Wells's international lending, at first thought it was too simple but sold the board, "and that is pretty much what the bank did."

Ford's risk formula, of course, had little or nothing to do with a country's ability to pay. (And the exposure-to-capital ratios used as guidelines were way out of line with the U.S. regulatory domestic bank lending limit of no more than 10 percent of capital to any one borrower.) But it was brilliant strategy. When the debt torpedos began to fly in 1982, governments in the major creditor countries rushed to save those large battleships that surely would sink or be badly crippled if they took the full hit. And in the process, they saved Wells, too. Wells Fargo used the time that government rescue efforts bought for Citibank, Chase, Bank of America, Manufacturers Hanover, Lloyds Bank, Midland, and the other vulnerable behemoths to gradually absorb the losses and shed virtually its entire troubled Third World portfolio—indeed, to shed most of its foreign business. Wells became one of the more profitable regional banks in the United States, and its stock has traded at a substantially higher price-per-earnings ratio than the stock of banks still heavily laden with dubious foreign loans.

EUROMARKET ALCHEMY: THE TRANSFORMATION OF RISK

Evaluating risk, as Walter Wriston, chairman of Citicorp through the international lending boom, said in his 1986 book, *Risk and Other Four-Letter Words*, "is what bankers get paid for," adding baldly, "Events of the past dozen years would seem to suggest that we have been doing our job reasonably well."[1] It is unlikely that his successor, John Reed, assaying the mass of problem loans left him by his predecessor, would fully endorse this statement.

Any bank loan carries risks, the most basic being credit risk—the possibility that a borrower will be unwilling or unable to pay. In a time of volatile interest rates, there is also interest-rate risk—the danger that the rate a bank pays for deposits or other funds will rise faster than the rate it earns on loans. Market risk is the possibility that the credit markets will suddenly turn against a borrower and shut off its flow of credit, creating a cash-flow or liquidity crisis for a debtor dependent on that flow to manage its affairs and service its debts. Lending across national borders entails additional risks: currency risk—the risk that the value of a loan denominated in one currency will fall relative to the currency in which the loan is funded or the currency in which a bank reports its earnings; and transfer risk—an inability to transfer earnings from one country, and perhaps one currency, to another.

The market in international loans in the 1970s seemed structured to protect the banks on all counts. Bankers dismissed the credit risk involved, pointing out that losses on foreign loans had been far lower than on domestic loans. "Where Citibank loses money is down the street, down at 42nd Street in the railroad," Jack Clark once told the Senate Banking Committee, "and where we don't lose money is in Brazil."[2] The bankers conveniently forgot that they had avoided losses on loans to Indonesia and Turkey and Zaire only through repeated reschedulings. A survey of international bankers by the Group of Thirty in early 1982 found that a majority of respondents expected "no significant change" or a "modest increase" in riskiness of international lending to the end of 1986.[3]

"Interest-rate risk," said Leland Prussia, vice chairman and former head of international lending for Bank of America, "was considered much more important [in international lending] than credit risk. The record on that was very good; there had been few losses in the post–World War II period. In that part of the portfolio there were no problems; that was the area to do business in. We didn't anticipate a world economic downturn." Interest-rate risk was a worry because international lending involved a substantial maturity gap. After the oil-price shock the principal source of funding for sovereign loans was the wholesale Eurocurrency money market, where depositors include other banks and large corporations, laying off excess cash or working capital to earn a few fractions of a percentage point of interest until more permanent use is found for the money. Deposits in this market typically range from overnight to a maximum of six months. A bank that is making five- to seven-year loans with this short-term money must constantly refinance the loan at current market rates and runs the risk that funding costs will rise sharply sometime during the life of the loan.

Banks solved the interest-risk problem with a technique that has now become routine in domestic lending—the variable or floating-rate loan. The introduction of the floating-rate system was "as crucial to international lending as the invention of the steam engine was to the industrial revolution," said Brazilian banker Fernão Bracher. Floating rates made it possible to reconcile the sovereign borrowers' need for long maturities with the banks' need to adjust interest income to short-term fluctuations in interest costs.

Floating-rate loans may have medium to long maturities, but interest charges are adjusted every three to six months to reflect current market rates. The interest charge has a two-part structure—a floating base that is reset periodically according to some agreed benchmark and a fixed spread or margin over the base. The benchmark that determines the floating-base rate in the Euromarket is the London interbank offered rate (LIBOR)—the rate banks charge each other for short-term deposits. In domestic lending the base is prime—the rate banks charge their best customers—or some treasury bill rate. Theoretically, the base rate reflects overall supply and demand for credit in the market, and the spread reflects the market's judgment of the borrower's creditworthiness.

Variable or floating-rate loans effectively shift most interest-rate risk from the lender to the borrower. Changes in the market where, say, Morgan buys its funds for a loan to Brazil, becomes Brazil's problem, not the bank's: Morgan's profit on loans to Brazil remains constant, roughly represented by the spread, whether interest rates rise or fall. (Since banks normally roll over funding for Euromarket loans between interest resets, the bank retains some interest risk.)

International loans were made in the currency in which they were funded—mostly Eurodollars, U.S. dollars moving among accounts outside the United States proper. Since borrowers owed the banks the same currency the banks owed their depositors, there was no currency risk to the lender. The borrower, whether the government or a private company, assumed the exchange-rate risk vis-à-vis the local currency in which its income—tax revenues or local profits—was denominated.

Transfer risk would loom only if the market turned against

borrowers and shut off the supply of hard currency. This market risk seemed negligible. In the 1970s everyone was eager to lend. Chuck Coltman of Philadelphia National admits there was some concern in 1977 to 1978. OPEC deposits were slowing to a trickle as the oil countries' spending caught up with their income, and the market was beginning to feel slightly pressed from the constant demand for credit from developing countries. A number of countries, including Turkey, Peru, and Zaire, were experiencing debt-service difficulties. In March 1977 David Rockefeller, chairman of Chase, warned, "Bank debt to a number of these countries has been expanding at a rate that should not—and cannot—be sustained."

"The 1979 oil shock," said Coltman, "saved us all. It widened margins and brought the last players in." The second sharp rise in oil prices in a decade restored the flow of petrodollar deposits into the banking system and produced another recession in the industrial countries. Some large U.S. banks slowed their lending but a new cadre of bankers joined the recycling game. Mellon Bank, for example, known then as "the Morgan of the Midwest" for its conservative banking practices, joined the fray for the first time in a big way as the steel industry, mainstay of the Pittsburgh economy, collapsed around it. Many other banks from the Midwest joined for the same reason. And Japanese banks, freed for the first time from tight ministry of finance limits on foreign activities and seeking to escape the tightly structured, government-guided domestic market, became aggressive lenders. So debtor countries that had grown totally dependent on new loans to service their old debts were assured an ample supply of credit a while longer. From late 1977 to mid-1982 commercial bank loans to non-OPEC developing countries nearly tripled.[4]

Federal Reserve governor Wallich's father had been a senior officer of Deutsche Bank and helped develop the Latin American market early in this century. The senior Wallich taught his son to always ask a borrower two questions: "What is the money for?"

and "Where is the repayment to come from?" When the answer to the first question comes back "debt servicing" and to the second "more loans," he warned, you have a problem. But modern bankers like Wriston argued that just like IBM or the U.S. government, Brazil should not be expected to repay its debts. Maturing debts would simply be replaced by new loans.

In March 1982 a senior economist at Morgan Guaranty was asked whether he was worried about Mexico. Oil prices were showing signs of weakening, and capital flight was said to be on the increase. The economist answered thoughtfully, "No, I don't think Mexico's need for financing will exceed the market's willingness to lend." At some point in the 1970s both sides decided that "creditworthiness" was a function of "the market's willingness to lend" and not the borrower's ability to pay. And "the market," it was generally assumed, would always be willing to lend.

Fernão Bracher, who served in a senior capacity in the Brazilian central bank in both the military government and the democratic administration of José Sarney, said of the attitude before the crisis, "It was clear to all that this was a medium-to long-term arrangement, that Brazil would continue to borrow and that the market would supply the money for debt servicing. Brazil didn't pay a penny out of its own pocket until 1982. The money was always provided by the market. Everyone assumed this would continue." As long as banks gave every sign of wanting to lend, borrowing governments saw little reason to restrain their spending.

Conversely, the rising demand for loans from developing countries prompted some banks to continuously exceed or raise their internal country lending limits. Lending limits became quotas to be filled and, if possible, exceed. Comerica Bank of Detroit was one of the regional banks caught in the Mexican moratorium. Vice president Richard Turner argued that some of the bank's international business was related to local strategy, serving Detroit clients, but was also "an exercise worth doing on its own." The bank, Turner said, placed a "special premium" on country-risk analysis and did its own. "If we waited for the money center banks to tell us things, we would be totally out of it." In the early 1980s the bank had started rating countries on a scale of A to F as it had rated domestic corporations for years. Rating countries, said Turner, was "tricky."

He was proud of having stayed out of Poland but admitted the bank didn't see trouble coming in Mexico and Venezuela, where it had substantial exposure. Growth in its international business was flat in 1978 and 1979 because the bank had liquidity limitations so that its lending was restrained by a funding shortfall. But in 1981 and 1982 the bank was once again liquid, and domestic loan demand was low. Comerica Bank's international business surged 40 percent in 1981 and again in 1982. "Syndications, club deals became available to us that hadn't been before." In 1982 the bank met its international growth projection for the calendar year by June. "We just kept going," said Turner, still cheerful in March 1983.

Not every second-tier bank was seduced by the new opportunities that became available as big lenders grew more cautious and the big debtors became more desperate for funds. Pittsburg National Bank was also a regional bank with strong international connections and substantial exposure in Brazil and Mexico when the debt crisis began. But the Pittsburgh bank read the tea leaves somewhat differently than Comerica Bank in 1981, according to the man then in charge of Third World loans, Jerry Alfano: "We knew Mexico was in trouble when we began to get opportunities which had been closed before. At Alfa, for example, suddenly the welcome mat was out. Alfa came to us. We said no; they were too willing to pay whatever we suggested." But, said Alfano, Alfa, which subsequently became Mexico's largest corporate bankruptcy ever, was able to do business "up to the day things closed down. Non-U.S. banks were still willing to take that risk."

In the end, of course, banks hadn't eliminated risk; they had merely disguised it. Paul Volcker's tight-money policy in the period 1979 to 1982 drove dollar interest rates worldwide into double digits, and if the banks at first did not see serious trouble ahead, the people of Mexico and Argentina and Venezuela did. They began shipping money out of their countries faster than the banks were putting it in (with both flows going through the banks). And in 1982 market risk reared its ugly head: the banks cut off countries that were now totally dependent on steadily larger infusions of credit to service their increasingly expensive loans. Suddenly these borrowers were unable to carry the interest-rate risk foisted on them by that wonderful invention, the floating-rate loan. And now there was credit risk: dozens of sovereign borrowers were unable to pay.

SALESMEN IN CHARGE

One says "banks do this and do that." But like all large institutions banks are composed of parts, subdivisions, and communities of interest that do not always view the world with the same eyes and do not measure success and failure by the same yardstick. The basic division at any commercial bank (until the dread Wall Street disease "suspender syndrome" struck and they began trying to transform themselves into investment banks) is between the liability side, the people who worry about funding the bank and therefore worry about its credit standing in the world, and the asset side, the officers who make the loans—and in their view, make money for the bank. But as retired Citibank chief George Moore argues in *The Banker's Life*, there is, overall, a matter of the philosophy that drives management on both sides of the balance sheet, the emphasis on risk taking versus prudence: "A banker has to be both a salesman and an analyst. If you let the credit

men, the analysts, run the bank, you won't have any customers; if you let the salesmen run the bank, you go bankrupt."[5]
In the 1970s the salesmen were in charge of international
banking.

"Wriston, Clausen, Deutsche Bank, and Lloyds after 1973
decided on recycling," charges an officer of Security Pacific.
"We had lots of visitors trying to make Security Pacific gear
up for more activity. They wanted us to co-manage loans. The
money salesmen in banks, who were not bankers, were so
successful that they began to decide bank policy. The wrong
people were making decisions by 1979. . . . Loan syndicating
groups producing all that income all those years came to wag
the dog. Anyone arguing caution was out or aside." As Peter
Walter, a German bank regulator formerly with the Bundesbank, recalled, "You went into a bank and had your reserva-
tions about sovereign lending. Management would say, 'It's
good business, and everyone thinks so. Everyone is doing it.' "

A senior international lending officer for Deutsche Bank
recalled, "There was always a dispute between the domestic
and the international side of the bank. The domestic side
argues that the real basis for going abroad is domestic savings
deposits and so on. But in the 1970s we could show how much
we could make on our big deals. The domestic side was
blamed for creating excessive, costly networks of people and
branches and computers. The international people were the
bright people, making big profits with just a few offices."

Peter Palmieri was vice chairman and head of the international division of Irving Trust before the bank was taken over
by the Bank of New York. Losses on the bank's $2 billion
foreign-loan portfolio were among the factors leading to the
takeover. As Palmieri admitted, "In the exuberance of the
moment, we lost sight of some of the basics of banking—that
is, portfolio diversification." Irving was known for the strength
of its correspondent banking relations around the world.
"Our international lending was deposit driven. We had all

this money coming in from foreign banks. They said, 'Hey, you have to lend some back if we are going to keep doing business.' "

Somewhat belatedly, in March 1982 a committee of bank supervisors from major creditor countries that had begun to meet under the auspices of the BIS in Basle issued an encyclical on "country risk analysis and country exposure measurement and control." It stated that "it is important that banks maintain a correct division of responsibility by separating the marketing function from the limit-setting function."[6] This separation did not exist in most banks at the time.

Country-risk teams typically reported to the lending officers. The latter did not always want to hear what the former had to say. In late 1977 or early 1978 Wells Fargo's credit committee conducted a routine review of a large loan to Iran. The loan was assessed on both political and economic grounds. The Hungarian economist in charge of political risk summarized his conclusion in one sentence: "The Shah is finished!" The week before, the same man had recommended against further lending to Poland. The Hungarian was fired, following a not-so-gentle reminder to the head of the risk group that the lending officer paid the salaries around there. The senior international economist at a New York money center recalls having his cautionary note about further lending to Brazil brusquely dismissed by the country-lending officer: "Don't tell me about risk. The spread is too good!"

An economist at the Frankfurt head office described Dresdner's risk-review system: "Our rating procedure was a combination of statistics, subjective views, and the 'brass knuckles interests' of Dresdner Bank. I would say this [the debt crisis] is the first time the bank has paid any attention to our views."

The drive to lend to Latin America swept all caution aside, explained a risk analyst at Security Pacific. "For two and a half years, Argentina was run by a chorus girl and a mystic on the mountain. When the generals took over, all the bankers, including here, were euphoric. 'Now, now everything is going to be OK, great. Let's lend!' They just forgot that the straight historic trend in Argentina was just craziness, one period after another. But they wouldn't hear of this argument."

There were in practice at least three layers of corporate culture at work in international bank lending—field representatives based in the borrowing countries, loan syndicators usually based in London or New York, and lending officers (and their subordinate country-risk analysts) at the home office.

Officers in the field run the banks' foreign branches and subsidiaries and "representative offices." The type of presence reflects bank strategy (Citibank opened branches wherever it could, whereas Chase acquired existing banks),[7] the relative importance of a particular country to the bank in question, or, just as often, the restrictiveness of local laws. Virtually every country in the world limits foreign participation in its financial sector, and since the 1950s the countries of Latin America have done so more than most. Only one foreign bank, Citibank, has full banking privileges in Mexico, for example. Most developing countries restrict foreign-bank branching and limit foreign participation to minority ownership of local financial institutions. Foreign-currency–based lending activity has therefore to be conducted mostly through representative offices that may range from a permanent staff of dozens of people to a single visiting fireman from the home office.

In the lending heyday, there were more than 150 foreign-bank "rep offices" in Mexico City. The king of bank reps was Bank of America's venerable José "Pepe" Carral, the only Mexican national to represent an American bank. "Pepe was the star of Bank of America, and there was a rumor he was going to be named ambassador to the United States. Banks believed it because he was so tight with the government," said Larry Rout, who covered Mexico for the *Wall Street Journal*. "Pepe and Bank of America set the pace, acted as liaison between foreign banks and the Mexican government." "Pepe Carral did a superb job in the growth environment," agreed Bank of America's Prussia. When it was over, B of A had the largest loan exposure to Mexico of any foreign bank.

Carral, retired in the late 1980s, defended his bank's level of lending: "Until 1981 we never had a major problem—maybe seven charge-offs in as many years, but all recovered 100 percent. By 1981 we were virgin—zero losses. So when people say, 'You overdid it—you went overboard for a better spread'—it's not so. We knew Mexico was a good risk. After fifteen years in paradise we said there will be no problems here. Wealth was created without oil, in one generation." Oil, he thinks, distorted the economy. Mexico undertook too many giant projects at once. "We wanted to be like Europe overnight. We weren't going to be like the Arabs, buying real estate and putting our money in Swiss bank accounts." If market conditions had remained stable, Carral argues, Mexico's economy would have remained on course.

Carral's boosterism not withstanding, those in the home office were often more enthusiastic than the field reps. A Citibank officer in Chile recalled the bank's director of country risk, Irving Friedman (a former World Bank and IMF official), coming to Santiago in 1981 or 1982:

I had a lending limit of $500 million. He said, "You can go to $1 billion, no problem." Thank God, we didn't! In fact, we started to reduce our exposure six to nine months before the restructuring. We did it by overpricing our offers, knowing someone else would be pleased to take that business away from Citibank. It was just a difference of a quarter or an eighth of a percent.

When you see the flow of money out of a country start to accelerate, you know something is wrong. Chileans started coming to me: "I have to go to the U.S. Whom do I see about opening an account?" That was part of our decision to cut our exposure 20 percent. If I had reduced it another 10 percent, I would have been comfortable.

MANAGING THE RISKS

The credit authority enjoyed by officers in the field varied widely from bank to bank. Lloyds Bank had 880 people in Argentina alone and only five people in the whole Latin American division in London. There was no credit committee. "Country limits were set by the Lloyds group board. So long as there was no problem, the group was willing to raise the limits annually," said E. Michael Hunter, an international officer for the bank. Individual officers had their own credit limits and could say yea or nay within those limits.

At Chase Manhattan Alfredo Salazar, the bank's man in Buenos Aires, explained in 1984, "The country manager was the basic unit. . . . The country-risk committee set a maximum level of exposure. But the country manager proposes the limit." Salazar noted that Citibank had a similarly decentralized operation. On the other hand, a representative for a German bank said, "We are just a marketing office. We have no loan officers, no final say on whether a loan gets done or not. All decisions are made in Frankfurt. I negotiate on behalf of Frankfurt." He described his marketing activities as "knocking on doors shopping around for public-sector loans." The Latin American region head for Bankers Trust, based in Miami, said, "I have no credit authority and wish to have none. The local rep offices report to me, and I report to New York. . . . Rep offices are a marketing tool and an information tool." John Donnelly, Manufacturers Hanover's representative in Mexico, had to submit all loans to New York for approval.

Bill Young, who became general manager of Bank of America's Latin American operation (except Mexico, which was run out of domestic headquarters in San Francisco) in 1981, was based in Coral Gables, Florida. He concluded that centralized loan decisions were a mistake: "We used to approve transactions at a very high level and that got us into trouble. . . . We tended to approve transaction by transaction. We lost sight of the overall picture."

Officers in the field, however knowledgeable, were rarely asked to make a rigorous assessment of specific loans or the overall level of lending to the country. Daniel Alberto Casal was a young officer at Argentina's Banco de la Nacion who dealt with foreign banks during the lending heyday. "Before 1982 foreign banks never looked at the asset-liability structure [of borrowers]. They lent on size, prestige—on the name. In June 1984 I asked a New York banker why they didn't ask countries for data. He said, 'You can't do that to a sovereign country.'

"When we made a syndicate borrowing, we prepared some figures, but a financial analyst never looked through the numbers. In 1979 we wanted to borrow. We said, 'What do you need to know of our projects?' 'No, we don't mind what you use the money for as long as the spread is right,' said a Japanese banker eager to get in on the loan.

"Banks were anxious to participate because they had high credit limits and some managers had trouble filling their quota. 'Please let me know next time you go to the market' was the attitude."

Jaime Pellicier served in Mexico's Office of Public Credit for most of the 1970s and 1980s. He recalls that disappointed bank suitors who did not win one mandate were easily steered to another: "Bank number four calls and says, 'Hey, we didn't win that deal. We still have room on the line.' We say, 'OK, go with Pemex on X project.' "

A Canadian banker with a lifetime of experience in Argentina explained, "You had Johnny-come-latelys who wanted to catch up with Manny Hanny in fifty days. The central bank had sharp guys who knew how to milk the market's demand for assets. If you asked too much, you lost your place in the lending queue. If you asked what the money was for, you lost your deal. Take the one-eighth spread and be happy."

The pressure on local reps not to lose a deal sometimes came from the bank's domestic interests. "All our business is linked to Swedish trade or multinationals," said Stig Dale, the PK Bank's representative in São Paulo. "We were involved in state enterprise projects which involved purchases from Swedish companies—for example, electrical equipment for Itaipu Dam. The loans were not legally linked to the project, but there would be a gentleman's agreement. We don't sign until they sign the purchase order from the Swedish companies."

A Mexican economist who served in a senior financial post in the presidency of Lopez Portillo agreed that the combined interests of foreign banks and their foreign corporate clients made the loan push even greater. "I tried to fight the exchange rate and rate of borrowing but to no avail. There was plenty of money and plenty of bankers. Borrowing was easy. They compressed spreads to historical levels. And many firms outside Mexico were interested in sustaining the boom because the boom meant big sales."

"We were pursuing a policy of supporting German exports and our bond issuers," explained an officer of Dresdner Bank. "We were not interested in balance-of-payments lending, though we did participate in the Golden Seventies—reluctantly. In Mexico we had to make balance-of-payments loans to the government to protect our lead management position for Nafinsa and Banobras [a public works agency] bond issues. And we had to make working capital loans to private companies to protect commercial relations." He added, "[Domestic] branch managers loved that kind of loan because it meant a profit stream on the balance sheet from the exporting company relationship." (German banks, like Japanese banks, are major shareholders in industry.)

The Deutsche Bank officer was embarrassed to discuss his bank's submarine loans to Argentina, only a small portion of which carried a German government export-financing guarantee: "It was a classic case of the exporters pushing us into lending. The firms argue, 'Here is a big sale. If you don't make the loans, we will lose the deal to U.S. or other competitors. It means a lot of jobs, etc., etc.' There was big pressure. So we made the loans."

But even the most conservative banks got caught up in a frenzy of sovereign-risk lending for its own sake. Deutsche Bank had branches in São Paulo, Buenos Aires, and Asunción and representatives in Santiago, Caracas, Bogotá, and Mexico City. "When Deutsche Bank was founded in the 1880s, the purpose was to help exports, to do international business. We started with supporting German businesses abroad. But in the roaring Eurobusiness years, there was a decoupling. It meant competing for mandates and losing if we didn't participate in certain loans. In 1977 to 1981 we did balance-of-payments financing rather than project lending."

The size and price of loans were not decided by the local rep but set elsewhere. Local reps had some input into those decisions, but, said the Latin American region head from Bankers Trust, "Those decisions get made in smoky New York meetings, drinking wine, bantering Harvard-Yale style—including the country reps. They lose sight of reality when they get to New York."

An international officer of Deutsche Bank was "the syndication manager for many big deals—Itaipu, Morocco, Mexico.... Now I enjoy the fascination of rescheduling some of the loans I helped syndicate." Luxembourg, where he served, was the "execution side" with no credit responsibility. Credit decisions were always taken at the head office in Frankfurt, even if they were within the country lending limit. Under German law each credit decision has to be approved by management. "We had country ratings that were shown to the board. But it was not too difficult to get the limit raised, say, for Mexico in 1980."

A former Mexican representative for Dresdner Bank said he reported "loan opportunities to the group head office in Frankfurt which would give the OK then decide if the loan should be done by the subsidiary in Luxembourg or home office or where." The funding-booking subsidiaries could act independently. "If one got a call from Chase to participate in a syndicate, it could say yes on its own hook. There was no country or regional limit, only regional 'aims.' " Now, he adds, there are centralized decisions: "The crisis accelerated the process of centralization."

American Express Bank International had $80 million in interbank placements in Brazil. But, said Robert Barbour, the Rio de Janeiro and São Paulo representative, "The deals were done by the Frankfurt treasury [of American Express Bank] with Brazilian banks in Germany and London. The Brazil desk didn't even know. We just woke up one day and found $80 million."

THE LUCRATIVE MANDATE

In most cases, the local representatives' primary function was not to exercise credit judgment but "to develop relations and to keep an ear out for lending opportunities." That is, they were to court the top officials of the major state enterprises and other government agencies that were potential borrowers and alert the home office when the next "big animal" planned to go to market—preferably before the competition got wind of it. The objective was not just to get a piece of the next loan: mere participations in a loan were usually taken in New York or London or other money centers, often after just a phone call or two with a colleague at another bank. A young officer with Fuji Bank in São Paulo recalled his own experience in London. "In the old days, there would be a telex: 'You have until Thursday to tell us how much of this loan you want.'" Such transactions might not involve the field officers at all.

The field officer's job was to "win the mandate"—the right for the bank to lead or co-manage a loan syndication and hence claim the bulk of the lucrative management fees the borrower paid in addition to interest on the loan. Hundreds of banks often competed for the nod from the same cluster of state corporations and borrowing agencies. A former field representative for Chemical Bank recalls, "You could sit in the Pemex waiting room with representatives from five or six banks who had all been given the same appointment time. We trooped in one after another to bid for the mandate for the next borrowing."

The lead bank or banks that win "the mandate" organize the syndicate and agree to raise a specific amount on specific terms, much as investment banks underwrite a securities issue. Or they may commit only to "best efforts." An oversubscribed loan may be increased. One manager is designated the agent responsible for collecting the payments from the borrower and distributing them to participating banks and receives an additional fee. (Syndication agreements bind all members to share equally on a pro rata basis any interest payment received from the debtor over the life of the loan.) The lead banks decide what other banks to bring in as co-managing underwriters or as providers of funds. The management group usually commits to make the bulk of the loan—and collects the management and commitment fees—

then sells down 30 to 40 percent to smaller banks in the market.

Regional banks rarely if ever got the mandate to lead a sovereign-loan syndication, but their willingness to take whatever exposure the large banks did not want to keep was crucial to the whole lending cycle. The lead banks, having made room on the balance sheet through the sell down, could then take on the next mandate. It was not a hard sell. "Back when banks were honest," said Barbour, "banks used to put together information memos for the syndicate. But as the pace of lending picked up, the practice stopped. It was not necessary, to get banks to participate." Only twenty-five banks knew what they were doing," said Allan Delf of First Chicago in London. "The others just jumped in and pushed down the price." Alfred M. Vinton, general manager of Morgan's London operation, agreed: "It was easy. There were lots of mediocre people on the rise, making the decisions. Other banks, sheep-like, followed the lead of what they think are prestige institutions. . . . If you knew the number of British banks who tell us they went into the syndicated market in the 1970s because Citi or Morgan led the deal!"

By 1982 at least 600 banks around the globe had taken part in the less-developed-country lending binge. In retrospect, the narrow spreads on balance-of-payments loans—Mexico paid as little as 0.6 percent over LIBOR in 1981, and Korea paid 0.52 percent over—seem inadequate compensation for the risk. But when compared to other lending opportunities, the attraction for smaller banks is understandable. "In a syndication," said Morgan's Vinton, "you send out 400 telexes, get 200 replies, draft the documents, and that's it." A bank in Michigan or Tennessee could put an exotic multimillion-dollar sovereign loan on its books with little more expense than a trans-Atlantic phone call or a few telexes, whereas a mundane car loan or a collateralized credit to a farmer or a construction loan to a small local company of a few paltry thousands involved many hours of labor and other overhead expense.

When smaller banks withdrew en masse from international lending in the 1980s, the lucrative international-loan-syndication market—and attendant fees—all but dried up, much as Wall Street's junk-bond-syndication business disappeared when savings and loan institutions that served as the dumping ground for high-risk securities became insolvent.

The structure of sovereign loans—interest rates, fees, maturities, grace periods after which amortization would begin—was the responsibility of the loan-syndication teams located at the head office or, more likely, in one of the international money centers like London or New York, where most petrodollars flowed and where banks gather and lay off their Eurocurrency deposits. The syndicator's expertise lay not in assessing the quality of the borrower but in reading the mood of the market and packaging and marketing a loan to suit that mood. If the market was receptive, as it was for most of the 1970s and early 1980s, the lead banks kept most of the fees for themselves. If the market showed some resistance to the loan, the fee pool might be used to sweeten the pot a little, with early commitment fees or special participation fees going to a large number of participating banks. The borrower could be charged a larger fee so there would be more to go around.

Brazil began experiencing political unrest and an economic downturn after the second oil shock, and banks became somewhat more reluctant to lend. Perhaps they were sated with Brazilian paper. (Brazil's net foreign debt had increased by more than 400 percent between 1974 and 1978.) Unlike Mexico, Brazil refused to shorten the maturity of its borrowings—except indirectly, through the interbank market—and therefore had to pay more. Between 1979 and 1981 the typical spread on a Brazilian state-guaranteed borrowing for eight years rose from 0.88 to 2.13 percent, and the fees increased from 1.2 to 1.9 percent of the principal amount of the loan.

Sometimes higher fees, which were confidential, were a sub-
stitute for higher spreads, which were almost always public.
For example, Nigeria's front-end fees rose from 2.75 percent
in 1980 to as much as 7 percent in 1983 while its spread
stayed around 0.88 percent.[8] Of course, when high fees were
a risk premium substituting for higher interest rates, only
banks sharing in the fees were being compensated for the
added risk of lending to a shaky borrower.

The syndicator's job was to do the deal, top the league book,
and get the tightest terms for the borrower. "The syndicators
were the high flyers in the business," said a Canadian banker.
"It was 'See you at the signing' and 'On to the next deal.' "
There was a certain machismo involved in ramming a half-
billion-dollar syndication through on fine terms, according to
the Canadian. "When the market resisted a syndication led
by my bank in late '81 or early '82 for BNDES, it was a pricing
problem. . . . People in headquarters thought they would play
tough, narrowed the price, and went for a ten-year maturity,
just to show it could be done. By mid-'82, the line among the
syndicators was 'Let's break that Brazil logjam!' "

Lending officers who bid aggressively and won new mandates, quarter after quarter, could amass quick profits for their
banks. Management fees could mostly be taken right down to
the bottom line as income for the quarter in which the deal
was closed.[9] A Bank of England study of fees and spreads
concluded, "For the credits that are drawn down, it is the
management and participation fees which . . . represent most
of the up-front return to the banks on their lending."[10] In the
1970s banks competed to be in the top ten on the "league
tables" published by magazines like *Euromoney*, ranking banks
by the number of Euromarket syndications they had led in a
given period. The ranking was not just a matter of prestige
but a reflection of profitability. An unpublished discussion
paper by the Federal Reserve Board staff found that front-
end fees accounted for almost 20 percent of the banks' an-

nual average return on sovereign loans syndicated from 1981 to 1983. In a year like 1978, when announced Euromarket loan syndications totaled $65 billion (60 percent to non-OECD borrowers), the leading international banks may have shared fees in the neighborhood of $650 million, in addition to their interest earnings and tax benefits for the year.[11]

A former senior officer with the Brazilian central banks commented that foreign bankers "had a one-year horizon. Come fall, they would look where their earnings were coming from, then decide to increase exposure where profitability would be the highest. A senior vice president tours, makes a judgment—then comes the pressure to increase returns."

A Canadian banker with many years experience in São Paulo who does not wish to be identified said, "I thought already in 1976 to 1977 this thing could not go on. I even said so to Bracher, at the central bank. He said 'Why not?' " When asked if he had also given this view to the home office, the Canadian responded emphatically, "No, I wanted to keep my job!" His bank had more than $1 billion in loans to Brazil when the crisis hit.

"We've learned that the lag in government statistics can be a serious problem," said an American bank representative heading a two-professional, two-clerical staff office in Mexico City. "In 1981 we'd be looking at end-1980 figures. We might sense that there was a lot of short-term lending but no sense of the huge rise." That year, his bank doubled its exposure in Mexico "from a low base. Mexico was eager to borrow at acceptable spreads and short term—six months. We didn't care very much which public entity we loaned to. Most were guaranteed by the central government. We couldn't imagine the government would not recognize its debt obligations." Nevertheless, the bank began to block renewal of short-term loans in spring 1982.

As John Donnelly of Manny Hanny in Mexico City concluded: "The problem was we weren't talking to our colleagues. If we had known in 1981 what was being lent, we would have done something. The government would ask us for $100 million for six months. We would say, 'They have no problem paying that in six months.' But they were asking twenty other banks at the same time.

"A lot of analysis was based on government budget borrowing projections. In 1981 the government budget showed $5 billion. We knew they were doing more, but we had no idea it was $18 billion."

Alfred Vinton, who for many years headed Morgan Guaranty in London, admitted the biggest management failure of the banks was their "unwillingness to ask tough questions and demand current information about reserves, the nature of a country's debt, etc. That was probably most critical. There was soft-headed management on both sides." And he added, "Banks that did ask tough questions were so big they couldn't get out. It was the 'stop the world I want to get off' syndrome."

In late 1981 and 1982, Mexico turned to the capital markets for financing. It went in first with Nafinsa and with Banobras, a public works agency. "It started with the acceptance credit market [a trade-financing mechanism]. Then in early 1982 we got the exclusive mandate to lead manage a bond issue," said an investment banker. "We took it. We had only co-led previous issues. We thought Mexico could pull back from the brink."

The bond issues "sold like hot cakes," according to an investment banker involved in the deal. "Mexico did three or four issues from January to April. They did very well for the managers. Mexico had no choice. Its last bank jumbo had collapsed so it had to pay a premium, accept fixed rates when interest rates were at their peak. But the market was hot. Others were paying 15 to 15.5 percent. Mexico paid 17 percent."

Resistance to a Bank of America–led jumbo loan was the first clear signal that the market was growing wary of Mexico. A February devaluation to slow imports may have increased the nervousness. When banks renewed credits, they did so for shorter and shorter terms. Mexico added $12 billion in short-term debt in the six months before the crisis broke.

Bankers were familiar with Mexico's policy cycles. In the first three years of a president's single six-year term, reforms and even austerity are possible. But the second half of a *sexenio* was invariably devoted to ensuring an overwhelming election victory for the next PRI candidate through increased public spending. Bankers apparently thought they could ride out the last stage of Lopez Portillo's term in office. Dr. Rinaldo Pecchioli, chief banking specialist for the OECD in Paris, remembered a meeting in Vienna in April 1982: "Bankers told me we all know Mexico will blow up, but not until February 1983 when the new government comes in. We are all preparing for that. A build-up of short-term loans had begun. In June I told a meeting of government officials here what they had said. They all said yes. But no one expected it in August-September."

CONGRESS WHISTLES IN THE WIND

To the end, home governments of the lending banks did nothing to stop or even slow the flood of credit. L. William Seidman, chairman of the Federal Deposit Insurance Corporation (FDIC), served on the White House economic staff in the Ford administration. He recalls an economic policy discussion there in 1975 or 1976 in which the question of petrodollar recycling came up. Everyone sang the banks' praises, Seidman says, including William Simon, then secretary of treasury, and Alan Greenspan, then chairman of the President's Council of Economic Advisors. The only dissent came from Arthur Burns, chairman of the Federal Reserve Board. "This isn't recycling," he grumbled. "It's bad loans." But even Burns's Fed did nothing to stop the lending.

The policy objective in both Ford's Republican administration and in Carter's Democratic administration was to keep the "recycling process" going. Banks were getting the oil deposits, so let them lend. When in 1977 there were indications some banks were having second thoughts and might pull back, the major industrial countries had cobbled together a $10 billion "Supplementary Finance Facility" for the IMF. Assistant secretary of treasury Anthony Solomon admitted in testimony to the Senate Foreign Relations Committee that the facility was modest in relation to the huge OPEC-related balance-of-payments disequilibria Treasury was predicting would continue indefinitely. Banks, Treasury assumed, would have to continue to finance 65 to 75 percent of the deficits. "It is not a substitute for bank credit and will not take over the banks' regular lending activities. . . . In fact, the facility is expected to encourage banks to continue to expand their foreign lending rather than cut back, by promoting sound economic policies on the part of borrowers."[12]

The late Senator Jacob Javits of New York challenged Treasury's conclusion that the economic condition of borrowing countries was sustainable, noting that the department's rosy scenario

fails completely to take account of contingencies—an increase in the price of OPEC oil, particular pressure in particular places because of political situations in those places, the burden of debt becoming so great compared to developmental needs—that is, Brazil—that situation which looked very good in credit terms may not look so good at a given time and the fact that if anything gives in the world, whether it is another Herstatt Bank or Franklin National, it is likely to bring the whole thing down with it.[13]

Senator Frank Church pointed to an American Express Bank International study showing that by 1981 one-half of the new loans being taken by developing countries would be used for debt servicing: "If they are borrowing this heavily just to repay old loans, how can they be investing in ways that expand their economies sufficiently to solve their problems? They are just borrowing their way deeper and deeper in debt." The Treasury official adamantly assured the subcommittee, "In my view, there is absolutely no prospect of a debt rescheduling in regard to Mexico or Brazil. And I would not want to leave any impression that there is."[14]

World Bank president Robert McNamara in his 1978 presidential address called for more funds to restore "a better balance" but also said "it is neither surprising nor undesirable that private lending accelerated."

Bank regulators also took a benign view of the lending activity. The Bundesbank occasionally sounded a cautionary note about "overrecycling" but did nothing to discourage German banks from participating. Of course, it had no way to know exactly how much they were doing. "We had branches and domestic figures, but not numbers on the subsidiaries," said Peter Walter, director responsible for banks in the Frankfurt region. "In fall 1982 we got to see numbers from the subsidiaries and learned the great bulk of these loans had been made by subsidiaries. This was the development that forced us to make a restructuring of the Banking Act." German banks were able to leverage prudential ratios like liquidity requirements and limits on large loans to a single borrower because a large part of their foreign exposure was not included in the calculations. The revised 1985 law among other things requires banks to report all activities on a consolidated worldwide basis—a proposal the banks had fiercely resisted.

Large banks in the United States were not held to a minimum capital-adequacy standard during the 1970s. The capital-to-asset ratio of the money-center banks slid steadily—to below 4 percent by the early 1980s—as these banks rapidly built up their foreign assets and liabilities without issuing more stock. The ever-larger loan book meant ever-larger dividends per share, even if many of the loans carried narrow interest margins (and high risk). The steady stream of foreign earnings disguised a progressive erosion of the competitive position of large American banks in their home market, where commercial paper and other sources of direct finance were displacing commercial banks as the principal financing source for leading corporations. Nonbanks like General Electric, General Motors, and Sears added to the erosion by setting up their own financing facilities—first for customer-related transactions and later as competitors to banks for commercial loans.

Bank regulators should have worried about the "moral hazard" of banks having ever less of their own (stockholders') money at risk relative to other people's money (deposits) at risk in foreign loans. But in March 1980 chairman of the Federal Reserve Paul Volcker could say, "The impression I get from the data I have reviewed is that the recycling process has not yet pushed exposure of either borrowers or lenders to an unsustainable point in the aggregate." Even as Volcker spoke, his anti-inflation policy (drastic but probably essential from a U.S. standpoint) was driving world dollar interest rates toward levels that would quickly bring the system to that unsustainable point.[15] When it was reached, two years later, Manufacturers Hanover's combined loan exposure in Brazil, Mexico, and Argentina was 190 percent of capital, Citibank's exposure in the three countries was 145 percent of capital, and Chase Manhattan's was 118 percent.

During the 1970s and early 1980s neither supply nor demand put any constraints on the flow of international bank credit to capital-hungry sovereigns, and neither did the finance ministers or central banks or the regulators. And the last important factor, price, that might have slowed the pace of lending—might have deterred either borrowers or lenders from going overboard—instead sent misleading signals to both sides. For the price factor was seriously distorted by the hidden tax bonanza.

5

The Hidden Tax Bonanza

The taxation—by both their own and borrowers' tax authorities—of the interest due to banks on their international assets can mean that the quoted spread on a loan may not be an accurate measure of either the cost to the borrower or the return to the lending banks.
—I. D. Bond, "The Syndicated Credits Markets,"
Bank of England Discussion Paper 22 (1985)

The tax credit issue is for the big New York banks. They've gotten a little spoiled over the years and think the world owes them a living.
—Charles Zwick, chair, Southeast Bancorp

The tax loophole was just there to be used. Get an ambitious manager here in the early 1970s—he sees the rate of return with the tax bonus and says "I'll be a king! I'll be a hero! Let's just bop up the portfolio."
—An American banker in São Paulo, Brazil, 1984

In May 1989 the Internal Revenue Service issued a tax ruling that brought howls of protest from several large American banks with heavy exposure in less developed countries (LDCs). The ruling concerned the allocation of losses on foreign loans, and unhappy bankers claimed the new rules would discourage them from participating in the so-called Brady Plan for reducing the debt burden of developing countries. Historically, U.S. tax rules had treated foreign and domestic income as two separate pools, and losses on foreign loans could be deducted only against foreign income. But since the 1986 Tax Act treated profits from *sales* of foreign loans as domestic income, a number of large banks decided that *losses* on foreign loans could also be taken against domestic income. The May ruling, retroactive to December 1986, said not quite. Losses on LDC loans would have to be allocated against both foreign and domestic income, according to the balance of foreign and domestic loans in a bank's portfolio.[1] Under the IRS formula, banks with mounting foreign loan losses might have insufficient foreign-source income to absorb all possible deductions. Worse, the IRS ruling threatened to retroactively wipe out billions in other tax benefits on Third World loans that banks had already claimed. To bankers, it seemed that once again the left hand of Treasury, the IRS, was sabotaging what the right hand of Treasury, Secretary Brady et al., was trying to do about the debt problem.

THE TREASURY GIVETH AND TAKETH AWAY

Back in the Reagan administration, in 1984, before U.S. Treasury secretary Don Regan changed places with White House chief of staff James Baker, the Treasury Department had proposed a radical reform of the nation's tax system that, in significantly modified form, became the Tax Reform Act of 1986. Among the loopholes Treasury originally proposed to close was one of critical importance to the overall profitability of U.S. banks' overseas lending. Treasury sought to curtail—sharply—the creditability of foreign taxes against U.S. corporate income tax.

Large banks with substantial loan exposure to Latin America would be among the biggest losers: foreign tax credits had provided a direct subsidy by the United States (and by the United Kingdom and Japan and other banking centers) of heavy commercial lending to Brazil, Mexico, Argentina, and many other developing countries during the 1970s. The excess tax credits generated by loans to these countries had been used by the lending banks to reduce taxes significantly on other overseas income, enabling them to earn a far higher post-tax rate of return on their global operations than would otherwise have been possible. Tax credits, in short, were one of the principal attractions of massive lending by banks to developing countries.

Before 1986, according to Marsha Fields of the U.S. Treasury Department's Office of Tax Analysis, "Banks [paid] almost no tax in the United States on foreign or domestic source income." In 1985, when the U.S. federal corporate income tax rate was 46 percent, Citicorp paid U.S. federal income tax of $30 million on pretax income of $1,716,000,000—an effective rate of 1.8 percent. Manufacturers Hanover paid $1,576,000 in federal tax on income of $597,209,000—a rate of 0.26 percent. Chase paid an effective rate of 3.1 percent. Bankers Trust paid 1.02 percent, and Chemical paid 1.00 percent to the U.S. Treasury. Among the big multinational banks only Morgan and First Chicago paid more than nominal U.S. federal tax in 1985—at 13 percent and 9 percent, respectively.[2]

The pre-1986 U.S. tax regime offered banks a number of ways to avoid U.S. tax: deferral, investment tax credits and accelerated depreciation on leasing operations, deductibility of interest on funds borrowed to acquire tax-exempt state and local government obligations, and deductions for bad-debt reserves taken into capital. By far the most important tax break for the large multinational banks that do most of the cross-border lending, however, was the foreign tax credit. And by far the most important source of these tax credits was loans to developing countries.

In 1985, twelve U.S. money-center bank holding companies claimed $1.3 billion in foreign tax credits—dollar-for-dollar reductions in their U.S. tax obligations to offset foreign taxes. These offsets were equal to 25.2 percent of the banks' net pretax income and 546 times their current U.S. federal taxes actually paid. Citicorp alone claimed $599 million in foreign taxes for the year, equal to 37.7 percent of its net pretax income for 1985. Morgan claimed $216.7 million in foreign tax credits, equal to 34 percent of net pretax income, and Chase claimed $158.9 million, or 21.7 percent.[3]

Banks don't publish detailed data on the source and allocation of tax payments and credits. But congressional testimony by Manufacturers Hanover's tax counsel Martin Hoffman in May 1986 briefly lifted the veil of secrecy that usually shrouds banks' tax affairs. What Hoffman said—as he was testifying in opposition to Treasury's proposed limit on the creditability of LDC withholding taxes—underscores the significance of tax credits generated by loans to LDCs.

Hoffman revealed that fifteen developing countries—the same fifteen heavily indebted countries U.S. Treasury Secretary James Baker had targeted for special assistance in his 1985 plan for solving the debt crisis—accounted for 96 percent of Manufacturers' total $86 million foreign taxes "paid" in 1985.[4] Bank officers and independent tax experts confirm that most of the tax credits claimed by large banks like Manny Hanny, the nation's fourth-largest bank holding company, are from Third World loans, even though such banks have more than half their foreign loans and substantial noninterest income in the industrial countries.

Understanding why the large U.S. banks appeared to pay taxes only to developing countries requires a little exploration of the general theory and practice of international taxation—especially how sovereign states divide up the revenue cake when the income to be taxed is earned in one country but is paid to a company resident or managed in another.

Interest on a cross-border bank loan, for example, is regarded as taxable income by the government in the borrowing country—the source country (source of the interest payment)—and that government will normally seek to collect the taxes before the interest payment is transferred abroad to or by the foreign lender. Once the interest is received by the lender, it is also subject, in principle, to taxation by the country in which the lending bank is considered resident for tax purposes. The U.S. government, in principle, taxes the consolidated worldwide income of American corporations, including banks. The same interest income stream may also be subject to taxation by a third country if the underlying loan is carried on the books of one of the bank's foreign branches or subsidiaries. Thus, the interest an American bank earns on a loan to Brazil that was booked by the bank's London branch is potentially subject to taxes in all three countries.

Fortunately for the banks—and for other multinational taxpayers—there are certain protections against such multiple taxation (usually referred to as double taxation, though that gives a misleading impression of simplicity). Most developed countries and some Third World nations have negotiated bilateral tax treaties that set out which jurisdiction has the right to tax what revenue. If it is agreed that the source country is to take the tax bite, the residence country will either exempt that income from taxation or will credit taxes paid at the source against taxes that would otherwise be owed to the country of residence. The United States generally relies on the credit method to avoid double taxation, whereas European countries tend to exempt classes of foreign-source income from residence-country taxation.

Where no treaty exists, a U.S. resident with foreign-source income may have to seek an exemption from the Internal Revenue Service or claim a credit for foreign taxes paid, against U.S. tax owed. A receipt from the foreign authority as proof the tax has been paid would normally be required to support the claim.

Industrial countries now tend to waive withholding of taxes on income sourced in their jurisdiction but paid to nonresidents. Many Western European countries exempt each others' banks from withholding on interest payments at the source. Thus there is no Dutch withholding of taxes on an interest payment by a Dutch borrower to a British bank, for example. It's up to the British to tax the income, if it wishes. And in 1984 the United States abolished its 30 percent withholding tax on interest and dividend payments to all nonresidents. Germany and Japan have since done the same. Consequently, interest payments in general are transferred freely among the industrial countries without being subject to taxation at the source.

Many developing countries, however, continue to impose high withholding taxes on interest payments to foreign banks and are not parties to double-taxation treaties that would exempt lenders from taxation at the source. The United States does not have double-taxation treaties with Brazil, Mexico, Argentina, or Venezuela, for example. In general, interest payments flowing from developing countries to industrial countries continue to be subject to withholding at the source.

The big banks with extensive operations in both the developed and the developing countries managed to turn this split between the two tax blocks—the OECD countries on the one hand and developing countries on the other—very much to their advantage, with the perhaps unwitting support of national tax authorities. Credits for *withholding* taxes imposed by borrowing countries outside the OECD effectively extinguished banks' *income* tax obligations in the countries where they reside or manage their operations. And the real genius of the arrangement, as will be explained, was that the banks in most instances didn't actually pay the withholding taxes that generated these valuable credits.

TURNING TAXES INTO PROFIT

Commercial banks began looking closely at the foreign tax-credit question after the first oil shock when the pace of lending to Latin America picked up and the Latin governments sought to extract more tax revenue from the transactions by increasing the withholding tax on interest paid to foreign lenders.

"The tax issue has been a mess for the last ten years," said an American who has represented a large U.S. bank in Mexico City for more than twenty years. "In the 1960s on a 6 percent loan and a 10 percent withholding tax, half the bank's profit went to taxes. In the early 1970s Mexico jumped the tax to 21 percent, at one point even 26.75 percent. This was totally untenable." The Mexican rate later went down to 15 percent. The Brazilian rate has gone as high as 25 percent.

A standard corporate income tax is owed on the *net* revenue, after expenses and allowable deductions. A typical withholding tax, on the other hand, is not a straightforward income tax on net profit after the cost of funds and overhead have been subtracted. It is a tax on gross receipts—on the total amount of interest a bank receives from the borrower. A source country normally has no way of calculating the net profit a foreign bank makes on loans to its residents—a bank's business presence in the country may be limited to a single representative and the borrower's tax authorities would have no access to the bank's books. Therefore, the source country will usually impose a flat withholding tax on the gross receipts *in lieu of* an income tax on the net profit. In the case of interest on a Eurodollar loan paid to a foreign bank, the tax would be levied on the entire interest payment—LIBOR plus spread. For example, on a Chase $100 million loan to Brazil, carrying 8 percent LIBOR and 2 percent spread, the Brazilian withholding tax would be 15 percent of $10 million, or $1.5 million, leaving Chase with a net spread of $0.5 million.

Fluctuating tax rates could defeat the principal benefit of "spread banking" that had become the norm in the Euromarkets in the 1970s—that is, lending at floating interest rates to guarantee the bank a fixed margin of profit or spread on a loan, regardless of changes in the cost of funds during the life of that loan.

If Brazil raised the withholding rate from 15 to 25 percent and a foreign bank was lending $100 million at 8 percent LIBOR and 2 percent spread, its spread, net of withholding, would go from +$0.5 million ($2 million less 15 percent of $10 million) to −$0.5 million ($2 million less 25 percent of $10 million). Assuming that LIBOR represents the bank's interest expense on the loan, it would actually show a negative cash flow on the loan.

One possible response by lenders to higher withholding taxes would have been to increase the spreads at which they were lending. Doubling the spread on Chase's loan to 4 percent would turn the bank's negative cash flow at 25 percent withholding into a positive $1 million cash flow. (Gross interest receipts would be $12 million. The net spread would be $4 million less 25 percent of $12 million.) Increasing the spread, however, might discourage customers from borrowing. And in Brazil the finance ministry at one point decreed that borrowers could not accept Eurodollar loans carrying more than a 2 percent spread. If that held, the banks would have done no business at all.

Banks instead found they could recoup the high withholding taxes provided they had sufficient taxable income elsewhere to absorb the tax credits generated. Tax authorities in the United States, the United Kingdom, and Japan, among other countries, have held that gross-receipt taxes such as the Brazilian withholding tax are comparable to an income tax for tax-credit purposes even though the base against which the two types of taxes are assessed is not.[5] Since the withholding tax generates credits on the basis of *gross* revenue, but the credits can be used by the banks to reduce their home-country taxes on *net* income, a foreign withholding tax is likely to generate credits far in excess of the home-country taxes on the profits from the loan. In countries like the United States and the United Kingdom, these excess credits can be used to offset tax obligations on other income. The United Kingdom permitted foreign tax credits, up to a notional 15 percent withholding tax rate, to be credited against U.K. taxes on all types of income.

The United States and Japan, among others, limited foreign tax creditability to foreign-source income. To determine its maximum usable foreign tax credits in a given tax year, a U.S. bank calculated its total foreign source income as a percentage of total worldwide income (including U.S.). If, for example, foreign income was 40 percent of total income, a bank could reduce its U.S. tax on *total* taxable income by up to 40 percent.[6] Moreover, foreign tax credits left over in a given year need not go to waste: they could be carried forward five tax years or back two tax years. The IRS also has allowed banks to allocate certain foreign interest and noninterest expenses against gross domestic income. This inflates apparent foreign-source income and shrinks domestic income, enabling banks to make greater use of foreign tax credits.[7]

In the example above, of Chase Manhattan Bank's $100 million loan to a Brazilian corporation carrying 10 percent annual interest, Chase comes away with $8.5 million cash and a tax receipt or other proof that $1.5 million in tax has been paid in Brazil.

Chase booked the loan in London and will be subject to U.K. income tax on the interest it receives. Unlike the Brazilian withholding tax, however, the U.K. tax is on profit, or net receipts, not gross revenue. If one assumes that LIBOR is the bank's expenses on the loan, Chase will have a U.K. taxable income—profit—of 2 percent, or $2 million, subject to a U.K. corporate income tax of, say, 35 percent, or $700,000. However, Chase has a tax credit of $1.5 million for withholding tax it has paid to the Brazilian government in lieu of an income tax—and this more than offsets the U.K. tax. Indeed, Chase has $800,000 of Brazilian tax credits left over to apply against other U.K. income taxes owed.

Since Chase's home base is the United States, it still has a U.S. tax obligation to contend with. Fortunately, the Brazilian withholding tax credits do double duty. Chase's U.K. income, including its profit on the Brazil loan, will of course be part of Chase's worldwide income that is subject to U.S. corporate income tax. It will claim no tax credits in the United States for U.K. taxes paid, since it didn't pay any. However, it will credit the Brazilian withholding tax against U.S. taxes. In effect, Chase transfers its income-tax obligation on the Brazil loan from the United Kingdom to the United States, which is highly desirable if the U.S. corporate tax rate is lower than the U.K. rate. This does not mean that Chase pays U.S. tax on that income: it just means the withholding tax credits will stretch a little further. (Chase's $2 million profit from Brazil will result in a U.S. income-tax obligation of $680,000—34 percent of $2 million—leaving an excess credit of $820,000 to be applied against other U.S. taxes.)

In this simplified example, the high withholding tax levied by Brazil is offset by a lower U.K. and U.S. tax burden. The bank comes out more or less even, but the U.K. and U.S. governments have lost tax revenue. This was acceptable in theory as long as these countries were in turn levying high withholding taxes on dividend and interest payments paid to Brazilians. Once the United States dropped its own withholding tax, the benefits flowed only one way.

"GROSSING UP"—OR HOW TO CREDIT TAXES WITHOUT ACTUALLY PAYING THEM

The real tax bonanza for the banks, however, came when they began "grossing up" the interest on their Third World loans. Grossing up is a loan-pricing method that effectively shifts the withholding-tax burden on interest from the lender to the borrowers—without depriving the lender of the tax credits it uses to reduce its tax obligations at home.

Grossing up works as follows, again taking Chase's $100 million loan at 10 percent and a Brazilian 15 percent with-holding rate. The stated—that is, publicized—terms on the loan would still be 8 percent LIBOR plus 2 percent spread, but the loan contract would stipulate that the total interest on the loan is actually 11.76 percent, or $11.76 million. To cover the Brazilian 15 percent withholding tax, the bank simply works backward and sets a gross rate that, with a 15 percent tax subtracted, will leave it with a net interest payment of $10 million. Fifteen percent of $11.76 million equals $1.76 million, and $11.76 million minus $1.76 million leaves $10 million, which is what the bank wants to come out with.[8] The bank has now ensured for itself LIBOR plus the desired spread, effectively insulating its profits from the Brazilian withholding tax.

When a loan is fully grossed up—that is, the borrower agrees to assume responsibility for the entire tax—the borrower pays Chase $10 million cash (LIBOR plus spread), stating that this payment is *net of all withholding taxes*.[9] On request, the borrower will provide the bank with a tax receipt or other proof that the withholding tax has been paid. Grossing up has the added advantage of swelling the size of the bank's tax receipts without any cost to the bank. In this case the tax receipt will be for 15 percent of the fully grossed-up interest of $11.76 million, or $1.76 million. The tax receipts are accrued like income: Chase's books will show income of $11.76

million, of which $10 million is cash and $1.76 million is "foreign taxes expense." The foreign taxes expense is the equivalent of an additional 1.76 percent spread on the loan. The "tax bonus" almost doubles Chase's return on the loan.

According to the senior foreign tax accountant at a major Chicago bank, most lending to developing countries after 1976 was on a partial or a fully grossed-up basis. Every developing country except the Philippines accepted the principle of grossing up and issued withholding-tax receipts on that basis.

The amount of grossing up on a given loan was a matter for negotiation. If the bank was to absorb some or all of the tax, it might insist on a higher spread as compensation; if the borrower agreed to absorb the entire tax, it might demand a lower spread. Jaime Pellicier of the office of public credit in the Mexican finance ministry said, "The banks began asking for receipts in 1974, and the next year we realized why and began asking something in return. Otherwise there would be windfall profits for the banks. We told Mexican entities that were borrowing, 'Don't give away the tax receipt for nothing. Get a break on spreads, fees, or something.' There are many different types of deals on taxes."

Paying the withholding tax is a cost to the borrower, provided he actually pays it. But unlike a higher spread, it is a local-currency expense rather than a foreign-exchange cost. (In the above example, the tax receipt shows $1.76 million, but whoever pays the tax, if it is paid, may pay the cruzeiro equivalent of that amount.) In fact, the borrower may not pay the tax either. Borrowing-country tax authorities sometimes issue tax receipts even though no withholding tax has been paid. It is not at all clear, for example, that state-owned companies always pay the tax, even though they have entered into loan agreements stating that they will and the requisite tax receipts are issued to the lending banks. According to one bank tax expert, the joke among foreign bankers in Brazil

was "You can buy a tax receipt at the neighborhood statio-
nery store." Indeed, any doubts about the fictitious nature of
the Brazilian withholding were inadvertently dispelled by
none other than John Reed, chairman of Citicorp, shortly
after his dramatic announcement in May 1987 that Citibank
was taking a $3 billion reserve against its troubled Latin loans
and would seek to convert a large part of its portfolio from
loans to equity. "I think it's not been appreciated," said Mr.
Reed, "that if you have an investment in the country that
produces revenue for the country, it's taxable. A loan doesn't
produce any taxes for Brazil."[10]

There also have been cases where the government insisted
in principle that the tax be paid but rebated a large portion
of the payment. At one point, the Brazilian government cut
its withholding-tax rate from 25 to 5 percent in the mistaken
belief that foreign banks would be encouraged to reduce their
interest rates to Brazilian borrowers. When the banks didn't
respond as expected, the government restored the 25 percent
withholding rate and began making rebates to the borrower—an explicit recognition that the tax is paid, if at all,
by the borrower, not the lending bank. The Brazilians understood that since the face value of the tax receipt rises with the
withholding rate, a high withholding tax is, perversely, more
likely than a low tax to encourage banks to reduce spreads
on their loans.

The IRS staff questioned the creditability of the rebated
portion of the Brazilian tax in the mid-1970s on the grounds
that it is "an uncollected bookkeeping entry"—a tax that has
no significance in the source country.[11] The only purpose of
the high tax seemed to be to take advantage of creditability
in other countries. The Brazilian government itself lobbied
the U.S. Treasury, urging that full creditability be retained,
and the staff was overruled by then–Secretary of Treasury
William E. Simon—who shortly after leaving office joined the
board of Citicorp. The Carter administration overturned Si-

mon's decision in 1979, holding that only the nonrebated portion of the Brazilian tax would be creditable. Brazil subsequently reduced both the rebate and the withholding rate to 15 percent.[12] U.S. banks challenged the Carter ruling. In 1989 the tax courts upheld the Carter administration's position.

Tax receipts have been a contentious issue in debt restructuring negotiations. In the first rounds, banks insisted that debtors continue to issue tax receipts even if the central bank took over the foreign debts of private-sector entities and state corporations. Brazil and Mexico argued that no tax receipts would be issued since a central bank was not going to pay tax to its own treasury. Citibank, among others, countered that loan terms would have to be renegotiated to compensate the banks for loss of the tax receipts. The fight with Brazil went on for a year. One U.S. banker in Brazil complained, "When we aren't getting the tax receipts, it means we are losing 50 percent of our income" on the loans.

According to banking sources, the U.S. Federal Reserve supported the banks on the tax question, and the debtors eventually relented. In more recent debt negotiations, banks have reversed themselves. Now that tax laws have changed and many banks lack the foreign income to absorb excess tax credits, they insist that interest payments be free of all withholding taxes.

AN INCENTIVE TO OVERLEND AND OVERBORROW

The tax aspect helps to clear up the mystery of why aggressive, profit-driven banks were willing to lend to high-risk borrowers at such narrow interest spreads. The tax game boosted the banks' earnings while holding down the cost of borrowing for Brazilians and Mexicans. When a bank shared its "tax bonus" with the borrower by lending at a lower spread, the home tax authority whose revenue was being reduced by the foreign withholding tax was, in effect, directly subsidizing lending by its banks to the developing country. The bank merely took part of its profit in the form of reduced tax payments to its home government rather than in a higher interest charge on the loan. The U.S. Treasury and American taxpayer, of course, bore the cost. This tax subsidy from the U.S. Treasury has amounted to tens of billions of dollars of lost revenue over the last fifteen years.

The bank withholding-tax situation bears a striking resemblance to the tax arrangement worked out between U.S. multinational oil companies and the Persian Gulf oil producers in the 1950s to ensure for themselves a constant per-barrel return regardless of "income taxes" imposed by the producing countries in the Persian Gulf. Indeed, the concepts are so similar that one wonders if some smart New York lawyer didn't just take the oil-company pricing model—which, as laid out in a series of Senate Foreign Relations Committee hearings, was developed with the help of the U.S. Treasury and State Departments in 1950 to funnel money to the Saudi royal family without having to go to Congress for an appropriation—and relabel it for the banks.

The "posted price" for a barrel of oil was, like grossed-up interest, an artificial construct against which the oil-producing country levied a tax. The tax was in fact a per-barrel charge—like Brazil's withholding, a tax on gross receipts—but was treated by the IRS as a creditable income tax. The American oil companies—the four Aramco partners—paid the per-barrel "tax" to the Saudis, then reduced their income taxes owed to the U.S. Treasury by an equivalent amount.[13] In effect, the oil companies served as the conduit for a transfer of revenues from the U.S. Treasury to the Saudi treasury.[14] Between 1950 and 1951, with the posted price set at $1.75 per barrel, the Aramco partnership's tax payments to Saudi Arabia rose from $66 million to $110 million while its payment to the U.S. Treasury dropped from $50 million to $6 million. Other Middle Eastern oil producers quickly adopted the Saudi tax system. Since that time the major multinational U.S. oil companies have paid hardly a penny of U.S. income tax on their foreign income.

According to witnesses and documents assembled by the Subcommittee on Multinational Corporations of the U.S. Senate Committee on Foreign Relations in the mid-1970s, the U.S. government knowingly subsidized the Saudi royal family (and the oil companies) via the U.S. Tax Code— (although Treasury hadn't expected to subsidize the whole Persian Gulf this way or to see oil prices go to $40. The price jump had the same effect on the rate of accumulation of oil tax credits that rising Eurodollar interest rates had on the banks' accumulation of foreign interest-withholding tax credits.) Treasury and the oil companies had jointly sent a team of lawyers to Saudi Arabia to draft the new tax law, and the National Security Council "recommended" to Treasury that the Saudi tax be held fully creditable against U.S. income tax. Congress was, of course, not informed.

The U.S. government subsidy for bank lending to developing countries was probably unwitting. There is no record of Congressional review of the matter. But a former banker remembers as a young lending officer, questioning the legitimacy of these tax credits and being told, "Don't worry about it, kid. Long knows all about it." The reference, apparently, was to Senator Russell Long, powerful long-time chairman of the Senate Finance Committee.

Revenue losses aside, the tax subsidy is troublesome. It created a hidden incentive for banks to overlend and countries to overborrow because much of the cost was paid by a third party. Perversely, the higher world interest rates went, the bigger the "tax bonus" in absolute terms and as a percentage of total profit. In the example used earlier, the profit with LIBOR at 8 percent and 2 percent spread, fully grossed up, is $3.76 million, of which $1.76 million is tax credits. When LIBOR rose to 18 percent (as it did in 1981), the grossed-up interest would be $23.53 million and the 15 percent withholding tax on that would be $3.53 million for a total yield for Chase of $5.52 million (tax credits plus spread). The surge in interest rates that followed the tightening of U.S. monetary policy in 1979 thus made lending to Mexico, Brazil, and other high-withholding LDCs even more attractive to certain banks at the very time that the sharp rise in debt-servicing costs was making these countries' economic situation increasingly untenable. At these interest rates, loans to high-withholding countries generated massive amounts of tax receipts that could totally wipe out bank income-tax obligations in the countries that were willing to credit them. Would lending to Brazil have been so attractive without the withholding tax credits? "Absolutely not!" was the emphatic answer of Dr. John Stavroupoulos, executive vice president and chief credit officer of First Chicago.

The tax factor makes the banking community's eagerness to lend to developing countries seem at least rational, if not prudent. For all the complaining in the late 1970s about cutthroat competition and hair-thin spreads, the returns on these loans were nothing short of spectacular: the combination of grossing up of interest rates and full creditability of withholding taxes (and substantial up-front fees) produced yields far better than anything the banks could earn on their domestic assets and more than double the profits one would estimate by looking only at the stated spreads on these loans.

Bank stock analysts and academics who unquestioningly accept the numbers served up by the banks may have consistently underestimated the importance of sovereign-risk lending to the banks' overall profitability. The banks' annual reports greatly understated foreign earnings because the method commonly used to compare foreign with domestic earnings obscures the role of foreign tax credits. "International earnings" are calculated net of "foreign taxes paid" and compared with "domestic earnings," shown net of domestic federal and state income tax. On this basis Citibank's 1985 foreign and domestic posttax earnings would appear to be roughly balanced—$545 million abroad and $453 million at home. What is misleading is that the "domestic" taxes subtracted from gross domestic earnings to get a domestic net figure have been reduced by the foreign tax credits being claimed by the bank—in Citibank's case in 1985, by $528 million. (Stated another way, the federal income-tax burden has been calculated on a consolidated basis, while all other computations in this formula are calculated on an unconsolidated basis.)

Since the bulk of foreign taxes paid comes straight back to the consolidated bottom line as a reduction in U.S. taxes, the creditable taxes should properly be counted as foreign income (which is precisely how the banks view them internally) when measuring the true importance of overseas operations to a bank. It then becomes apparent that foreign earnings for the large banks have, until recently, been much higher absolutely and as a proportion of total earnings than reported. And within that, the high-withholding-tax developing countries that generate most of the credits have been much more significant than one would judge on the basis of more common measures, such as the percent of a bank's total assets in LDCs, for example. (In 1985, $24 billion out of Citibank's $160 billion average total assets, or 15 percent, were in Third World countries.)

THE END OF (THIS) TAX GAME

The foreign tax-credit bonanza has become a thing of the past, however. The Chicago tax lawyer admitted that throughout most of the 1970s and 1980s big multinational banks didn't pay much tax anywhere, "but more and more countries are catching on to that fact." The two most important "resident" countries for multinational banking—the United States and the United Kingdom—have taken steps to limit the creditability of high withholding taxes.

In considering the 1986 tax reform, Congress dropped Treasury's original idea of a country-by-country limitation on foreign tax credits (credits generated by loans in one country creditable *only* against other income generated in that same country). Congress decided there would be "baskets" of income—one for shipping income, another for oil and gas income, another for financial services income, and still another for interest income that is subject to a foreign gross-basis tax of 5 percent or more. Tax credits generated by income in a basket could be allocated only against other income from the same basket. This modification would hit the banks hard since their game had been to credit taxes from high-withholding countries against income from low- or no-withholding jurisdictions. Putting income from high-withholding countries in a separate basket would effectively preclude this kind of tax play. The banking industry lobbied hard against the tax change and used the debt crisis as its strongest argument.

U.S. Treasury Secretary Baker had listed fifteen heavily indebted countries for special attention under his 1985 proposal for ending the debt crisis. As part of this plan, commercial banks would be asked to commit new money to those countries. But the "Baker Fifteen," not coincidentally, are also the "Manny Hanny Fifteen"—the developing countries that have generated most of the tax credits for the big multinational banks. Take away the tax credits as Treasury and Congress proposed, argued the banks, and you take away any incentive to lend more money to these countries and thereby jeopardize the whole Baker Initiative. Worse, you might force banks to renegotiate old loans at higher spreads because the old terms were based on calculations that incor-porated the value of the withholding tax credits in estimating the return to the banks. Baker apparently bought the argu-ment and overruled his own tax policy people ("All I can tell you is, it wasn't their idea," said a congressional tax aide), reversing Treasury's position on closing the withholding-tax creditability loophole.

To help the banks—and presumably, keep them lending to Brazil et al. and committed to the Baker Initiative—Congress, at Treasury's strong urging, agreed to exempt interest income from loans to thirty-three developing countries from the new tax-creditability limitation until 1990. (The Senate had listed only the Baker Fifteen for transition treatment.) Old and new loans to those countries would be fully creditable. Then there would be a five-year transition starting in tax year 1990, in which an increasing proportion of the interest income on pre-1990 loans would be subject to the "basket" rule. (A 1989 amendment ended the transition period in principle—but let it stand for "qualified banks" with loan-loss reserves equal to at least 25 percent of troubled LDC exposure.)

The United Kingdom moved at about the same time to curb banks' tax breaks. In 1987 Inland Revenue charged after a two-year investigation that banks resident in that country were structuring their overseas lending to take unfair advantage of British tax laws. Margaret Thatcher's 1987 to 1988 budget draft included plans to curtail sharply the creditability of for-eign withholding taxes. The Finance (No. 2) Act of 1987 changed the law so that withholding tax credits can be cred-itable only against the loans that gave rise to them—an even narrower concept than the U.S. "income basket." Tax author-ities estimated the change would increase tax revenues by £60 million in 1989. U.S. banks that reportedly were the prime target warned that the tax limits would make London far less attractive as an international financial center, but to no avail.[15] (London remains a premier banking center.)

The final blow for U.S. banks on the tax front came not from legislation but from the changing composition of bank earnings and the relative decline in foreign-source income as a share of total big-bank income. These changes were the result both of the debt crisis and structural changes in financial markets that were unrelated to the debt problem. Mounting interest arrears and loan losses have meant a sharp decline in foreign-source income for most large banks. Since banks have recently concentrated more of their activities in the home market, the domestic share of total U.S. bank earnings has increased. Consequently, many large U.S. money-center banks no longer have enough foreign-source income to absorb both the accumulated excess foreign tax credits *and* foreign loan losses. Loan losses are deducted against income and must be used before foreign tax credits. If large loan losses wipe out foreign income, then the foreign tax credits that banks may already have accrued as income could be wiped out. The 1989 IRS ruling discussed at the beginning of the chapter gave banks only partial relief by allowing some foreign loan losses to be taken against domestic income.

Evaporation of the extremely valuable foreign-tax credits has forced banks to look for other ways to reduce their potential U.S. tax liability—or at least to boost *reported* posttax income—to avoid investor panic. One approach is to deal creatively with the losses a bank figures it might have to absorb sooner or later anyway—for example, Third World loan losses.

In 1987, when Citibank and the others announced large losses resulting from an increase in reserving against developing country debt, they reassured shareholders that they would quickly recover some of the losses through the U.S. Tax Code. As far as the IRS is concerned, a general loan-loss reserve is strictly a "book reserve" for reporting purposes—that is, reporting to investors. Since 1986 there has been no tax deduction for this reserve. A bank must

pay its taxes currently and may not reduce its taxable income until there is an actual loss, an actual writing down
of a loan, a reduction in the asset. Banks, however, can
embellish their income statements that go to shareholders
by reporting "anticipated tax losses." That is, they may
claim tax benefits—in this case, deductions from taxable
income for losses on their foreign loans—before they actually take the losses. These anticipated tax benefits reduce
the *reported* tax liability of the bank and boost the bank's
reported after-tax income (called "book income"). The de-
ception is possible because our fragmented regulatory system requires banks to keep three sets of books—one for
the shareholders, one for the regulators, and one for the
tax collector. Each is kept according to a different set of
accounting rules. The Securities and Exchange Commission (SEC), which sets the rules for what bank holding companies must report to shareholders, inexplicably tolerates
such misleading reporting practices.

A bank can distribute the tax "benefits" over several years
following the increase in loan-loss reserves, provided it has
sufficient taxable income to absorb the deduction and provided it can make a plausible argument to its accountants that
there will eventually be real losses commensurate with the
deductions being claimed currently. Bankers call this "tax
benefitting the reserve." First Chicago estimated that it would
take eight quarters for the tax benefits from its $800 million
addition to the reserve to flow through the financial statement; Chemical estimated four years. One admiring competitor said, "In three years, it will be as if Citibank never had a
loss in 1987." Most large U.S. banks bathed in a sea of red
ink in the summer of 1987 because of LDC loans. But in
October of that year, *American Banker* reported, "Tax benefits
from the losses that ruined bank earnings in the second quarter helped to dress them up in the third." *American Banker*
noted "a flood of non-recurring items . . . including markedly

lower tax bills."[16] It did not explain that a bank must come up with the cash to pay its current taxes even while telling shareholders its tax burden has been reduced or eliminated thanks to supposed tax benefits growing out of its loan-loss reserve. The income statement thus does not give an entirely accurate picture of a bank's financial situation for the period covered.

It is too soon to say that banks will now have to begin paying taxes at home. But many of the tax benefits of lending to LDCs have disappeared, accelerating the pace of bank disengagement from sovereign lending. Changes in the U.S. and U.K. Tax Codes since 1986 have reduced the appeal of traditional cross-border lending for American banks, even if most of the borrowers miraculously recover their "creditworthiness" in the next decade. But loss of the hidden tax subsidy should mean that cross-border loans will in future be more honestly priced. The risk premium will have to be included in the spread where it belongs and not hidden away in arcane manipulations of the Tax Code. And that may put the bank-borrower relationship on a more realistic footing. Said the Chicago tax expert, "We can still be creative in our tax accounting, but we probably won't be quite so successful."

6

Capital Flight: Their Savings and Ours

Life is so sad, without Miami Beach.
> —Refrain from popular song in Caracas, summer of 1984

Private international banking is also a growing area. . . . It may be the best business there is. Maybe we should make no loans [to Latin America], just take deposits.
> —Head of international operations for a large U.S. regional bank

If capital flight is given a free ride in the caboose of the LDC debt train, the train has little hope of making the station. It is both necessary and feasible to deal forthrightly with issues affecting capital flight.
> —Morgan Guaranty Trust, *World Financial Markets* (September 1986)

THE PHENOMENON OF PRIVATE CAPITAL EXPORT

"Poverty is the inability to generate wealth," says the opening line of a World Bank report on Bolivia. By this definition, Latin America is not poor: the estimated $200 plus billion of

Latin American deposits in foreign banks and other foreign assets attest to the continent's ability to generate wealth.

Capital flight is loosely defined as an outflow of capital from a country where capital is relatively scarce. This outflow defies economic theory, which holds that money goes where capital is scarce and thus yields greater returns. Capital-scarce countries may impose controls on the movement of capital out of the country. Flight capital is thus sometimes illegal capital.

A Federal Reserve study concluded that for eight major debtor countries in the period 1974 to 1982, private capital export was the second-largest use of foreign exchange after debt servicing.[1] In the case of Latin America, the accumulation of foreign assets may be as much as 43 percent of the total build-up of foreign debt in the period 1973 to 1987.[2] The World Bank has estimated that by 1987 Venezuela's flight capital exceeded its foreign debt by perhaps 40 percent, Argentine flight capital was probably equal to at least 70 percent of the country's foreign liabilities, and capital flight from Mexico was equal to about 50 percent of its foreign debt. These accumulated billions are not dollars that were clipped from foreign bank loans, off the top. They are for the most part the domestic savings of individual Mexicans, Uruguayans, Argentines, and so on that have been converted into foreign savings. The vehicle for this conversion was the dollars and other foreign currencies accumulated in their respective central banks from export earnings and, in the 1970s and early 1980s, from loans by foreign banks to the government, domestic banks, companies, and individuals.

The phenomenon of capital flight is at once the most disturbing and the most encouraging feature of the international debt crisis. The rule for any debtor, as stated by the World Bank, is that "the rate of return on all investments must exceed the cost of borrowed funds." The wealth that has been accumulated abroad indicates the borrowing has yielded ample returns. The problem is that these returns are not reinvested at home, are not taxed at home, and are mostly not available for debt servicing. This accumulated wealth has been deployed in other economies—financing real estate development in Colorado, providing equity capital for Fortune 500 companies, financing the debts of the United States and other governments whose IOUs are held a better risk than the home government paper. And, of course, flight capital has helped fund the lending operations of large multinational banks. This last might be a wash except that a depositor usually gets less for his deposit than the bank charges for its loans. Third World flight capital financing Third World loans is "recycling" with a negative rate of return for the debtor countries.

The root causes of capital flight can be found in the political and economic conditions of the home country. But foreign banks have contributed to the problem, first by lending governments in the debtor countries the wherewithal to support overvalued currencies, then by providing easy avenues of escape and safe haven for the expatriate funds. The spectacle of a debtor country's citizens taking domestic savings out as foreign lenders were transferring foreign savings into the country should have caused banks to question seriously the underlying economic rationale for their lending. Capital flight clearly short circuits the development process bank loans were supposed to advance. Yet the banks carried on happily for years as the principal intermediaries in both channels of this two-way traffic.

A return of flight capital is said to be the solution to the debt crisis. But if in the early stages capital flight is a principal cause of excessive borrowing, capital flight in the later stages of the crisis is at least in part a product of an excessively high debt-servicing burden resulting from that borrowing.

MIAMI VICE

As Ralph Llop escorted me to his compact twenty-ninth floor office with a spectacular view of Biscayne Bay, we passed a room on the left crowded with people and desks. "There we have private international banking," he said and then gestured to the room on the right, where all fifteen desks sat bare and unused. "That side is corporate banking. I understand those desks used to be filled at one time."

It was 1986, and Llop had just become manager of Morgan Guaranty International Bank in Miami, Florida, an Edge Act corporation wholly owned by Morgan Guaranty Trust of New York. (This office was closed in 1990.) Edge Act subsidiaries are an exception to the long-standing ban on interstate banking in the United States (in effect since the National Banking Act of 1863, restated under the MacFadden Act of 1927, and now gradually being lifted). Since 1919 banks have been allowed to establish special subsidiaries outside their home state and abroad to conduct foreign banking business. Domestic Edge Act subsidiaries manage foreign-related accounts for U.S. corporations and local accounts for foreign residents doing business in the United States. Large domestic banks have used the Edge Act loophole to establish a presence in their competitor's home markets, with California having the largest number and Florida ranking second. Foreign banks may open U.S. Edge Act subsidiaries, too.

The Edge Act subsidiaries in Miami are a logical organizational complement to banks' lending offices around the world and their booking centers in London, Paris, and other major financial centers: the latter put money into foreign countries; the former help take it out. In certain respects, the Miami Edge Act operations resemble the offshore "brass-plate" banks in the Cayman Islands, the Bahamas, or the British Channel isles—so called because these offices consist of little more than the shiny brass name plate on the door and a couple of telex machines with operators. Like the offshore havens, Miami serves primarily as a parking place for expatriate funds and offers confidentiality and certain tax benefits.

Seventy-seven percent of the deposits at Miami Edge Act corporations in 1979 were from non-U.S. individuals, partnerships, and corporations. This compares to a 5.6 percent foreign share of deposits at New York Edge Act corporations and 54 percent in all other cities.[3] Llop explained that Morgan's Edge Act subsidiary used to do a good corporate business with Latin America—short-term lending and letters of credit. (Another Miami banker pointed out that doing a letter of credit for a Latin American client is much cheaper in Miami: "Our overhead costs are lower. In New York, it goes directly to translation; here, there is no need.") But since medium-term commercial lending to Latin America dried up in 1982, much of the ancillary short-term commercial activity ceased. By 1985, said Llop, the subsidiary's business had become almost exclusively "private international banking"—the banking community's euphemism for the solicitation and investment of flight capital.

Retired senior economist John D. Wilson writes in his history of Chase Manhattan Bank that the Miami office "engaged principally in gathering deposits from customers in Latin America—chiefly funds seeking safe haven in the United States."[4] It is Chase's most profitable domestic Edge Act corporation. Many foreign banks opened offices in Miami in the late 1970s, too: one major European bank office in Miami has more than $2 billion in deposits, mostly Latin American flight capital. "It's absolutely flight capital. It's here and it is still coming, although the new flow is much less. Most of it has already come out," said the Miami manager for a New York bank who like most bankers willing to be interviewed about capital flight asked not to be identified.

Why Miami? "It's a question of customer preference. The alternatives are Panama or New York," explained one banker,

"but we run the portfolios out of New York or Switzerland."
"Here they feel they are still in Latin America, they feel at
home," explained another banker. Gregorio Obregon, general manager of Bankers Trust International, said that because of Venezuela's chronically overvalued currency, "What
happened for ten years was that the cheapest commodity in
the market was U.S. dollars, so cheap that it was less expensive
[for a Venezuelan] to fly to Miami for a vacation than to stay
at home. And condominiums were cheaper here than in Caracas." Mexicans, Venezuelans, Colombians, and Ecuadorans
especially, favor Miami; Chileans and Argentines are said to
prefer taking their money to New York or to Switzerland.
Statistics suggest Brazilians mostly kept their money at home
until the country began to struggle with hyperinflation in the
mid- to late 1980s. Since then, the government estimates, more
than $30 billion has left the country, some of it no doubt
landing in Miami.

Relatively little lending to Latin America was done by the
Miami Edge Act subsidiaries. Loans to foreign governments
or commercial customers are only 16 percent of their total
loans. "Commercial transactions originating in Latin America
would be handled here only if they involved one of our individual customers," said one Edge manager. This subsidiary
of a large New York bank has loans equal to only 10 percent
of its deposits. "We have an entirely different customer base
than our local branch or rep office [in Latin America]. They
have the borrowers." Florida banks as a group are large net
suppliers of funds to affiliated and unaffiliated banks in other
regions.

Nevertheless, the flight haven and the lending office work
in tandem. According to one Miami banker, "The customers
have usually been referred to this office by our local rep. He
sets up the appointment. But the customer has to get the
money here himself." A U.S. banker in Buenos Aires said,
"We don't solicit dollar deposits for accounts abroad. We

chose not to do so even while it was legal. But lots of people deposit their money in our branch in Uruguay [which had strict bank secrecy laws] or in Miami. We don't encourage it or discourage it. Anyway," he added, "Swiss banks probably have most of it."

Sometimes banks take a more active role. A senior officer at a large German bank commented in 1986, only half joking, "We have a guy down in Mexico with two empty suitcases right now." He does not think his bank is unique. An official in the Alfonsin government of Argentina with close ties to the central bank commented that there wasn't a single major bank in Buenos Aires, foreign or domestic, that didn't have a back office to help people convert and transfer money out of the country. Kent Atkinson, head of Bank of London and South America, one of the oldest and largest foreign banks in Argentina (part of Lloyds Bank), said, "Even now [1984] there is no law against an Argentine opening an account in the Caymans. And lots of people are doing it. We have a little department that does nothing else." He added, "We're just acting as a post office. Nothing illegal about it." Brazil, Chile, Colombia, and Peru had capital controls for most of the 1970s and 1980s, while Argentina, Mexico, Uruguay, and Vene-zuela did not. Apparently, the first group suffered far less capital flight than the second. (If tax avoidance is involved, subterfuge may be necessary even in the absence of capital controls.)

A lot of hard cash gets carried around. Venezuelans coming through Miami customs in 1981 who filled out the requisite Treasury forms reported bringing in more than $2 billion in cash.[5] One Miami banker claimed, "We almost never take cash. Well, occasionally, if we know the customer. But there is no way the first time someone comes in off the street. If we know [the party], an existing client, we might.... We even had a guy who told me he had sold a farm to a Colombian mafioso and part of the payment was U.S. dollars, cash.... We told him to deposit it. But all forms are signed. I doubt any of the big banks would do it differently." But in 1985 more than forty U.S. banks—including Chase Manhattan Bank, Manufacturers Hanover, Chemical, Irving Trust, Crocker National, Bank of Boston, and Bank of America—pleaded guilty to the charge of failing to report large cash transactions, a violation of the Bank Secrecy Act that requires banks to report to the U.S. Treasury all cash deposits of more than $10,000. Bank of Boston was fined $500,000 in 1985 for failing to report $1.2 billion in large international cash transactions, mostly with Swiss banks;[6] Bank of America was fined $4.75 million for failing to report 17,000 large cash transactions from 1980 to 1985; Crocker National had failed to report transactions worth $3.9 billion over four years.

Of course, a lot of flight capital never comes out of the home country, strictly speaking, because it never went in. Dummy invoicing is a well-known device for accumulating savings outside the country without alerting tax and monetary authorities. An exporter that wishes to build up bank balances abroad without signaling this intention understates the price of what it is selling when reporting to its home government. It remits the reported foreign-exchange receipts to the central bank for conversion into local currency and asks the foreign purchaser to credit the balance—the difference between the reported and the actual selling price—to a foreign bank account. Such transactions may show up as discrepancies in international trade statistics. For example, Mexico reported $14 billion in exports to the United States in 1984, while the U.S. Commerce Department said U.S. imports from Mexico for the year totaled $18 billion.[7] Similarly, an authorized importer can overstate the price it has paid and purchase more foreign exchange than necessary from the central bank, depositing the excess abroad. (Global balance-of-payments data had a total excess of imports over exports of as much as $100 billion that many experts attribute, at least in part, to capital flight transactions.)

False invoicing is used particularly for tax avoidance. Understating the export price reduces the burden of high export duties prevalent in many developing countries. (Taxes on foreign trade are 28.9 percent of central government revenues in middle-income developing countries compared to 3.7 percent of government revenues in industrial countries.)[8] And the U.S. Internal Revenue Service is currently investigating whether Japanese companies and other foreign multinationals have underpaid U.S. corporate income taxes through the manipulation of prices on intracompany exports and imports.

In a variant of the discounted debt swapping that became common in the 1980s, those wishing to stash assets abroad can find, with the help of a bank or another intermediary, some multinational corporation or other party needing local currency and swap local assets for foreign-currency assets to be kept abroad. No foreign-exchange license or other recourse to the central bank is necessary to execute such a swap. The foreign investment inflow produces no net increase in domestic investment: the foreign multinational invests in the domestic economy, while the local resident invests abroad.

Identified bank deposits held abroad by nonbank residents of Latin America stood at $80 billion as of June 1990.[9] If one includes Panama—where a lot of Latin flight capital is laundered before making its way to the United States and Europe, and the only important offshore banking center not participating in the Bank for International Settlements (BIS) reporting system—total Latin American nonbank deposits rise to $100 billion. (The post-Noriega regime continues to protect bank secrecy. During the years of political turmoil, Panama lost interbank business but remains the biggest offshore haven for nonbank depositors.)

This $100 billion does not include fiduciary or custodial accounts managed by banks on behalf of residents of these countries. Fiduciary accounts are considered off–balance-sheet loans and deposits because they are for the account of and at the risk of the customer with respect to currency, transfer, and credit risk. The omission of such accounts from international banking data, including BIS figures, may result in significant understatement of the foreign exposure of commercial banks. Fiduciary accounts are 44 percent of the total external assets of Swiss banks, for example. In 1984 Swiss banks reported to the BIS data-base deposits of $1.9 billion from Argentina and Brazil, but they had an additional $2.7 billion of Argentine and Brazilian money in fiduciary accounts. As an IMF report on the Swiss market pointed out, "Notwithstanding the fact that the customer carries the full risk of a fiduciary transaction, the customer does not always know where the funds are placed. Equally, if the funds are placed with a foreign bank, that bank is usually not aware of the underlying fiduciary transaction but considers it a normal transaction with a Swiss bank."[10]

Swiss banks have more than $200 billion in trustee deposits from all over the world. It is reasonable to assume that at least $15 billion to $20 billion of this is Latin American flight capital. Then the total amount of private deposits in the banks, just from Latin America, would be at least $120 billion. Some portion of identified bank deposits is the legitimate working balances of businesspeople and corporations. But the bulk of these billions is probably private flight capital: deposits from "residents who decide to keep a portion of their liquid assets outside their own country," as one Miami banker put it.

DRIVING SAVINGS OUT

The reasons for capital flight are not hard to fathom. The now almost commonplace examples are corrupt politicians who systematically plunder the economies they rule and then secretly invest their gains abroad. The deposed Marcoses and

President Mobutu Sese Seko of Zaire may have accumulated foreign assets of at least $5 billion. Mobutu's real estate holdings include chateaus in Spain and Belgium, a townhouse in Paris, a villa in Monte Carlo, an estate in Switzerland, a horse ranch in Portugal, and a villa in the Ivory Coast. (There was some embarrassment in Washington, D.C., in early 1987 when Mobutu visited President Reagan to plead for help in managing Zaire's $4.5 billion foreign debt and, on departing, rented a Concorde to fly his daughter to her wedding in Abidjan.)[11] Haiti's Baby Doc Duvalier reportedly secured $1.5 billion, enough to buy a comfortable exile, Panamanian dictator Noriega's foreign assets have yet to be determined, and the hunt is on for Saddam Hussein's overseas stash.

Tax evasion—at best, sometimes tax avoidance—is another reason for capital flight, from rich countries as well as poor. Argentine officials estimate that before 1981 tax evasion was the primary reason people put money abroad. George Moore, retired but ever-active former chairman of Citicorp, started a new bank, the Gibraltar Trust Bank, with Crédit Suisse as principal shareholder. Its purpose, Moore wrote in his memoirs, "is to provide a tax-efficient residence where top-quality service can be given to the multiplying billions of homeless dollars in today's world."[12] For this purpose, Gibraltar has the distinct advantage of being the only Common Market jurisdiction without a dual-taxation treaty with the United States.

But the extravagances of the kleptocracy and the visibility of the wealthy ducking the tax collector tend to obscure the extent to which capital flight has become a way of life for virtually the entire moneyed population of certain countries.[13] An overvalued currency that makes foreign assets cheaper than domestic assets and also raises expectations of an eventual devaluation, hyperinflation that rapidly erodes the real value of savings, political instability that may result in a sudden loss of property or value—all these are reasons why people may seek to convert their domestic savings into foreign savings. All of these conditions were manifest in Latin America at one time or another during the last two decades.

Over the years, the citizens of Argentina and other unstable economies have become expert at protecting themselves against and even profiting from the vagaries of government economic policy. The lavish spending of the Perón regime in Argentina led to a public-sector deficit equal to 16 percent of gross national product (GNP) in 1975, which was financed by printing money. The resulting inflation was followed by a maxidevaluation, and Argentines with foreign bank accounts enjoyed a 1,202 percent rate of return on their investment. Financial manipulation is not just a pastime of the rich but a necessity for the common citizen. The publisher of the newspaper *La Prensa* related how a mix-up with his wife about who was to pay the maid led the maid to receive her salary two days late and then to complain bitterly that she had lost two days' interest. Kent Atkinson, of the Bank of London and South America, describing the country's volatile financial structure, remarked, "Thirty days is an eternity here. We lend money for three days." A term loan in Argentina is two weeks. By 1989, 90 percent of Mexico's domestic government debt had an average maturity of twenty-eight days. Brazil's government in 1990 was rolling over more than $80 billion of domestic debt every night.

High inflation has been chronic and a prime motivation for capital flight. The specter of hyperinflation produces one of two responses in people. Those who can afford to do so buy a car or other tangible asset that will retain its value in an inflationary environment. In the summer of 1984 when Argentina was in the midst of a severe austerity program but the annualized rate of inflation was running at 700 percent, people were lining up to buy every Fiat, Renault, VW, and Ford that came off the assembly line. A new Ford Falcon— the Argentine-produced model that has not been updated for more than twenty years—cost about $20,000.

Those without enough cash now but who hope someday to buy a car scramble around for a way to protect the purchasing power of their savings while they accumulate. Speculative investments in the local currency are one way to protect purchasing power; converting one's local-currency savings into foreign currency is another. When foreign banks are lending billions of dollars without asking what the money is to be used for, there is plenty of foreign exchange available for such conversion. From 1974 to 1982 Argentina had a cumulative current account deficit of only $10 billion but borrowed $32 billion[14]; in other words, the country was borrowing three times as much foreign exchange as it needed to pay for foreign goods and services. Some of the surplus constituted the exchange reserves of the central bank and of Argentine companies engaged in foreign commerce, but the bulk became a vehicle for Argentines to transform domestic savings into foreign savings.

Small investors probably buy dollars for cash on the black market and store them in a safe place—a process that might be called internal capital flight. Alfredo Salazar, manager of Chase Manhattan's bank in Buenos Aires, said in the mid-1980s, "This is a dollar economy. We pay our people pesos. They save by buying dollars in the black market, then keep them in their mattresses. Local banks are out of the peso business because they have no funding. Peso savings are way down." There is plenty of cash around, mostly dollars, to fill both bedding and foreign bank accounts. A Federal Reserve survey tracing the use and locale of U.S. dollar bills and coins concluded that perhaps as much as 70 percent of the U.S. currency in circulation was outside the United States.[15] According to the Fernand Braudel Institute of São Paulo, by 1989 Argentines held an estimated $5 billion to $7 billion in dollar currency—more than double the local currency narrow-money supply (cash and checking accounts).

Bigger fish—the Argentines call them *patria financiera,*

"those who are above the nation"—who are on good terms
with a friendly local or foreign banker have always been able
to arrange to send their money out of the country. Indeed,
sometimes they have arranged to have their cake and eat it,
too. Consider the self-loan or *auto-prestamos*, as the Argentines
call it. One of the Miami bankers explained how it works:
"Say some big Venezuelan industrialist took out $10 million.
He deposits it in Miami and asks for a hypothecation agreement [pledging a deposit as security for a loan], creating a
two-year deposit as collateral. We give him a two-year, $10
million loan. He takes the check to Venezuela, deposits the
dollars, and gets a peso account on the books." This self-
lending has several advantages. Most important, it allows the
depositor-borrower to safeguard his or her savings abroad
and at the same time have the use of them at home. Further,
since only the loan is reported to the Venezuelan authorities,
the Venezuelan gets a tax break: interest on the debt is deductible from domestic taxes, while interest earned on the
deposit in Miami is free of home taxes (and, most likely, host-
country taxes as well). The Miami bank, of course, has a completely risk-free loan on its books and makes something on
the spread between what it pays on the deposit and what it
charges on the loan. The bank earns the currency-exchange
fees, telexing fees, and so on associated with these transactions as well.

For the Venezuelan central bank this transaction appears
as a future claim against the country's foreign-exchange resources (when the loan is due to be repaid) and a current-
account outflow in the form of interest paid on the debt. But
the foreign loan does not represent any net addition to domestic investment: the industrialist simply has chosen to invest domestic savings in the international capital markets and
is using foreign financing for domestic investments.

Back-to-back loans are particularly attractive when real interest rates are high at home. In 1978 Argentina joined an

experiment with Chile and Uruguay to open the economy to foreign competition in order to eliminate inflation from the economy. Integral to the liberalization scheme was a steady exchange rate vis-à-vis the dollar, with a predetermined, preannounced rate of devaluation. (Chile switched to a fixed rate in mid-1979.) Domestic interest rates were also decontrolled, and both deposits and interest paid by banks were fully guaranteed by the government to attract funds. The economy did not respond as planned. There was heavy public investment and expenditure, especially on armaments, financed by borrowing at home and abroad, but disinvestment by the private sector, which could not compete with the cheap imports pouring into the country because of an overvalued peso. The textile industry, makers of semi-manufactures (products such as steel wire that are made from raw materials and used to manufacture finished goods), and producers of household wares and cars were overwhelmed. It cost less to import a Mercedes-Benz than to buy a locally produced Ford.

Private-sector activity concentrated on financial intermediation and exploiting the opportunities offered by high interest rates and predictable devaluations. Argentine speculators discovered *la bicicleta* ("the bicycle"): an investor borrowed dollars, converted them into pesos, deposited the pesos in a bank paying 20 percent per month, knowing from *la tablita* (the central bank's devaluation schedule) that the peso would be devalued by 10 percent during that month. Then the investor would take the money out with interest, buy dollars, and repay the loan, making a handsome profit on the whole transaction, with no risk: the deposits and the exchange rate were guaranteed by the government. Juan Sommers, director of international economics at the Central Bank of Argentina in the mid-1980s, estimated that almost all of the private foreign debt accumulated in the period 1979 to 1982 were *autoprestamos* by Argentines wanting to take advantage of high real interest rates at home.

But in a pattern much like the S&L bust in the United States a decade later, money flowed into the Argentine banks that offered rates their assets could not cover. A massive bank collapse in 1980 created a crisis of confidence, and money poured out of the country again. Rather than seek to stem the flow with capital controls, which would have been antithetical to the Chicago school monetarist doctrine still guiding economic policy, the government stepped up foreign borrowing to replace lost reserves. An exchange-risk-guarantee program was instituted to encourage the private sector to borrow abroad, and Argentine banks borrowed dollars and used them to buy government paper to boost official reserves.

A government assessment in mid-1982 summed up the results of Argentina's borrowing binge and failed liberalization effort: Argentine gross domestic product (GDP) had grown 2 percent since 1974, industrial output was at the level of the 1960s, consumption per capita had dropped 8 percent in the previous three years, and many enterprises were on the verge of bankruptcy. The country had gone from almost no foreign debt to owing $35.6 billion, with annual interest charges of $4.5 billion.[16] The main uses of these funds, in order of magnitude, were outflows of funds—capital flight—of around $22 billion, tourist expenditures, and purchases and nontraditional imports such as armaments.[17] According to the economist Manuel Pastor, Jr.,

These two-way flows can be explained largely by the discriminatory treatment of locally-held versus foreign-held assets, along with "loan pushing" by the multinational banks. Loans by international banks were often explicitly or implicitly guaranteed by Latin governments. . . . Most local investors, however, had no such explicit guarantees. It was possible that when the bills came due for the rapidly growing debt, local governments might seek to acquire a share of domestic wealth through either direct taxes or the "inflation tax." It was rational, then, for local elites to export capital even as the country as a whole imported it.[18]

THE WELCOME MAT FOR "HOMELESS MILLIONS"

Bankers and their governments have taken to making pious statements about the need for debtor countries to halt capital flight (see the quotation from Morgan Guaranty Trust at the beginning of the chapter). The Baker Initiative said, "As a practical matter, it is unrealistic to call upon the support of voluntary lending from abroad, whether public or private, when domestic funds are moving in the other direction."[19] Yet neither the banks nor their governments have taken concrete steps to discourage funds from "moving in the other direction." On the contrary, under the guidance of Treasury Department Secretary Baker, the United States in 1984 dropped the withholding tax on interest payments to nonresident owners of U.S. securities, including negotiable certificates of deposit (CDs). To remain competitive, France and Germany quickly followed suit. Switzerland does not withhold taxes on fiduciary accounts.

Professor Rudiger Dornbusch of the Massachusetts Institute of Technology charged,

> The administration, in an effort to fund our own deficits at low cost, has promoted tax fraud on an unprecedented scale. The only purpose one can imagine for the elimination of the withholding tax on nonresident asset holdings in the United States is to make it possible for foreigners to use the U.S. financial system as a tax haven. To compete with the tax-free U.S. return, anyone investing in Mexico and actually paying taxes there would need a yield differential, not counting depreciation and other risk, of quite a few extra percentage points.[20]

The Reagan Treasury added the appeal of anonymity when it began selling bearer U.S. government bonds to non-U.S. residents in 1985—just in time, said James S. Henry, a former bank management consultant with McKinsey & Co., for large Mexican depositors who "have begun to shift their holdings into U.S. government securities because of concern about the health of U.S. banks that have loaned too much money to places like Mexico!"[21]

The commercial banks that have so much at stake are curiously sanguine about their own role in promoting and facilitating capital flight. They cite organizational factors, competitive pressures, and the "Swiss defense" to explain what on its face appears to be suicidal behavior. A Miami banker admitted, "There has been no debate inside the bank on our dual role because the banks are run by people who are domestically oriented. They don't see the day-to-day international business activities. . . . There is no moral issue. If we don't do it, the Swiss will." Another Miami Edge Act subsidiary manager agreed that capital flight was "one clue that was missed. A bank that saw a big jump in outflows should probably have shut down lending to that country." But he explained that the "marketing-lending side of the bank is not coordinated with the depositing side of the bank, which operates independently. There is no feedback."

Managerial structure may perhaps explain banks' failure to recognize the dangers of capital flight or to do anything about it before 1982. Officers in the private international banking division operate in great secrecy and are supposed to maintain discretion even within their own institution. Some of what they do has a cloak-and-dagger quality involving dummy corporations and secret codes. But Atkinson's comment in 1984 about the bank "acting as post office" and the joke of the German banker about colleagues going to Mexico with empty suitcases in 1986 suggest that bank behavior has not changed, even though bankers now readily acknowledge the direct and damaging relationship between capital flight and debt-servicing problems.

The basic reasons for banks' continued complicity in capital flight is that private international banking is extremely profitable. Bank management consultant James S. Henry, who examined banking practices from inside, estimated that Citibank had 1,500 people dedicated to its private banking business worldwide and over $26 billion in such funds, over half from Latin America. Citibank, he suggested, may owe more to the major Latin American debtors—or some of their citizens—than these countries owe to Citibank. The private banking divisions concentrate on large accounts. According to Henry, Citibank courts a list of 5,000 or so people, the "Global Elite," who are each worth more than $100 million, and American Express competes by offering a "Black Card" with a $500,000 credit line and "services such as private planes, bodyguards, and access to Fifth Avenue stores in the wee hours of the morning for solo shopping. At this level the key function of the card is not credit but identity: 'Do you know me? I may look like a twit, but I own Paraguay.' "[22]

Not only are George Moore's "multiplying billions of homeless dollars" a major source of funds for the banks, but management of this money on behalf of the customer yields considerable fee income to the banks in an era when banks emphasize fees over interest income. Swiss banks earn a commission of 0.25 to 0.5 percent per year on fiduciary accounts that entail no risk and no liquidity or capital requirement.

American banks seem to worry less about repatriation than about offering clients the same level of confidentiality as Swiss or other banks bidding for these deposits. When the Venezuelan government insisted on knowing whether foreign loans taken by Venezuelan companies had been collateralized by deposits outside the country, "we had to certify to company accountants whether there was a deposit in the name of the borrowing entity," said the Miami manager of a New York bank. "But we certify only exactly what is asked. We don't volunteer information. That might violate confidential client relations." He added that deposits in a name other than the borrower's can be used as collateral for a self-loan. In theory, the bank has collateral to secure the loan in the event of a default; in practice, the banks are reluctant to invoke it. "In cases where a commercial borrower has collateral but cannot pay because of an exchange shortage, we wait. We don't off-set," explained another U.S. banker. Instead of pressing val-ued customers to pay up, banks pressured the public sector to assume private-sector debt.[23]

Another Miami banker worried that U.S. banks are at a competitive disadvantage in trying to hold flight capital. "When the Mexicans and other governments cracked down, some Latin Americans got concerned about the safety of their money in the United States because there might be records of their transactions at home. . . . Mexicans became concerned after 1982 about a repeat of the Iran situation, that there would be offsets, or if there were no collateral for a loan that the banks would use personal deposits to offset."

The Latin American clients' anxiety stemmed from the be-havior of U.S. banks during the Iranian hostage crisis. In No-vember 1979 President Jimmy Carter froze Iranian assets, including $7.5 billion in deposits held by U.S. banks in for-eign and domestic branches, in retaliation for Iran's seizure of fifty-three hostages in the U.S. embassy in Tehran. Large U.S. banks moved with unseemly haste to use those deposits to repay themselves the billions in loans they had made to the shah's Iran and whose repayment had been in doubt since the Islamic fundamentalist revolution.[24] The banks concocted the "Big Mullah Theory" to justify the offsets. The theory was that because the Islamic revolution had so totally reorganized Iranian society, every Iranian entity was now identical to every other Iranian entity and deposits in the account of one party therefore could be used to pay off the debts of another. Iran challenged the legality of this argument in the courts of several countries but never obtained a final ruling. The offsets and legal challenges were superseded more than a year later by the hostage release agreement, under which the assets were unfrozen and most of Iran's bank debts were paid off.[25]

Not surprisingly, there was a clear shift of new deposits by the Arab oil states away from U.S. to European banks. Many Latin American depositors also moved their money out of U.S. banks. Swiss banks, for example, increased their share of Argentine and Brazilian flight capital in banks reporting to the BIS from 12.5 percent at the end of 1979 to more than 30 percent at the end of 1983. Additional sums may have gone into fiduciary accounts. Officials in Argentina confirm that Argentines also moved their funds out of U.S. banks during the Falkland War, fearing the United States would join the United Kingdom in freezing Argentine assets. Bankers in Buenos Aires and Miami say there was another shift of funds away from U.S. banks when 1983 Argentine stabilization talks with the IMF broke down and depositors worried that U.S. banks might again resort to offsets.

The biggest threat to banks' lucrative private banking business now comes from the antidrug war. Government regulations on unreported large cash transactions have already curtailed large financial transfers, but section 4702 of the 1988 Anti-Drug Abuse Act, sponsored by Senator John Kerry of Massachusetts, and subsequent regulations require banks to ascertain the identity of the true beneficiaries of large financial transfers, including international wire transfers. The United States has negotiated a tentative agreement with fourteen other countries, including Switzerland, to impose the same requirements on their banks. The agreement recommends that banks be required to keep records on such financial transactions and identifying documents for five years. Switzerland has already enacted money-laundering legislation making it a criminal offense to fail to take adequate steps to identify third-party beneficiaries of banking transactions, deposits, investments, or transfers. Most surprisingly, Swiss authorities in the spring of 1991 announced that they would abolish the famous numbered bank accounts. The object of these efforts is to curb drug money laundering and hence drug sales. The potential of the new record-keeping and client-identification requirements as a tool for tracking flight capital is obvious. So far, however, neither the banks nor their government have shown the slightest inclination to use it for that purpose.[26]

REPATRIATION

Debtor countries, then, are pretty much left to their own devices in dealing with capital flight. But convincing the flight capital to come home—and that means convincing people to reconvert their foreign assets into domestic assets in such a way that these become part of the official as opposed to the underground economy (internal flight capital)—is no easy task under current economic conditions.

Foreign banks used to finance Latin American government budget deficits. But with credit flow constricted, governments have had to turn to domestic sources to raise budgetary revenues to finance debt servicing and other fiscal expenditures. High real rates of interest on the order of 3 to 5 percent per month cause the domestic debt service to balloon—requiring still more borrowing, making investors still more nervous, and demanding still higher risk premiums to keep their money in the country. Interest payments on the Mexican government's domestic debt in 1990 were higher than on the foreign debt, although the latter is larger. Brazil's domestic public-sector debt grew 47 percent in 1989 alone. High interest payments and depressed imports generate enormous inflationary pressures, and weak governments feel compelled to permit at least partially offsetting wage and price increases. In 1989 inflation in Brazil hit 1,000 percent and, in Argentina, 1,800 percent. Since the public sector is absorbing virtually all savings and using them for public wages and debt servicing, investment in new productive capacity virtually stops.

In 1989, faced with a desperate situation, the governments of Argentina and Brazil halted domestic debt payments— having virtually stopped servicing their foreign bank debt some time before—and froze domestic financial assets. This drastic action temporarily halted private capital export, but the precedent served only as a further blow to confidence and a stimulus to capital flight.

The standard prescription for reversing capital flight offered by classical economists is simply to get interest rates and exchange rates right. This may work for developed, stable economies with a high degree of investor confidence: when the price is right, the money returns home. But residents of poor, historically unstable economies are looking for security perhaps even more than for returns. The price that would be sufficient to overcome these concerns may be antithetical to other economic policy objectives. High interest rates and extreme domestic credit stringency have forced some repatriation of funds by businesspeople needing to finance their domestic operations. Mexico's conclusion of a debt settlement with its banks and elimination of capital controls combined with high real rates of interest have attracted a reflow of capital in recent years. But even now, much of this is what Mexicans call "swallow money"—repatriated flight capital invested in very liquid instruments and ready to fly out at the slightest provocation. President Salinas's reforms are beginning to attract long-term investment, too. But the process is slow.

Economist Charles P. Kindleberger points out that there is little incentive for people to repatriate flight capital because these assets are highly liquid. That is, in the dollarized economies of Latin America and other developing countries, foreign-currency holdings are useful not only as a store of value but also as a means of payment. An American may wish to keep some savings in yen instruments, but those assets have to be converted to dollars to be spent at home: one cannot use yen to pay a New York cabbie, buy an apartment, or settle the rent. Not yet, anyway. Dollars, however, are an acceptable, even preferred means of payment throughout Latin America and many other economies plagued by capital flight.

The wealth accumulated abroad by citizens of the debtor countries suggests that the billions borrowed during the 1970s were not so much wasted as mismanaged. The debt has yielded real, large returns that under the right conditions could make a large contribution to economic recovery in these countries. But while creditors say that the debt problem cannot be solved until the flight capital comes home, the reverse is more probably true.

7

Sovereign Risk

A sovereign risk was no risk, none at all.
—Michael Rose, division head, Bankers Trust, London

Banks have learned that the weakest, poorest country is stronger than the strongest financial institution in this country. A sovereign state is always sovereign.
—Richard Huber, head of equity finance and global securities group, Citibank

PLEDGING THE CROWN JEWELS

When James II of Scotland borrowed 60,000 florins from Christian I, king of Denmark and Norway, he had to pledge his title to the Shetland and Orkney Islands as security. The creditors of Maximillian I required him to surrender the royal jewels of the house of Burgundy as collateral. And in 1340 Edward III of England, having already pledged his crown to the moneylenders of Brussels, asked Parliament for additional funds from the Estates of the Realm lest he be obliged to surrender his royal person as "hostage" to foreign lenders to secure his royal debts. Sovereign borrowers often had to pay usurious rates of interest in addition to offering security for the loans. Interest charges of 25 to 100 percent were not unknown.[1]

Heads of state no longer rule by divine right, and most have neither crown jewels nor royal lands to pledge to the money-lenders. The offer by an Argentine general or a president of Mexico to make himself hostage to his country's lenders would probably have no takers. Instead, a loan to a modern government ultimately becomes a claim on the public treasury. Early in this century bonds were often backed by explicit pledges of government revenue, primarily import and export duties, which were the principal source of funds for many governments—and in many developing countries continue to be. (Fifty percent of Argentina's tax revenue today comes from export taxes and a tax on oil products, and only 3 percent from income taxes.)

Countries with rich exportable natural resources—Peruvian guano, Brazilian coffee, Argentine hides, Chilean copper—were considered good risks for foreign investors because the tariff revenues they generated could be counted on to service the loans.[2] This, of course, turned out not to be so. A 1925 restructuring of Mexico's prerevolutionary debts, for example, stipulated that all taxes on Mexico's oil exports and production—Mexican oil at that time being in private, mostly foreign, hands—should be allocated to the payment of current interest on the debt starting in 1926, with full debt servicing to resume in 1928. Mexico paid about $24 million in interest, then abrogated the agreement in 1927. It is clear from the current list of "Top Ten" borrowers that, despite the frequency of such defaults, resource-rich countries have never really lost their luster as favored borrowers. It is equally clear from the performance of Korea and Taiwan, not to mention Japan, that creditworthiness may have nothing at all to do with an abundance of natural resources.

The most common form of sovereign default is currency debasement, either directly through devaluation or indirectly with inflation. Dionysius of Syracuse decreed that all money in circulation be turned in to the government, with refusal punishable by death. The coins turned in were reminted, and the two-drachmae symbol stamped on one-drachmae coins. Dionysius then repaid his outstanding debts to the people of Syracuse with the new coins. The rulers of Rome regularly reduced the precious metal content of their coin for the same purpose. Modern governments cheat their creditors by increasing the supply of paper money in circulation, producing inflation and reducing the real burden of the government's debts.

Default through currency debasement is possible, however, only when the debt is owed in the government's own currency. Denominating international loans in a "hard" foreign currency over which the sovereign borrower has no control not only allows the lender to match assets and liabilities (if the lender's source of funds is dollars, it wants its claim to be in dollars) but protects the lender against the deliberate debasement of its claim. (In countries where high inflation tends to be endemic, local investors who lend to their government prefer bonds that are indexed to some foreign currency, usually the dollar, for the same reason.)

Of course, international creditors have learned that even "hard" currencies may be debased by the actions of the issuing government. The pound sterling isn't what it used to be, and in 1971 President Richard Nixon took a series of steps that in effect forced a devaluation of the dollar. The practice of lending internationally at floating rather than fixed interest rates offers some protection to the lender—not only against being squeezed by a rising cost of funds but also against this kind of devaluation. In periods of heavy U.S. inflation or a weakening dollar exchange rate, dollar interest rates are likely to rise, and, with them, interest charges on floating-rate debt, preserving the present value of the lenders' loans. Thus protected against hidden default, lenders are left with the more basic risks that the sovereign borrower will be unable or unwilling to repay.

Moneylenders during the Middle Ages recognized that lending to a sovereign was an inherently risky business. Those who ruled by divine right could not always be counted on to respect the claims of mere bankers, and something more than a promise to repay was necessary to secure such credits.

The basic problem is the imbalance of power between a private lender and a sovereign borrower. Private individuals and corporations enter into a contractual borrower-lender relationship more or less as equals—equally subject to a body of law and courts that can punish violations of the agreement and can protect both parties. When one of the parties to the contract is a sovereign state, however, the relationship is inherently unequal. *Sovereign* means just that—"supreme controlling power, having absolute and independent authority," according to Webster. A sovereign state, by definition, is not subject to any other law unless it has surrendered some part of its sovereignty in specific situations—by treaty, contract, or under duress. And even then, it may abrogate such agreements. Ultimately, a private lender has parity only with the implicit or explicit backing of another sovereign. The lender alone has no power to hold a foreign state to either treaty or contract.

Courts of law historically offered little comfort to the creditor, generally holding that anyone foolish enough to assume the "notorious risk" of lending to a state was on his own when it came time to collect. In the annexation of Cuba after the Spanish-American War, the U.S. government took the position that it had no obligation to assume Cuban debts from Spain: "The creditors, from the beginning, took the chances of the investment. The very pledge of the national credit, while it demonstrates on the one hand the national character of the debt, on the other hand proclaims the notorious risk."[3] The United States made the further argument that there was no moral obligation to repay because the loans had been of little benefit to the people of Cuba—an argument that if applied today would wipe out a substantial portion of the Third World's indebtedness.

The traditional doctrine of sovereign immunity virtually barred private suits being brought against a foreign power. The opinion of the British High Court in 1851 sums up the prevailing attitude of Anglo-Saxon courts: "To cite a foreign potentate in a municipal court ... is contrary to the law of nations and an insult which he is entitled to resent."[4] Continental views were not much more sympathetic to private creditors. The Abbé Thierry, an eighteenth-century French minister of finance, held that every government should default at least once every 100 years to restore equilibrium.[5]

GUNBOAT DIPLOMACY

In the days of "gunboat diplomacy" sovereign loans were often enforced by violating the sovereignty of the debtor, with the help of the private creditors' own governments. This was sometimes done under the guise of a treaty forced on the hapless debtor. It became common practice in the late nineteenth century for the European powers to put weaker defaulting states' revenues under international receivership to the benefit of creditors. Between 1880 and the 1920s Egypt, Greece, Germany, Hungary, Bulgaria, and Poland all had commissioners appointed by foreign creditors to monitor their internal fiscal affairs for the protection of foreign bondholders.

In a modern version of receivership, the International Monetary Fund (IMF) in the late 1970s sent a retired German bank regulator named Irwin Blumenthal to the Zairian central bank to try to ensure that some of Zaire's considerable wealth would be available for the servicing of its substantial foreign debt. Blumenthal discovered that among the channels for transferring foreign exchange out of the country were special accounts with banks in Switzerland, Belgium, France, Germany, and the United States on which only President Mobutu and the head of the central bank could draw. Blumenthal managed to close down those accounts but soon found that there were others. Although Blumenthal as principal director of the bank had nominal control over the disbursement of the country's foreign-exchange reserves, he gave up in exasperation after less than a year, later telling the IMF in a personal letter,

> The corruptive system in Zaire with all its wicked and ugly manifestations, its mismanagement and fraud will destroy all endeavours of international institutions, of friendly governments, and of the commercial banks towards recovery and rehabilitation of Zaire's economy. Sure, there will be new promises by Mobutu, by members of his government rescheduling and rescheduling again of a growing external public debt, but no (repeat: no) prospect for Zaire's creditors to get their money back in any foreseeable future.[6]

The expression "gunboat" diplomacy grows out of a 1902 naval blockade of Venezuela by Britain, Germany, and Italy to help their banks and bondholders collect on loans to the local dictator, Cipriano Castro. The blockade prompted U.S. president Theodore Roosevelt to add what was later called the Roosevelt Corollary to the Monroe Doctrine—to the effect that henceforth the United States would assume responsibility for the external financial affairs of "backward" states in the Western Hemisphere and the European powers need no longer concern themselves.[7]

Having asserted the Western Hemisphere's freedom from

European interference, the United States shortly began dis-
patching its own fleet of gunboats southward, often for the
purpose of collecting on U.S. loans (after pressing the Central
Americans, in particular, to refinance their European debts
in New York and thus give U.S. bankers a leg up in their
competition to end Europe's dominance of international finance). U.S. Secretary of State John Hay declared in 1902,
somewhat prematurely, that "the financial center of the world,
which required thousands of years to journey from the Eu-
phrates to the Thames and Seine, seems passing to the Hud-
son between daybreak and dark."[8] Cuba was under U.S.
military rule from the end of the Spanish-American War until
1909; Haiti was occupied in 1915, and U.S. control over the
island's affairs lasted until the 1930s. U.S. troops remained in
Nicaragua from 1912 to 1933.

The Dominican Republic was governed by the U.S. military
from 1916 to 1924, but its finances had actually been in U.S.
hands since 1907. Even before sending an invasion force to
Santo Domingo, the United States had negotiated a Treaty of
Customs Receivership with the Dominican government giving
the United States authority to oversee the collection of customs revenue to ensure that sufficient sums were diverted to
service Dominican foreign debt. The customs receipts, in
other words, served as security for these countries' foreign
loans—with collection guaranteed by the U.S. Navy. When
Kuhn, Loeb arranged a $20 million loan to the Dominican
Republic in 1907, one of its officers wrote to the Secretary of
Treasury "that for all practical purposes the bonds referred
to will be based upon the faith of the United States to carry
out its treaty obligations." The reference, of course, was to
the Treaty of Customs Receivership.[9]

Although troops remained in Central America until the
1930s and the United States did not relinquish its customs
receivership in the Dominican Republic until 1940, the practice of collecting private debts by public force had already

become unfashionable by the early 1920s. When virtually the whole of Latin America went into default in the 1930s, no one sent gunboats.

The heyday of imperialism was over, Franklin Roosevelt declared a Good Neighbor policy toward Latin America, and most important, this time Latin Americans were in good company: just about everybody owed the United States money after World War I, and many European states were having trouble paying their debts, too. As a result of these World War I debts, which included considerable government-to-government lending, the national interest, as defined by Washington, was no longer seen as necessarily identical to the interest of private creditors. Indeed, private claims were seen as possibly competing with repayment of official loans.

Popular sentiment did not change as quickly. When the U.S. government finally relinquished the customs receivership over the Dominican Republic in 1940, the *New York Herald Tribune* wrote a bitter denunciation:

> Collection of the Dominican customs is to be turned over to a native Dominican, although an American has acted in that capacity since 1907, for good and sufficient reasons. Those customs receipts are the real basis for continued service on $15,250,000 Dominican dollar bonds. In place of this sound assurance, the bondholders are to receive an "irrevocable" pledge of general revenues of the Dominican regime ... The whittling down of bondholders' safeguards in the new convention illustrates once again the antagonism toward strictly American interests displayed by this Administration, when the interests happen to be those of investors.[10]

The split between Washington and Wall Street was apparent even in the early 1920s. Herbert Hoover, while Secretary of Commerce, proposed that the U.S. government adopt a formal loan-control policy and set "definite and firm standards" for foreign loans. Hoover and others in government were concerned that rising private claims on European states would eventually interfere with repayment of official war debts and reparations.

Hoover also worried that an unknowing American public was eagerly snapping up bond issues of governments with a long history of defaults and that in the event of new defaults, there would be popular pressure on the U.S. government to intervene to ensure repayment. He argued that many of the borrowers were squandering America's surplus capital on excessive consumption and, in Europe especially, military expenditures. Loans should be judged in terms of "their security, their reproductive character, and the methods of promotion." In Hoover's view loans that were used for arms, for balancing spendthrift budgets, or for supporting inflated currencies "generally would be disastrous" because such loans would not increase domestic productivity or aid in the "economic rehabilitation of the world."[11]

Under Hoover's plan, loans would have been submitted for approval by three departments: the Commerce Department would judge the economic soundness of the loan; the Treasury Department, the creditworthiness of the borrower as determined by the status of its war debts to the United States; and the State Department, the political implications of the credit. Hoover also toyed with the idea that some portion of the proceeds of a foreign loan should be tied to purchases of U.S. goods or services. His plan was strongly opposed by the banks, of course, but also by the New York Federal Reserve, which argued that formal government approval might be construed as a government guarantee. Moreover, Benjamin Strong, governor of the Federal Reserve Bank of New York, warned that Hoover's standards for "reproductive" loans "might well mean that foreign governments with unbalanced budgets and which are spending money for unproductive purposes will be unable to borrow in this market, and in consequence the American export trade will be cut down by the exact amount of all such loans as are thereby prevented from being placed here."[12]

The State Department preferred its own limited informal arrangement with the financial community by which banks (sometimes) voluntarily informed the State Department of impending loans and that department then announced whether or not the U.S. government had any objections.[13] Hoover's plan was never adopted, and the pace of foreign lending by American banks and American investors accelerated.

Foreign government issues were particularly sought after in the investment mania of the late 1920s. Two-thirds of all the foreign bonds floated in the United States in the 1920s were for governments or government entities. Latin America and the defeated enemy, Germany, were favored. Germany got almost half the money loaned to Europe in the latter half of the decade, and U.S. capital accounted for the bulk of the borrowing by German government entities and large corporations in the period. Banks acted as underwriters and salesmen. "Loan pushing" was common. Cleona Lewis reports that thirty-six American investment institutions competed to handle a Budapest municipal issue and that a Bavarian village was encouraged to borrow $3 million when it had only intended to borrow $125,000.[14] Even Morgan's Thomas W. Lamont in 1927 criticized "indiscriminate lending and indiscriminate borrowing" and "American bankers and firms competing on almost a violent scale for the purpose of obtaining loans in various money markets."[15]

Commercial banks and investment banks shared the business. Before the Glass-Steagall Act of 1933, there was no prohibition in the United States on commercial banks engaging in what is called investment banking. In the 1920s, National City Bank was one of the biggest securities underwriters on Wall Street through its investment banking offshoot, the National City Company, which originated or participated in over one-fifth of all bonds issued in the United States during the decade. This included 150 foreign bond issues for borrowers from twenty-six countries.[16] National City Company had a network of fifty-one offices spread over the country to "make connections with the great new bond-buying public . . ." through which it could market foreign and domestic issues.[17] Investment houses like Morgan, which originated many of the foreign government issues sold in the United States, relied heavily on National City Company's branch network to distribute them.

National City and other banks engaged in securities underwriting were not above peddling securities to the public that they thought too risky to hold for their own account. Congressional hearings in the 1930s revealed, among other things, that National City floated three loans totaling $90 million to Peru while its own experts described the credit position of its government as "an adverse moral and political risk"; National City Company's public prospectus for a $8.5 million bond issue for the Brazilian state Minas Geráis in 1928 praised the administration of the state's finances even though one of its own officials had described the borrower as lax, negligent, and entirely uniformed of the responsibilities of a long-term borrower. Half the proceeds of that issue were used by Minas to repay short-term credits from National City Bank. The hearings also showed how National City Bank through a complex maneuver managed to dump $25 million in worthless Cuban sugar loans on National City Company, whose public stockholders had to absorb the loss.[18]

The Scripps-Howard columnist Heywood Broun commented on the National City hearings that "The only thing that some of our great financial institutions overlooked during the years of boom was the installation of a roulette-wheel for the convenience of depositors."[19]

There was little official sympathy when many of these bonds went into default—and no government retaliation against

Latin America. And when Hitler's central banker, Hjalmar Schacht, came to Washington in 1933 to tell President Franklin D. Roosevelt that he was about to forbid the remittance of foreign exchange for the servicing of private foreign debts (Germany was the largest foreign issuer of bonds in New York in the 1920s), Schacht claimed the president exclaimed, "Serves the Wall Street Bankers right!"[20] The British attitude also changed. The first postwar Chancellor of the Exchequer, when pressed in Parliament to do something about the Japanese suspension of payments to British investors, responded "to the effect that it served the British bondholders right to lose their money—why did they lend to Japan?[21] Larger political considerations now outweighed the individual concerns of private investors.

SOVEREIGN IMMUNITY

In the post–World War II period international lenders have taken refuge in the intricacies of contract law. A standard loan contract sets out with considerable specificity the conditions under which the lender may declare the borrower in default. From a legal standpoint default is in the eyes of the beholder: it hasn't happened unless the creditor formally declares the loan in default. The major grounds for declaring default are failure to pay interest or principal on time, which in turn entitles the lender to pursue remedies—among them accelerating the due date, using any of the borrower's deposits in its control to offset the loan, and bringing suit in a court of law.

When the parties to a contract are citizens of different states, there is normally a clause in the contract stating whose laws shall govern in the event of a dispute. Eurodollar loan agreements usually designate U.S. federal law, New York state law, or U.K. law, even when neither party is a U.S. or British citizen, because execution of the loan agreement is likely to take place in New York or London, the two principal international banking centers.

Despite the care taken in drafting international loan contracts, especially when the borrower is a government entity, legal action in cases of cross-border default is rare.

Conditions of sovereign default have clearly been present repeatedly during the 1970s—Indonesia and Zaire, for example—and massively since 1982, yet banks have almost never formally declared a borrower legally in default or brought suit under the terms of their loan contracts. On the contrary, large lenders have exerted considerable pressure on smaller banks *not* to pursue legal remedies, which because of cross-default clauses could force other lenders to do the same. Even when Poland fell behind on its payments in 1981 and U.S. government guarantees covering some loans could be activated only with a formal default declaration, the banks were reluctant to take the step. Cross-default clauses might have triggered a cascade of default declarations on noninsured loans and eventually forced the banks to recognize some losses on their Polish portfolio.

The U.S. government let the banks, and Warsaw, off the hook by waiving the default requirement and paying off the government-insured loans. Reagan administration officials explained that while they wanted to keep financial pressure on Poland to protest the imposition of martial law and suppression of the Solidarity movement, they feared that a formal default declaration would disrupt the financial system—in 1981 a $14 billion bank debt still looked huge—and create political strains within the Western alliance. Germany, in particular, wanted to avoid a complete break with Poland.[22]

Outright repudiation, which would force the lenders' hand, has been rare historically and has not happened in the 1980s debt crisis. Failure to live up to loan agreements has instead taken the form of what Anatole Kaletsky calls "conciliatory defaults." The debtor assures its creditors that although it isn't paying now, it has the very best intentions and will pay when it can.

The banks' reluctance to pursue legal remedies against a sovereign debtor is understandable. Britain and the United States have recently tried to make it easier for private parties to take a foreign government to court by enacting legislation that distinguishes between purely commercial and other official activities of foreign states in their jurisdiction. But both the U.S. Sovereign Immunities Act of 1976 and Britain's State Immunity Act of 1978 leave formidable obstacles to the successful pursuit of legal remedy.

A foreign state remains immune from the jurisdiction of federal and state courts throughout the United States except when there is an implicit or an explicit waiver of immunity. The law states that there is an implicit waiver of immunity for commercial activity, but only if it has "direct effect" in and "substantial contact" with the United States. It is not at all certain from court rulings under the Act that a Eurodollar loan to a foreign government from a New York bank negotiated in London, or even in New York and payable in U.S. dollars, would constitute "substantial contact" sufficient to establish U.S. court jurisdiction.

Banks often insist on an explicit waiver clause on immunity against suit or attachment of property pursuant to a court judgment. But the Act recognizes such waivers as applying only to attachment of property "used for a commercial activity in the United States." Embassies, military property, personal property, and assets with international financial institutions such as the IMF or the World Bank are protected.

And the Act gives special status to the property of a foreign central bank or monetary authority—likely the most attractive attachment target for a creditor. The law recognizes an explicit waiver of immunity against execution by a central bank but is silent on the waiver of immunity from prejudgment attachment a court may issue to prevent the target of a suit from moving assets out of the court's jurisdiction before a final ruling is issued.

The New York Federal Reserve, where many foreign central banks keep their gold and foreign-exchange reserves, has argued that this legislative omission is deliberate, giving foreign central banks irrevocable—even after voluntary waiver—immunity from prejudgment attachment.[23] During the Iran hostage crisis U.S. courts issued injunctions blocking the transfer of Iranian assets out of the country. But even then a court order (*Pfizer v. Islamic Republic of Iran*) specifically excluded the foreign-currency reserves of the Bank Markazi Iran. Britain's State Immunity Act recognizes waiver of immunity by a central bank, but no prejudgment attachments ("Mareva injunctions" in Britain) have ever been imposed in a case involving a foreign central bank.[24]

Even if the legal obstacle of sovereign immunity could be overcome, large debtors are unlikely to have sufficient attachable assets in any one jurisdiction to make whole the creditors as a group. A debtor planning to default can move to protect itself by moving its assets out of reach first. Brazil, before declaring a moratorium on interest payments to foreign banks in 1987, moved its central-bank assets out of commercial banks and the Federal Reserve Bank of New York to the neutral and inviolable Bank for International Settlements in Basle. (The resulting loss of substantial interest income was reportedly one factor in Brazil's decision eventually to rescind the moratorium and negotiate with the banks.) With the possible exception of Mobutu Sese Seko's Swiss bank accounts, suit against a defaulting debtor would have to be brought in many jurisdictions, with different laws, years of litigation, and an uncertain outcome. Litigation might impede certain commercial activities but would by no means tie up a defaulting debtor's entire foreign commerce in the courts.

The threat of seizure of Brazilian coffee shipments or Mexican oil in a foreign port as payment for some government debt is clearly unrealistic. A debtor has only to arrange transfer of ownership in its own ports—already standard practice in the oil and grain trade—or in a jurisdiction where the creditor has no legal standing. Even direct commerce with the creditor country need not be disrupted. The People's Republic of China (PRC), for example, bought jumbo jets from Boeing before it had settled its prerevolution debts to the United States. China simply had Boeing fly the planes to the PRC (with U.S. government approval) and took legal possession only on delivery.

Shortly after the debt crisis broke in 1982 the New York Federal Reserve produced a volume of exhaustive analysis several inches thick on the legal remedies banks might pursue against Latin American defaulters and concluded there weren't many. "We sent it out to all the banks saying, 'Don't get carried away; it might not stand up in court,'" said a senior Fed staff member. Clearly, the big banks had already reached this conclusion. Virtually the only time a major legal action has been taken by the large banks against a defaulting sovereign debtor in recent times was against Iran, and that only under the extraordinary circumstances of the 1978 to 1979 hostage crisis, when the U.S. government revoked Iran's sovereign immunity under the Economic Emergency Powers Act and froze its assets, including deposits in U.S. banks.

The Iran situation was also unique in that the country was both a large depositor in and a large borrower from U.S. banks and the banks moved immediately after the freeze was announced—indeed within hours—to seize all Iranian deposits in their overseas branches (Washington ordered that deposits in the United States proper were to be reserved for awards to nonbank claimants) to pay off their outstanding loans to Iran.

It was not at all certain that foreign courts would uphold the extraterritorial reach of Washington's freeze decree or the legality of the banks' offsets. Iran could argue that the offsets were unjustified because it had faithfully serviced its debts until the freeze made this impossible. Furthermore, as already noted, the banks had invoked a dubious "Big Mullah Theory" that the Islamic revolution had so roiled Iranian society that every Iranian person or entity was now identical with every other. The funds belonging to one Iranian depositor could therefore properly be seized by a bank to satisfy a claim against an unrelated Iranian borrower.

As Kaletsky points out in his excellent analysis *The Costs of Default*, this theory goes against the legal doctrine of "the veil of incorporation." Even "nationalized corporations, wholly owned by the government and central banks, are recognized by the courts of most countries as distinct legal entities, separate from their governments and liable only for their own defaults."[25]

To further secure their claims, some banks moved in foreign courts to attach other Iranian assets—Morgan Guaranty to attach Iranian shares of the German company Krupp, Chemical Bank to hold up a payment by the British Water Council on a loan from Iran, and so forth. Iran, of course, challenged the attachments and the offsets, as well as the extraterritorial reach of the original asset freeze, in courts around Europe.

Iran might even have challenged the legality of the bank loans themselves. At least one New York lawyer had warned his client Chase Manhattan Bank in the mid-1970s that a jumbo $500 million syndicated loan contract with Iran was not properly documented because the borrowing had not been approved by the Iranian parliament as required by Article 25 of the Iranian constitution. His warning was ignored. Apparently Chase's close ties to the shah were considered sufficient guarantee.

Had the Iranians successfully challenged the loan, Chase would not only have been out its own share of the syndication but possibly also liable to other lending banks. As manager of the syndication—for which it earned an extra fee—Chase was responsible for preparing the credit documentation and might have been charged with negligence leading to a loan loss.[26]

Since this was the first loan that Chase moved to declare in default within hours of the U.S. Treasury's freeze announcement and without consulting other syndicate members, there has been some suspicion that the freeze was encouraged by Chase and other large U.S. banks, which felt their interests threatened by the new regime in Iran. Chase, whose chairman, David Rockefeller, was a friend of the shah and played a crucial role in bringing the shah to the United States for medical treatment after his exile, had already lost the Iranian oil account, and other deposits were being withdrawn. With some Iranian officials arguing that loans that had ultimately been only to the personal benefit of the ruling Pahlavi family need not be repaid, Chase risked being left with loans the new government in Tehran repudiated and no opportunity to offset.

Key Carter administration officials and bankers alike deny that there was a deal on the freeze. However, there is no doubt that the big banks knew it was coming, welcomed it, and were ready to take immediate advantage. According to the Citibank lawyer who carried on nine months of secret negotiations with Iran after the freeze, the banks had started looking for a way to offset their loans with Iranian deposits shortly after the revolution. Since the Iranians were scrupulous about paying on time—a payment order had even gone out for the loan Chase declared in default on the morning of the freeze—there were no legal grounds to do so, absent the freeze. The freeze made it virtually impossible for Iran to transfer dollar funds for any purpose, including debt servicing, and thus gave the banks an opening to declare a default, which in turn opened the way to the offsets. (It should be noted that banks that had loans out to Iran but no deposits to seize as an offset were far less enthusiastic than the big banks about a freeze. They were stuck with a nonpaying asset that had to be funded and had to wait for the hostage settlement to collect anything at all.)

Neither the banks (which feared troublesome legal precedents) nor the European governments (which worried about undermining the U.S. government's efforts to secure release of the hostages) were eager to see the courts proceed to a final ruling on Iran's challenges to the asset freeze, offsets, and other attachments by the banks. Litigation was delayed until the cases were dropped as part of the final hostage settlement—in which Iran agreed to pay off its loan in full, immediately. Thus the underlying legal issues were not settled at that time.[27]

In 1987 Britain's High Court held that a 1986 Executive Order by the Reagan administration freezing all Libyan assets did not extend to Libyan bank deposits in the London branches of U.S. banks. Bankers Trust had argued that it could not legally transfer $131 million from its London branch to a Libyan account with another bank because such a dollar transaction would normally be cleared electronically through the Clearing House Interbank Payment System (CHIPS) in New York and the freeze order barred any transfer of Libyan funds from one account in New York to another. Libya argued that, in theory, it had a right just to back up a truck to the London branch and demand its dollars in cash. Therefore, U.S. law was irrelevant. The U.K. court held for Libya.[28]

The British ruling has important implications beyond the issue of the extraterritorial reach of U.S. freeze orders. It would seem also to limit lenders' opportunities to retaliate against an errant debtor by barring its access to the international dollar payments system. A U.S. court order attaching dollar transfers between the defaulter would complicate the commercial life of the target country but would not necessarily compel it to pay.

Giving the banks permission to offset complicated the final

hostage settlement with Iran. Since the agreement was in effect to restore the *status quo ante*—hostages released, money returned—all the bank offsets had to be undone. However, the banks that held the deposits insisted that Iran should agree to pay off all loans before any frozen funds were returned. The negotiations dragged on until the waning minutes of the Carter administration before Iran and the banks could finally come to terms on a debt settlement and the exchange could proceed.

The Bush administration apparently learned from Carter's experience. When it and its allies froze nearly $20 billion in Iraqi and Kuwaiti deposits after Hussein's invasion of Kuwait, banks were told that under no circumstances were they to offset. Iraq owed banks in the industrial countries more than $10 billion (that is not guaranteed by the banks' own governments) and had deposits of roughly $3 billion. Banks thus will have to await the outcome of the crisis and the evolution of Iraq's debt-burdened economy. (The country is thought to owe a total of at least $80 billion to private and government creditors.)

Back in the early 1970s, a leading New York investment firm was called in to help untangle the messy financial affairs of the Indonesian state oil company, Pertamina, which had piled up more than $7 billion in debts it couldn't pay. The investment bankers were shocked to find that many lenders had almost no documentation to back up their claims. The sole documentation for one $25 million loan was the scribbled signature of General Ibnu Sutowo, the powerful head of Pertamina, scrawled on the inside cover of a matchbook from one of Djakarta's more famous nightclubs. In light of the legal experience of the 1980s, perhaps that is all the documentation banks should bother with when making a sovereign loan.

"COUNTRIES NEVER GO BANKRUPT"

Without a lien on the crown jewels, without gunboats, and without courts of law for protection, what security is there for the modern banker who ventures to lend to sovereigns? Why did bankers insist so confidently in the 1970s that "sovereign risk was no risk, no risk at all"?

Under Roman law a person who failed to pay his debts could be dismembered and the limbs distributed to his creditors. Modern societies have provided less drastic means to satisfy one's creditors—through bankruptcy. Bankruptcy law carries forward the Roman principal of dismemberment, but less bloodily. An insolvent corporation will be liquidated, or dismembered, and its assets distributed to the creditors pro rata. An individual debtor does not lose his limbs, but may be forced to give up most of his wealth while keeping some basic necessities, like a house and a car. Painful though this may be, once the debtor has gone through the legal bankruptcy process its debts are permanently discharged. Even if the liquidation yields the creditors little or nothing, the creditors have no further legal claim. From the creditor's standpoint, it is as if the debtor had died.

But the discharged debtor, even a company, can be resurrected in a new incorporation and can live to borrow another day. To be sure, its past poor payment record may be an impediment, but its old debts will *not* be. By one important measure of creditworthiness—debts outstanding—the borrower will now look like a good risk.

It is also possible, under Chapter 11 of the U.S. bankruptcy statute, for example, for a near-insolvent company to seek the protection of a court without going through a full liquidation. In a Chapter 11 reorganization, the company loses managerial autonomy, the old stockholders may lose their investment, and the creditors become the new owners, substituting equity for the loans. But the entity continues to operate under the court's protection and may even contract new loans that are prior to the old claims. That is, the new lenders will be paid off first.

Sovereign debtors, however, do not have these legal avenues of escape. Although country-debt restructurings linked to an IMF stabilization agreement have sometimes been compared to a Chapter 11 reorganization, they are different in two vital areas: the IMF does not have the authority to force a substitution of assets or to permit the debtor to permanently discharge its debts through partial payment; nor does it have the power to order that old loans will be subordinate to new loans secured under the reorganization.

This absence of a recognized international bankruptcy procedure for sovereign states has been seen by the banks as their best guarantee against permanent sovereign defaults. Winkler described the age-old belief in his 1933 study of sovereign bonds:

> Now no matter how well a man may be regarded as a credit risk, he may die and leave his creditors at an impasse, their moneys unrecoverable. A State, on the other hand, with its government taking no matter what form, may continue to exist through the ages, and continues to hold out hope, however vain, of settlement of its debts.[29]

The modern version is Walter Wriston's dictum that "countries never go bankrupt." (In fact, what Wriston said was that countries "don't go out of business.")[30] That is, although the condition precedent to bankruptcy may exist (a country may be insolvent or near-insolvent), as long as there is no internationally recognized bankruptcy court whose protection a sovereign debtor can seek—no independent arbiter with the power to say, "Pay X percent of your debts, and that settles the matter"—banks can keep pressing their claims.

When the debt crisis broke in 1982, it was therefore of vital importance to the lenders to try to convert as many as possible of their private-sector loans into sovereign loans. Banks began pressuring debtor governments to assume the foreign-exchange burden of bank and private nonbank debts whether or not they carried explicit exchange guarantees when the loans were contracted. Mexico nationalized the banking sector outright, much to the relief of foreign creditors, who didn't see how the banks were going to repay them. The Pinochet government assumed the foreign obligations of Chilean banks after pressure from foreign lenders. Other debtor governments have been pressured into accepting responsibility for the foreign debts of failed local banks and for many corporations that might have been wiped out if they had to pay off their foreign loans at postdevaluation exchange rates. In 1982, U.S. banks' cross-border claims on developing countries were evenly distributed one-third each on banks,[31] private nonbanks, and the public sector. By 1987, roughly two-thirds of all bank claims were on the public sector.

Loans to multinational corporations, however, posed a difficult problem. Much of the foreign-bank lending to the private sector, perhaps the bulk—though there are no good statistics—were loans to subsidiaries of multinational corporations. Multinationals, like local companies, found that tax policies, high interest rates, and underdeveloped capital markets in the host countries made foreign sources of capital attractive. And parent companies preferred to have their subsidiaries borrow rather than commit parent-company capital. A survey by a Mexican academic found that 55 percent of the investment inflow to that country from foreign multinationals he polled was financed with bank debt.

When such borrowings are done in the name of the LDC affiliate, which is usually the case, the company's liability becomes part of the host country's foreign debt. These obligations accumulated by multinationals were no small part of Latin America's foreign debt problem. Roberto Bonder Bornhausen of Unibanco, one of Brazil's largest commercial banks, estimated that the biggest part of Brazil's private-sector foreign debt when the crisis began consisted of loans from MNC parents to the local affiliate or of local affiliate borrowing. Brazil had about $30 billion in private sector foreign debt, and MNCs may have accounted for as much as $20 billion of that.

These loans were a special problem for the banks since they could not compel debtor governments to assume the obligation. When the debt crisis hit, many multinational companies insisted their LDC affilliates should be treated like local companies and their debts rescheduled like everyone else's. SAAB's 100 percent-owned Brazilian manufacturing subsidiary had 40 percent of the truck market in Brazil and a substantial share of the bus market, with virtually all the vehicles produced in its factory outside São Paulo. According to financial officer Håkan Frisk in 1984, "All our foreign loans are part of Brazil's rescheduling. The banks wanted head office to pay, but the parent said no." SAAB's position, he thought, was the rule among multinationals rather than the exception.

"Comfort letters," in which the parent company acknowledges certain parental responsibilities and which in recent years have accompanied foreign-bank loans to a local MNC affiliate, have in fact given little comfort to the lenders. Stig Dale, head of Sweden's PK Bank office in São Paulo admitted, "MNC guarantees from the parent companies have not been air tight." Alfredo Salazar, manager of Chase Manhattan in Buenos Aires, said the bank considered loans to multinational subsidiaries to be non-Argentine risk because of the comfort letters. "But when we go to ask for payment, the parent says this is sovereign risk, and we only agreed to cover commercial risk." In 1988, according to Kimberly-Clark de Mexico's chief financial officer, major foreign banks including Morgan, Citi, and Chase allowed the company to pay off $62 million in loans at discounts of 30 to 50 percent rather than have the loans included in Mexico's 1987 jumbo 14-year restructuring of private sector debt. Other multinationals have reportedly been offered similar deals. Much of the debt reduction that countries carried out in the two years before the Brady Plan involved prepayment of bank debt by multinational affiliates. In May, 1989, the British high court upheld the MNCs' bargaining position. It ruled that a comfort letter is "accepted on both sides as indicating a moral rather than a legal liability to ensure payment" and "cannot be legally enforced as a contractual promise to ensure repayment of a loan."[32]

With a government as the counterparty on most loans, banks could continue to press their claims. No court may be able to adjudicate the claims or, if it does, to execute settlement. But creditors could continue to deny the debtor country legal standing. And new lenders were unlikely to step up with fresh credits as long as the old claims remained unsettled, for fear that their own claim might become entangled. Sooner or later, the banks reasoned, a sovereign debtor will have need of its good name in order to borrow again and will have to come to terms with its creditors. So bankers convinced themselves that even without the aid of gunboats, as long as private creditors stuck together and controlled the debtor's access to the credit markets, and their own governments backed them up, they could bring the debtor to heel. On this basis the banks went into the debt-restructuring phase of sovereign lending.

8

Stop the World

The debt has been rescheduled for a hundred years. It's just a question of how often we have to meet.

—Carlos Lemgruber, São Paulo, 1984

BRAZIL AND CITIBANK PULL THE PLUG

The board of directors of Citicorp, Citibank's parent holding company, is said to have chosen John S. Reed over his more senior colleagues to succeed Walter Wriston as chairman because of Reed's superior ability to make strategic decisions. It didn't take Reed long to prove their point. On 20 May 1987 the young chairman of Citicorp stunned the financial community at a news conference called after the stock market had closed and with only two hours' notice to the press. He announced that his institution was increasing its loan-loss reserves by $3 billion and as a result would show a $2.5 billion loss for the quarter—the biggest loss ever reported by an American bank.

Reed offered as an explanation the generally bleak payments prospects for developing countries to which Citibank had lent $15 billion. (Citibank's total Third World loan port-folio was closer to $25 billion. The lower figure was for coun-tries that had rescheduled since 1982.) The announced increase in loan-loss reserves amounted to a 25 percent pro-vision against an anticipated drop in the value of Citibank's troubled Third World loans.

Citibank later explained that the precipitating event lead-ing to Reed's decision had been Brazil's unilateral interest moratorium announced three months earlier. In late Feb-ruary the Brazilian government had declared that it would not—and could not—continue to pay the interest on the country's $100 billion foreign debt and that it wanted a deal on the debt new and fundamentally different from what had been negotiated since 1983. Brazil's "temporary" morato-rium left creditor banks no choice but to put their Brazil loan portfolios on nonaccrual—that is, to stop including an-ticipated interest income from Brazil in their reported earn-ings. Virtually overnight U.S. banks had to add more than $23 billion to their stock of nonperforming loans, a further blot on the multinational banks' already shaky standing with investors.[1]

Reed's action, however, was in part merely an accounting change. Of the $3 billion allocated to loan-loss reserves, only the $500 million that came out of current earnings consti-tuted a real increase in the bank's cushion against losses. The other $2.5 billion involved a balance-sheet transfer from col-umn A, *equity*, to column B, *loan-loss reserve*. Under U.S. reg-ulation before 1989 both A and B counted as primary capital for capital-adequacy purposes. The $2.5 billion shift had to be accounted for on the income statement as an operating loss (not recognized as a real loss by the Internal Revenue Service since no write-off of assets was involved). But the bank expected to recover that on future income statements by claiming tax deductions in advance of future write-offs (see chapter 5). The magnitude of the fakery may have spurred the Fed to try to tighten the definition of bank capital. But Reed's move had the desired public relations impact.

With the announced increase in loan-loss reserves, the biggest commercial lender to developing countries appeared to draw what the Germans call a *schluβstrich*, or bottom line, under its sovereign loans, recognizing losses that Reed's predecessor Walter Wriston always adamantly denied would ever have to be taken. Although Reed insisted that his bank would continue to participate in country-debt restructurings and to lend to troubled debtors, he added, "This idea of getting the countries back to the voluntary market without a blip just isn't there"—thereby knocking the intellectual supports out from under the debt-rescheduling process as it had been conducted since 1982.

Reed also stated that Citibank hoped to convert, swap out of, sell, or otherwise dispose of up to one-third of its troubled developing-country loan portfolio. The loan-loss reserve would enable the bank to dispose of loans at below face value and nearer the going market rate—Brazilian debt was then trading for around sixty-three cents on the dollar on the small secondary market that had developed since 1982—without significant penalties to future earnings. Losses incurred in selling or converting the loans at a discount would be charged against the reserve.

Between them, the second-biggest international borrower (Brazil having just been surpassed by the United States) and the biggest international commercial lender had altered the terms for solving the international debt problem. Although they refused to admit that they were doing so—indeed, insisted they were not—Brazil and Citibank were violating the basic tenets of the global debt-restructuring policy that had been followed since 1982: that important steps pertaining to the debt must be taken collectively; that debtors must maintain interest payments in full; that consequently, these loans continued to be worth 100 cents on the dollar and therefore

no extraordinary reserving by banks was required. These tenets were meant to preserve the appearance of near normalcy
and to support the assertion by both sides that voluntary
lending would soon recover.

CASSANDRA ANSWERS WRISTON

In 1982 the idea that banks would soon be back to sovereign-
risk lending as usual (well, maybe not at quite the same volumes as before) did not seem absurd. The full implications
of OPEC's fall and Japan's rise as the world's biggest saver
and principal source of market liquidity were not yet obvious.
The well-spring of the massive Eurocurrency lending of the
previous decade—an ample supply of cheap petrodollar deposits—was drying up. The locus of international financial
activity was shifting to the securities side of the market, to
Eurobonds and notes and eventually to equities, where investors are said (at least until the advent of the junk bond) to be
more risk averse and where commercial banks are not the
dominant players. And the United States was just beginning
its own sovereign borrowing binge.

But in 1982 the prevailing view among creditors was that
the international debt problem was short-term and that the
relationship between the debtor countries and the commercial banks would soon be back to "normal." All that was required was for the debtors to tighten their belts and continue
paying interest and for banks to agree to wait for repayment
of their loans, regardless of maturity, while continuing to
"keep the conduits open," in the words of Walter Wriston—
that is, lend enough to enable debtors to maintain interest
payments.[2]

Normal meant a gradual return to the market by Mexico,
Brazil, and the other major debtors and a resumption of voluntary lending by the banks. (Bolivia, Nicaragua, Sudan, and

some other African borrowers were put in a separate category of hopeless cases.) "Mexico had a plan," said a California banker, "to go back to the market in late 1985 or early 1986, at the latest, with Pemex and NAFINSA, then the United States of Mexico." Brazil, it was said, would be back as soon as the transition from a military to a civilian government was completed.

In this scenario, debt relief through concessional interest rates or outright debt forgiveness was out of the question: if debtors did not live up to market principles during the crisis, bankers argued, the market would never welcome them back voluntarily. Washington economist William Cline—whose prediction that a 3 percent growth rate in the OECD industrial countries would solve the debt problem was often cited in support of the short-term approach[3]—put the argument succinctly: "Debt forgiveness," wrote Cline, "is incompatible with improving the debtor country's creditworthiness and returning the country to normal access to international capital markets. Any improved capacity to service reduced debt would tend to be more than offset by the deterioration in creditors' perception of the country's willingness to pay.... Credit reputation is crucial in sovereign borrowing where physical collateral is absent."[4]

Commentators who dared to suggest the debt problem was more than temporary and that big losses lay ahead for the banks were dismissed as Cassandras by Citibank chairman Walter Wriston. (Wriston apparently forgot that although the Cassandra of Greek legend had been condemned by the gods to have her predictions ignored, her prophesies came true; Troy was destroyed as she had warned.) Any suggestion that banks should build a cushion against possible losses on their foreign loans was consistently rejected by Citibank and other U.S. banks. Citibank's chief spokesperson on the debt problem told a congressional committee in 1983, "The first proposal that really worries me is the suggestion that the commercial banks would be asked to establish large reserves against our sovereign risk loans in specific countries. . . . The establishment of reserves for sovereign loans would be to apply a process that is well-developed for corporate and consumer lending, but which basically does not apply for sovereign risk lenders. . . . The only norm that I can think of for sovereign lenders is that the record bears out that governments do pay their international debts."[5]

Many members of Congress were critical of the debt strategy almost from the start. Senator Bill Brady of New Jersey cautiously suggested a negotiated debt reduction of 3 percent for the banks. That was dismissed by both the administration and the banks. Congress itself had little leverage except to hold up appropriations for the IMF and the multilateral development banks. But that seemed too drastic a step even for the strongest critics.

James Robinson III, chairman of American Express, at one point proposed that an intergovernmental entity buy up the bank debt at a discount. That, too, was dismissed by bankers and by governments. The latter had no desire to pick up more of the banks' troubles than they had to.

Despite the forced nature of post-1982 lending, bankers continued to insist that all solutions had to be market based. Deferring some interest payments by incorporating them in rescheduled principal "poses no serious problems for us," said a German banker in mid-1985, "except that it undermines the ability of Mexico and the rest to return to the free market. You can't have an image of steady progress if you go to interest capitalization because that is a nonmarket element."

Only when it came down to the question of how troubled debtors should treat their bondholders did the commercial banks decide a "good name" was less important than making sure no one got paid before themselves. According to Rodolfo Silva, who was Costa Rica's chief debt negotiator in

1982, the bank steering committee told Costa Rica, "If you are not paying interest to the banks, you are not to pay anyone—bondholders, suppliers, governments." When Costa Rica continued to pay on its foreign bonds anyway, some U.S. banks threatened to go to court and call a default. The situation was awkward, however, because several Swiss and German banks on the steering committee had acted as bond underwriters as well as lenders. They were not so eager to see a default on bonds behind which they had put *their* good name. When Mexico and Brazil decided to continue servicing their bonds—and default must have been very tempting for the Mexicans at a time when interest rates had dropped below 10 percent and their bonds were paying a 17 percent coupon—the heat was off the smaller debtor. One German bank even made a loan to Costa Rica so it could pay the bondholders and avoid being in arrears on the bonds the bank had underwritten in the German market.

There are several explanations for the initial insistence by a majority of banks that this was a short-term problem in the face of strong evidence to the contrary. The bankers who had made these loans were quite naturally reluctant to admit that they blundered colossally in making them. During the 1970s international lending was the fast track to top banking positions, and by 1982 management at the biggest banks was firmly in the hands of those who had made their careers on the international side of the bank—Wriston, Angermueller, and Theobald at Citibank; Preston and Weatherstone at Morgan; Rockefeller and Ogden at Chase; Herrhausen, one of the two cospokesmen at Deutsche Bank; Bank of America's Clausen. Said a leading investment banker in London in 1986, "U.S. banks by all classical accounting are bust, and instead of making reserves that would sack management and lose stockholders' money, they drag it out to justify their past actions."

The middle managers most directly charged with handling

the problem were usually the people who had made the loans. Rodolfo Silva points out that the steering committee for Costa Rica was composed of "just those bank officials who in '79, '80, and '81 made all those imprudent loans to Costa Rica. Imagine how they felt: they had been part of the process. How can they be a reasonable negotiator? They're just trying to get the money back to save their careers."

In a variation on this scene, Carlos Rodriguez Pastor for a time headed international banking at Wells Fargo and among other deals put together a large syndication for the Peruvian oil pipeline. A few years later Rodriguez found himself on the other side of the table as one of Peru's principal debt negotiators in the Bellaunde government—seeking a stretch-out of the very loan he had made as a commercial banker. A former colleague said, "He told the bankers around the table, 'I know what you were thinking when you made the loan, and you're not going to get paid right now.' "

Some young lending officers at first found their careers enhanced by the crisis. "I liken this to the REIT [real estate investment trust] crisis a few years ago. People who were responsible for bad lending were thrust into the limelight because they knew the most about it and were put in charge of restructuring. Some thrived and advanced as a result of the successful salvage. It's the same in international," said one young New York banker, adding, "I've had more fun at these countries' expense in the last two years than in all my other years of banking."

The principal reason for this misplaced euphoria was that the debt strategy seemed at first to succeed beyond all expectations where it counts the most—on the bottom line. The profits of the big multinational banks soared in the first years of the debt crisis because in keeping with the "liquidity problem" approach, interest spreads and fees on the restructured and new loans were raised substantially, making them even more profitable than before. Banks tripled the spread on their new loans to Mexico, for example. And the December, 1982 rescheduling of $20 billion in Mexican debt gave bank $260 million in front-end fees. The gleeful comment by an American banker about Poland soon after its rescheduling—"They've become a cash cow for us. We hope they *never* repay!"—could just as well have been spoken about Mexico, Brazil, et al. Citibank made $163 million on Brazil alone, in 1983 and again in 1984, roughly 20 percent of its total world-wide earnings for those two years. In 1984, two years into the crisis, the big U.S. money center banks paid shareholders double the dividend they had paid in 1980. Charge-offs were only 0.3 percent of international loans.

The multiple, protracted debt negotiations themselves were hugely expensive to the debtors. The debtor was required to reimburse the Bank Advisory Committee, which negotiated on behalf of the banks, for all "reasonable" expenses incurred by the committee over the months of negotiation. These expenses included legal and accounting fees, air fares, hotel accommodations (at the best hotels, of course), meals, documentation cost, et cetera. An Argentine government lawyer complained that they were even being asked to pick up baby-sitting expenses for one of the bank negotiators.

Security Pacific was one of the few banks to dissent from the prevailing bank view. Robert M. Lorenz, chairman of the California bank's credit committee, said, "We took an opposed position to the principal steering committee banks. . . . They take the position that this is a short-term, liquidity problem. We say they have a medium-term insolvency.

"The definitional difference is very important. If General Electric comes to its bank and says, 'We have a cash-flow problem and we need to stretch out our payment schedule,' you make them a loan and charge a premium because they are no longer quite a prime risk.

"But if they come to you and say, 'We are nearly insolvent,' you take an entirely different approach. You give relief; you take equity, bonds, other forms of assets. You don't increase the interest or tack on big front-end fees."

Security Pacific's "Chapter 11" approach would most probably have meant taking some losses immediately, and that was something most lenders were not prepared to accept. The sovereign-lending merry-go-round instead kept going 'round for another five years, propelled by collective fear of the consequences if it stopped altogether. To be sure, Bolivia and Nicaragua fell by the wayside early, and Peru bailed out under the new civilian government of Alan Garcia, who stated flatly his country would pay for debt servicing only an amount equal to 10 percent of its export earnings. But these dropouts were too insignificant by themselves to force a reconsideration of the policy.

THE COMMITTEES

The IMF and the U.S. Federal Reserve insisted from the beginning that no government funds would be committed to the rescue unless the banks also continued to lend. "Concerted" or "involuntary" lending replaced spontaneous lending; collective bargaining replaced individual bank deals and international syndicates. With the IMF, the U.S. Treasury, and various central banks looking over their shoulders, a country advisory committee of twelve to fourteen banks negotiated new repayment schedule for old loans and terms for new loans to enable the debtor to continue to pay the interest. The debtor government negotiated on behalf of virtually all borrowers in that country—state enterprises, municipalities, and often, even the private sector. Credits of all kinds were thrown into the same rescheduling pot, much to the dismay of some bankers, who felt that they had acted prudently by concentrating on short-term trade credits and had dealt mostly with the private sector.

Large banks ran the show. "We'd just as soon not have some other bank play our cards, if possible," said a Morgan Guaranty spokesperson. The Mexico committee had thirteen large banks negotiating on behalf of 480 institutions. One of the big British clearing banks represented other British, Middle Eastern, and African lenders (there were such); a French bank represented the French, Spanish, Portuguese, and Belgian banks; Deutsche Bank spoke for the Dutch and Scandinavians as well as the other German banks; six large U.S. banks spoke for the banks within their own region of the United States; and so on.

Although country chairs were distributed among the biggest U.S. lenders—the Europeans regarded the Latin American debt as first and foremost a U.S. problem—Citibank characteristically dominated the restructuring process. William Rhodes, a Citibank vice president who for eight years headed the negotiations for the three most important debtors, Brazil, Mexico, and Argentina, is widely credited with holding the banking community together and propelling the process. "Bill Rhodes played a unique role, not just for the banks but for the world monetary system. I don't know any other banker who could have done it," said Guy Huntrods, former head of the Latin America division at Lloyds Bank and later a consultant on reschedulings. (Rhodes's previous claim to fame was a successful rescheduling of Nicaraguan debt after the fall of Somoza. Although the banks made concessions that they refused to make to other less radical debtors, they considered it a success because the Sandinistas did not, as they feared, follow in the footsteps of other revolutionary governments to repudiate outright the debts contracted under the Somoza dictatorship.)

Most of the talks have taken place in New York. (Bank-debtor negotiations are called "London Club" in reference to where most of the loans are booked. Government-to-government debt talks are dubbed "Paris Club" negotiations because the French usually host them.) Some weeks, country negotiating teams were stacked up at Citicorp Center in New York like airliners circling over Kennedy Airport at 6 P.M. on a Sunday night. Rhodes and Robert Carswell, the senior managing partner of the bank's outside counsel, Shearman & Sterling, moved back and forth making sure everything was on track. (Carswell learned how to knock bankers' heads during the Iranian hostage crisis when he was Undersecretary of Treasury and played a key role in negotiating the release of the hostages in return for the banks' release of frozen Iranian deposits.) Despite the bankers' public and repeated assertions that every restructuring is independent of every other and is considered on a case-by-case basis, Carswell rode close herd on the negotiators, meeting every Friday afternoon with the Shearman & Sterling lawyers on the various country teams to make sure that no unfortunate precedent was allowed to slip into one agreement that would affect the others.

Although it may not always have its way on every point, Citibank is big enough so that it did have a veto. "Citibank usually got the rest of the New York banks except Morgan to go along with its positions," said Bank of America's Latin American division head. According to Costa Rican debt negotiator Rodolfo Silva, "Citibank totally intimidated all the others, even when it was ten banks against one."

Committee members were responsible for keeping nonmember banks in their region informed and for making sure no smaller bank broke ranks by taking a debtor to court or cutting a separate deal—they called it "babysitting." "A few smaller ones tried to abandon ship," said a German participant in the first phase of the debt crisis. "This brought a strong reaction from the big banks.... We design the concepts with the other big banks then try to get other banks in our area to join the concept. We can't force them, but we argue that the whole system must be kept going."

Other creditors were expected to endorse the framework-restructuring agreement and to contribute pro rata to any new loan based on their exposure at the time the debt crisis broke. The late Joseph Kraft in his excellent account of the first Mexican rescue called this "the seven percent solution."[6] That was the portion of its 1982 Mexican exposure each participating bank was asked to lend in 1983.[7] This did not necessarily mean that banks were increasing their net exposure; U.S. banks as a group held their Latin exposure more or less constant from 1982 to 1987 through loan sales, offsetting the new loans with sales of older loans, write-offs of some private-sector debt, and cashing in the U.S. government guarantees—mostly Export-Import Bank and Commodity Credit Corporation guarantees—that had covered certain types of trade credits. However, as more and more small banks dropped out, the debt became increasingly concentrated in the twenty or so large banks with too much exposure to exit.

Once an umbrella agreement had been accepted in principle by all creditors, it was up to the debtor government to make the final arrangements with each bank or syndicate. Their representatives might have to circle the globe for months to actually pry loose the new money from a growing list of increasingly reluctant creditors—a process Mexican government officials cynically called "diving for dollars," evoking the image of poor children diving for coins tossed into the water by amused tourists aboard the luxury cruise ships that anchor off Acapulco.

DIVIDE AND RULE

The banking community's greatest tactical triumph in the early stages of the debt crisis was to divide the debtors while maintaining a reasonably unified front among creditors. The first was a good deal easier than the latter, and Washington's support was crucial to both.

The old Keynes line—"If you owe the bank 100, the bank owns you; if you owe the bank 100 million, you own the bank"—was often recited after 1982. But the Latin debtors, even the very biggest with tens of billions owing to the banks, never quite believed it. A senior policy official in Brasilia explained in 1984, "The government said a moratorium or tough position would risk very costly retaliation, so we took a minimum-risk situation. We couldn't afford to gamble if shortages would result. This government is not politically strong.... There is no internal political cohesion to back a tough negotiating stance."

The ruling elites in Latin America—the democratic revolutions in Argentina and Brazil were less class upheavals than the replacement of a conservative military by a more liberal elite—have traditionally identified more closely with Europe and the United States than with the nations next door. Moreover, an Argentine foreign ministry official commented that "We are divided among ourselves.... Finance ministry negotiators become bankers, act and think like them. The people who contracted the debt have interests and ties with the banks. They don't want to misbehave with the banks."[8] Just as many bankers found themselves renegotiating the loans they had so eagerly booked a few years earlier, some debtor-government officials were confronted with the problem of not being able to meet the terms of borrowings they had themselves encouraged or approved. Like the bankers, they had a vested interest in putting the best face possible on past borrowing and, up to a point, playing down the seriousness of the current difficulties.

Just as the inflow of credit had helped shore up weak governments in the 1970s, the loss of credit standing threatened to undermine weak governments in the 1980s. Perhaps almost as painful as the economic deprivation that befalls a nation that has gone too deeply into debt to foreigners is the loss of autonomy that is sometimes brought home in small but humiliating ways. An immediate response by Mexico to the lack of foreign exchange in 1982 was to impose sweeping import restrictons and to bar imports of anything that smacked of "luxury item." Among the items banned for import were substances used in the production of toothpaste. "Suddenly, there was no toothpaste in the country!" exclaimed Francisco Suarez Davila, undersecretary of finance. "How could we be in a position not to be able to make toothpaste?"

In Brazil Lars Janér, the wealthy owner of an import company, found out quickly what the loss of credit standing meant: "I orderered the book *Country Risk* from a foreign publisher and said, 'Bill me.' They refused to send the book unless I paid cash!"

The International Monetary Fund came to symbolize the loss of national autonomy. Official loans to troubled debtors were conditional on an acceptable agreement with banks, and both were conditional on an economic program acceptable to the IMF. Before negotiations with banks or official lenders took place, a team of IMF economists would descend on the debtor government to negotiate the terms of a letter of intent in which the government pledged to meet certain economic and monetary targets, usually for a period of three years. The IMF took the position that its mandate was to help countries stabilize their balance of payments. Long-term economic development or social welfare were not its institutional responsibility. The IMF targets included adjustments in the annual level of government borrowing, rate of growth of the domestic money supply, subsidized prices, inflation, exchange rate, and current account deficits. Domestic growth and internal rates of investment were not targets.

Only after the IMF executive board had voted to approve the letter of intent would IMF and other official moneys flow and commercial banks settle down to discuss terms for their debt restructuring. Breach of the letter of intent during the three-year period was grounds for the IMF to halt its loans and would trigger a halt of financing from other lenders as well. The IMF was in a sense, therefore, the creditor community's enforcer. The presence of one of its teams in a country was rarely welcome. Some missions were undertaken under deep secrecy and with heavy security. In one round of negotiations with Argentina, IMF economists had to travel to and from their meetings in Buenos Aires in an armored truck.

The IMF is not insensitive to political considerations, however. The Fund was sometimes willing to renegotiate letters of intent when a debtor—particularly a large debtor country—could not meet the original targets. In the first years of the crisis, Brazilian economic chiefs signed seven letters of intent in a row without living up fully to any one. A first priority of the debt strategy was to avoid exposing the banks to losses. Too tough a stance by the IMF could create the conditions where losses would be unavoidable. In 1983, after lengthy and heated debate over the debt issue, the U.S. Congress finally approved a quota increase for the IMF. But it moved simultaneously to tighten regulatory standards for U.S. banks' overseas lending. The International Lending Supervision Act of 1983 includes a provision that banks be required to build special allocated transfer risk reserves (ATRRs) against LDC borrowers that were falling behind payments. The ATRR would not be tax deductible, nor would it count as capital, and loans would have to be written down by the amount of the ATRR. One trigger for the ATRR was the absence of an IMF stabilization agreement.

Debtors learned that there were no alternative sources of financing. The governmental lenders pressured banks to participate in rescue packages. But the IMF, the World Bank, and even the Inter-American Development Bank (IDB), also made clear to the debtors that no official financing would be forthcoming for debtors who did not come to terms with their commercial lenders.[9] The largest contributor to these organizations, the United States, was adamant that maximum pressure be kept on debtors to come to agreement with the banks. The debtor countries saw themselves as over-matched. Countries like Peru, or Brazil in 1987, that did not keep up interest payments to the banks were summarily shut off from development funds. Brazil had hoped the pressure of a moratorium would compel banks to give it better rescheduling terms. But faced with a common front on the creditor side, Brazil backed down. Brazilian president José Sarney told *New York Times* reporter Alan Riding in 1988, "The fact is that we cannot destroy the international system. . . . We can scratch it, but it can destroy us." Sarney called off the moratorium.

An Argentine official said resignedly, "We came to the conclusion that the consequences of not going along would be magnificent. The U.S. government would harass us in every way and push the Europeans into not supporting us." According to an Argentine foreign ministry official, "In the U.S. power game with Latin America, there are three to five countries which set the tune for the region. The U.S. tells them, 'You will survive, you will do well—if you play by the rules. Don't worry about what the small countries do.' " The popularly elected government of Raoul Alfonsin had taken office in Argentina talking tough and promising a new deal on debt, but soon it too was vying for the title of "Model Debtor of the Month." (Each time a new candidate was selected, the financial press declared the debt crisis over.)

The creditors' divide-and-rule tactic was helped by timing. The important debtors—Mexico, Argentina, and Brazil—did not at first experience their most acute payments problems simultaneously. Large payments that could not be met came due at different times; IMF stabilization agreements expired—or were withdrawn by the Fund for noncompliance—at different times. Banks therefore could settle with one large debtor before tackling the next, and sweeten the precedent-setting agreement just enough each time to keep the others in line, or at least prevent them from joining forces. Any large debtor that talked tough thus quickly found itself isolated, its potential allies bought off with a better offer than the previous "benchmark" rescheduling—reduced fees and spreads here, longer maturities and grace periods there, and of course new money.

The closest the Latins ever came to forming a debtors' cartel was a meeting of heads of government in Cartagena, Colombia, in 1984 to discuss common debt issues. That meeting was instigated by junior foreign ministry officers and young political reformers in Brazil and Argentina to counter what they saw as the finance people's excessive acquiescence to the demands of foreign banks. A senior civil servant in the Brazilian foreign ministry explained: "Finance ministry officials decided to do business as usual and rely on their longstanding links with the banks. They tried to accommodate them as much as possible.... When domestic repercussions began to be felt, there were demands for a different approach and the foreign ministry began to take a stronger position— play a bigger role in the problem. The Cartagena meeting was one result."

Two factors played against the effort. Mexico was seen by the other Latin American debtors as the one best able to win special consideration in Washington. Perhaps for that very reason, Mexico was unwilling to take part in any collective approach to the debt issue. It could do better on its own. Other Latin American governments, says Jerome Levinson, long-time general counsel of the IDB, were deeply distrustful of the Mexicans because of their "special relationship" with Washington. The other factor was the strong reaction from those within the Reagan administration. An Argentine official explained, "This government thought that as a new and democratic government and one that had already undertaken economic adjustment, the IMF, the United States, France, and others would be more flexible, helpful. We came to realize that isn't so. The Europeans were flexible, but the U.S. was very tough." According to one Alfonsin adviser, an angry Assistant Secretary of State for Western Hemisphere affairs Langhorne Motley warned the Argentine foreign ministry, "We know you initiated the Cartagena group. We don't like it, and you keep that in mind." The Argentines protested that the purpose of the meeting was dialogue and not confrontation—but to no avail. The officials Motley had confronted came home "furious and scared." The debtors' cartel never materialized.

VOLCKER IN CHARGE

Perhaps not since the days of gunboat diplomacy has a U.S. government so carefully tailored public policy to suit the interests of large private banks. Despite President Reagan's free-market rhetoric and supposed devotion to keeping the government out of the affairs of private business, Washington involved itself almost immediately in the debt crisis, and it chose to side with the banks.

True to the Reagan rhetoric, Under Secretary of the Treasury Beryl Sprinkel at first told the banks flatly, "You made the loans, you collect them." Treasury showed equal disdain for the debtors. Sprinkel's boss, Treasury Secretary Don Regan, a former Wall Street broker and chairman of Merrill Lynch, reluctantly accepted the necessity for the government to play a role in the Mexican rescue in 1982 but was quite prepared to charge for the service. Carlos Tello, head of the Mexican central bank at the time, said, "The U.S. Treasury wanted to kill us. They had no understanding. Regan took the position we had to pay for our sins. He preached morality at us."

Washington agreed to give Mexico an emergency infusion

of money. According to a former senior State Department official, $2 billion cash, freshly printed, was flown directly from the New York Federal Reserve to Mexico City in the first days of the crisis. Part of this was to be called a prepayment by the United States for oil it was buying for the national emergency oil reserve. But Regan insisted that the Mexicans—whose foreign-exchange reserves were *minus* $100 million at the time—sell the prepaid oil at a deep discount from the world market price. Regan recounts proudly how he later told the president, "I just wanted to give the American taxpayer the same kind of service I gave the stockholders of Merrill Lynch."[10]

The banks' most important ally in Washington at first was not part of the Reagan administration at all but Federal Reserve Board chairman Paul Volcker, a Democrat appointed by President Jimmy Carter and later reappointed by Reagan. More than any other individual, the Fed chairman is credited by both bankers and debtor governments with holding things together in the first crucial months of the crisis. Volcker lowered dollar interest rates, stretched banking regulations, pressured regional banks, and urged foreign central bankers to push *their* banks to participate in the restructuring process. Years later, on leaving the Fed and, after the requisite cooling-off period joining an investment bank, Volcker was asked what he knew about Wall Street–type deal making. Referring to the Third World debt Volcker said, "I don't know who you thought was making all those deals. I was."[11]

Volcker's tight money policy from 1979 to 1982 had pushed interest rates into the high teens and helped precipitate the debt crisis. In 1982, shortly after Silva Herzog's ignominious appearance at Treasury, Volcker gave in to the long-standing arguments of Fed staff and other board members that it was time to ease the anti-inflation squeeze on the sagging U.S. economy. (The U.S. unemployment rate was then over 10 percent.) According to Fed and Treasury Department staff mem-

bers, what finally tipped the decision in favor of loosening
monetary policy was Volcker's concern that Mexico and the
other debtors could not continue paying interest to the banks
at double-digit rates.

Volcker, said Fed staff members and bankers, saw a mortal
threat to the U.S. banking system and was willing to do whatever he thought necessary to hold things together. The Fed,
in concert with IMF executive director Jacques de Larosière,
at first let the banks exact harsh terms from already desperate
borrowers on the grounds that this was the only way to keep
smaller banks in the game. According a senior Federal Reserve Board staffer, "We're unhappy the banks are charging
so much, but we wheedled them down from their original
position." Volcker admitted in late 1982, "We're all being induced to close our eyes to loose banking practices. We can't
force terms on bankers now without creating a crisis of confidence. If there were a God in heaven, the banks would not
profit from the current crisis. If it were only an isolated problem, we could pressure the banks more, but there is no time;
the problem is too widespread."

Largely at Volcker's insistence and over the objections of
Todd Conover, the comptroller of the currency, who wanted
the banks to start writing off some loans, government regulators adopted an accommodative stance. When interest payments from sovereign borrowers were delayed or interrupted,
the regulators looked the other way and let banks report interest payments as received even when arrearages exceeded
the regulatory ninety-day limit. When the Mexican private
sector had trouble meeting its dollar debt payments after several maxidevaluations of the peso, the Mexican government
arranged for companies to make the payments in pesos to an
escrow account, and the government assumed responsibility
for paying the banks dollars, eventually. Regulators let the
banks accrue these payments, too, as interest earned, even
though the payments were in pesos and had never left Mex-

ico. This policy continued until Congress began questioning the regulators.

The Fed agreed with the largest creditors on the need to keep all exposed banks in the negotiating process and participating in new lending. It was important to discourage so-called free riders—banks that refused to put up new money but would benefit from the restructuring package by continuing to receive interest on their loans. (Sharing clauses in syndication agreements entitle all lenders to a pro rata share of any payment received.) Free ridership would limit the pool of money available to debtors (without which they would be unlikely to pay interest) and would gradually shift exposure to the banks that already had the biggest piece.

Banks like Security Pacific that would have preferred debt relief over new lending got no support from regulators. On the contrary, "No bank goes ahead on its own to make an interest-rate reduction or write down a loan because you know eventually you will be forced to join whatever the group decides and you might end up with a double hit," explained Robert Lorenz—that is, both taking a loss and having to put up more money.

Smaller banks received a clear signal from the government that they were expected to accept the restructurings and participate in new lending. "We asked the Fed early on about its attitude to our Mexican exposure," said Richard Turner of Comerica Bank in Detroit. The bank was concerned that if all its loans were pooled as claims against the central government, it would be in violation of the legal lending limit. "The unique thing is how the government and the regulatory people have come down in support of increased exposure. They are so committed it's been made clear that any 'technicalities' would be resolved. We were told that hiding behind aggregations was just an excuse to bug out."

Even banks that were barely above water were asked to step up with new money. As part of the government's effort to salvage Continental Illinois Bank in 1984, the Chicago bank was permitted to transfer to the Federal Deposit Insurance Corporation $1.5 billion of its worst loans—loans considered least likely to be good over time. Continental used this to get some of its sizeable Third World private-sector loans off its books and onto the FDIC's. When it came time to put up new money for Mexico in the 1986 rescheduling, Continental at first took the position that its share should be based on its current exposure, not its 1982 exposure. After all, the bank was just regaining respectability in the market; the last thing it needed was more doubtful Latin loans. When British banks then threatened to scuttle the deal because U.S. banks were not putting up their full share, however, the pressure became too great, and Continental had to put up an amount that more nearly corresponded to its original Mexican exposure.

The perceived vulnerability of some large banks was one of the principal, though unpublicized, arguments made by U.S. Federal Reserve Board chairman Paul Volcker and others as to why the borrowing-lending game must go on even under duress. "It's like the FDIC [Federal Deposit Insurance Corporation] keeping banks alive rather than paying off depositors," explained Marc Leland, assistant secretary of treasury for international affairs in the Reagan administration. "It's better to help the borrowers keep paying." (As Treasury learned later in the S&L disaster, it ain't necessarily so.) Recalcitrant banks were warned of the consequences if they refused to play along. "I'm so fed up," said an exasperated Swedish banker in fall 1986, "with these phone calls in the middle of the night from Reed or Preston [chairman of Morgan Guaranty] telling me that if my bank doesn't participate in the new loan for country X, the Western banking system will collapse and it will all be my fault!" He added, "Dammit, this Mexican package is the last time!"

Each rescheduling round seemed to involve more old loans being stretched out for a longer period of time. Banks grew increasingly reluctant to put up "new money" as well. In 1986 Mexico was knocking at the door again for another stretch-out of its repayment schedule and a new loan to help it make the interest payments. But now the common bank front was crumbling. Even the biggest lenders disagreed among themselves and with the Fed and the IMF about terms. During the World Bank–IMF annual meeting in Washington, D.C. in October 1986, Federal Reserve chairman Paul Volcker and IMF executive director Jacques de Larosière (the two principal architects of the debt-restructuring strategy on the government side) mounted a full court press on the attending commercial bankers to close the new loan to Mexico as part of the package. Bankers joked, "It would, after all, be a lot cheaper to bail out Mexico than to bail out Bank of America." Mr. Reed, however, was not amused to be shut in a room with Messrs. Volcker and Baker until 9:00 P.M., while he was supposed to be the host at his bank's traditionally lavish bash for official delegates and the international coterie of private bankers (who use the Bank-Fund meeting as a sort of trade show to display their wares).

Officialdom said the commercial lenders together should put up $6 billion in new money, while Reed was prepared to concede only $3.2 billion. He also wanted a bigger spread over London interbank offered rate (LIBOR) than the Mexicans were prepared to pay. In the end, Reed gave in, and the $6 billion package was eventually closed—though with great difficulty and many defections among the smaller banks. Angel Gurria, director of public credit for Mexico's Ministry of Finance, said at the end, "It's been push and pull all the way. And there are so many wounds, scars, and broken arms that it's going to have an effect on the other negotiations that are going forward. The whole process has been very tortuous and inefficient."[12] It is clear, in retrospect, that this titanic struggle marked the end of the first phase—one might call it the denial phase—of the debt crisis.

Some observers say that this unpleasant experience was the beginning of Reed's resolve to get out from under the sovereign-loan legacy left to him by his predecessor, even if the cost was high. The creation of a large loan-loss reserve the following summer was perhaps Reed's declaration of independence, as much from Washington as from the debtors: never again would Washington dictate loan terms to the nation's biggest bank.

THE COMMON FRONT CRUMBLES

Citibank's decision in 1987 to increase reserves massively was widely praised on the editorial pages of the world's financial press as wise and courageous, and the markets reacted favorably by pushing up the price of Citicorp's stock despite the red ink. But comments of other bankers were tinged with bitterness. Citibank's about-face had come without warning— not even the Fed was informed in advance—and it caught most other banks with their reserves down, so to speak. Because the banks' strategy since 1982 had been to tell the world there would be no losses, U.S. banks—which unlike European and Japanese banks in those days, had to disclose at least some of what they were doing—had no incentive to provision against them. The 1986 Tax Act eliminated the deductibility of general reserves. But once Citibank admitted that the value of its sovereign loans was impaired, others had little choice but to build up comparable reserves or see their stock values trashed in the markets. The consequences of Reed's move were felt immediately, from the Bank of Montreal to the Old Stone Corp., a Rhode Island thrift holding company with $93 million on loan to developing countries. Salomon Bros. called Citicorp's announcement "the shot heard around the world." Altogether, the fifteen largest U.S. banks reported second-quarter losses of almost $11 billion. Many so-called super-regionals also reported losses or sharply lower earnings as a result of increased reserving for Third World loans.

Intentionally or not, Reed's preemptive strike exposed the institutional weaknesses of many of Citibank's competitors. West Coast bankers went so far as to privately accuse Citibank of having taken the step to destroy Bank of America and thereby seize the competitive advantage in California, the nation's most important retail banking market. (Reed did appear to quite deliberately turn the spotlight on the two bank rivals that would have the greatest difficulty emulating Citibank's loan-loss reserve build-up. Toward the end of his press conference, Reed said other lenders had been informed, but he had personally telephoned only two banks that day to warn their CEOs of Citibank's impending announcement—Bank of America and Manufacturers Hanover.)

Bank of America had the second-largest LDC loan portfolio after Citibank, with $11 billion. Its ratio of loan-loss reserves to assets was already the highest of any major U.S. bank, but this was a cushion against its disastrous domestic real estate, energy, agriculture, and silicon valley loans, not foreign loans. The bank hadn't paid a dividend to shareholders for many quarters and in 1987 hoped to report a small operating profit for the first time in three years.

The combative B of A chair A. W. "Tom" Clausen, who had recently returned to that post after an undistinguished term as president of the World Bank, at first assured an annual meeting of hostile shareholders that the bank's reserves were "appropriate" and no additions would be necessary following the Citibank announcement. (Clausen said of that meeting, he felt a little like a Christian going in to face the lions.) Five days later, Clausen announced a $1.1 billion addition to reserves that would result in a $1 billion second-quarter loss for the bank. The reserve build-up further depleted the bank's shallow pool of shareholders' equity, leaving Bank of America with only $2.6 billion in common equity supporting more than $100 billion in assets.

Bank of America wasn't the only bank threatened by Citibank's move. Manny Hanny had the dubious distinction of carrying the largest Latin American loan exposure relative to capital. Reed's announcement had reverberations abroad as well. Two of the four large British clearing banks, Lloyds Bank and Midland Bank, were also badly overexposed and underreserved. Lloyds was one of the biggest lenders to Latin America through its Bank of London and South America (Bolsa), the oldest foreign bank in Brazil and one of the biggest in Argentina. Bolsa, renamed Lloyds Bank International, in good years accounted for about 50 percent of the bank's profits and operated as a separate entity until 1985 when it was consolidated with the then more profitable, largely domestic Lloyds PLC.

Midland bought into Latin America's troubles when it acquired Crocker Bank of California. It eventually sold off Crocker to Wells Fargo, but had to keep the Latin loans. The half-year losses reported by the four British clearers after additions to reserves totaled $1.2 billion—far less than the $5.7 billion reported by the four largest U.S. banks but sufficient to force Lloyds and Midland, like some second-tier U.S. banks (Wells Fargo, First Chicago, Bank of Boston) to pull in their horns internationally for years to come. Barclays, with far less Latin American exposure, nevertheless reported a loss for the first time in its history. And National Westminster, also with relatively few Latin loans, dissolved its international division in London. Canadian banks, too, took large losses after the regulators belatedly prodded them into establishing reserves of 30 to 40 percent of their exposure to thirty-four developing countries.

Only the continental European banks could afford to shrug off Citibank's action. Favorable tax treatment and pressure from their regulators early in the crisis had encouraged the Germans and the Swiss to take large reserves early on. Swiss authorities gave the banks a list of troubled debtor countries and ordered them to take a 50 percent reserve against all loans outstanding to those countries, including new loans made in the reschedulings. According to Peter Walter of the Hessische Landescentralbank, German banks were told "when their provision is not on the average" and were expected to make provisions for troubled debtors "at least as high as the interest that comes in on that loan per year." In 1987 that would have been about 10 percent.

Deutsche Bank set the standard with a 70 percent reserve against $3.1 billion in developing-country loans. German loan-loss provisions are charged against securities trading income and need only be reported if provisions exceed that noninterest income. Since Deutsche Bank had an admitted "hidden reserve" of securities with a market value of $7.5 billion, which it carried at the book value of $543 million, DB is not likely to report embarrassing losses any time soon.[13] Other German banks also have large undervalued securities holdings.

The Japanese banks, with the second-largest LDC exposure after the Americans, had made few provisions against their loans. Since March 1983 banks had been permitted to create a "reserve for specified overseas receivables" equal to 5 percent of exposure to countries meeting certain criteria as troubled debtors. Up to 1 percent of loans rescheduled or refinanced was tax deductible. Japanese banks are an important source of tax revenue for the Japanese government, and the powerful ministry of finance was opposed to large debt write-offs. Both the government and Japanese banks have taken the basic position that the LDCs should pay. Nevertheless, perhaps not wanting to appear too far out of step with other banking centers, the ministry of finance allowed the banks to increase their reserves to 10 percent of outstanding troubled loans after 1987 (and raised the limit to 15 percent of exposure in 1989).[14]

Citibank's drastic action triggered a wholesale abandonment of the debt process by regional American banks. In December 1987 several New England banks upped Citi and made reserves of 55 to 100 percent against LDC loans and were followed by Security Pacific and American Express Bank International. American Express and Bank of Boston went one step further, actually taking real losses by writing off some of their loans and putting all the rest on a status that subsequent interest received would be used to pay down principal and get the banks out. American Express announced simply that it was making "an orderly exit from cross-border lending."[15] These banks would no longer participate in any "new money" package for troubled debtors. From then on, the Third World debt problem would be a big bank problem.

The reaction of regulators was not what one might expect. Rather than applaud this apparent display of prudential initiative on the part of banks, the Federal Reserve and the Bank of England urged the large banks *not* to follow suit. "Excessive" provisions would "send misleading signals to the debtors themselves," warned Robin Leigh-Pemberton, governor of the Bank of England. Gerald Corrigan, president of the New York Fed, told banks that they would create "self-fulfilling prophesies." Large loan-loss reserves would encourage debtors to think they did not have to pay their debts and further diminish the willingness of banks to extend new loans. Another worry was never addressed publicly: only some banks could afford to allocate still more earnings or equity to reserves, which would further isolate and expose the banks that could not.

The money-center banks heeded the regulators' pleas for the time being. And Brazil—after months of losing trade credit lines from banks, getting cold-shouldered by official lenders, and growing unhappiness in the Brazilian business community—returned to the fold, canceled its moratorium, and sought a conventional agreement with the banks. But everyone recognized that perpetual restructurings offered no lasting solution to the sovereign-loan problem. Debt restructuring had become a trap for the banks, which found them-selves with a huge bloc of questionable assets frozen on their books for the foreseeable future. Mexico had been granted a twenty-year postponement on the repayment of $44 billion in public-sector debt and $9.7 billion in private-sector debt originally falling due between 1988 and 1991 (including loans with earlier maturities that had already been rescheduled once or twice). And it had seven years' grace before any payments would be due. The multiyear agreement with Argentina re-scheduled $30 billion of bank loans for nineteen years. Sim-ilar stretch-outs had been negotiated with the other major Latin American debtors and with the Philippines.

In the first round of debt negotiations, 1982 to 1983, thir-teen Latin American debtors, including all the big countries except Venezuela, had rescheduled $50 billion of loans ma-turing in 1982, 1983, and 1984, and had received $33 billion in new loans. Slightly less than half came from the banks. The commercial new money carried six- to eight-year maturities and spreads ranging from 1.88 to 2.50 over LIBOR. Fees were additional. In 1983 to 1984, five Latin American debtors re-scheduled $20 billion in debts coming due through 1985 and received $11.5 billion in new bank loans. In the third round, 1984 to 1985, reschedulings of Latin American commercial debt covered thirteen countries and $113 billion in debts—including some previously rescheduled loans—coming due through 1990. $5.5 billion in concerted lending accompanied the restructurings. The fourth round, 1986 to 1988, took care of $180 billion in loans maturing mostly through 1990, but as late as 1993 in the case of Brazil. Banks put up $15.2 billion in new loans.

Each round covered more outyears, and the spreads and fees became smaller and the new maturities longer with each rescheduling. The average margin over LIBOR on resched-uled debt was about 1 percent in 1987 and 0.8 percent in 1988. Maturities were stretched to an average nineteen years.

The Brazilian 1988 deal included a new menu of instruments to satisfy the increasingly divergent regulatory, tax, and strategic concerns of the country's 700 creditor banks. The menu included avenues of exit for banks that wanted out permanently. Up to $1 billion in rescheduled debt could be exchanged for inflation-indexed cruzado securities that could be sold in Brazil. Many small banks took that option to sell out their position.

The rescheduling of such vast sums involving such a large number of debtors was unprecedented and an accomplishment. But the fact remained that the international financial system was just treading water. Each new round was in a sense a mark of failure, an acknowledgement that the previous reschedulings had not done the job. The debtors still had more debt than they could support, and banks still had an uncomfortably large block of questionable loans on their books.[16] Worst of all, these debtors had taken on billions in additional loans for the sole purpose of making interest payments.

No one believed that even these massive restructurings constituted a final settlement. Many debtors were having trouble paying the interest even with single-digit interest rates. Since the debt still carried floating rates—albeit with lower spreads after the latest rounds—any rise in world interest rates would trigger a new crisis. When one New York bank tried to sell interest-rate hedging instruments to Mexico to cover some of the floating-rate debt, its representative was told, "Why should we pay you a fee for that? If the rates go up, it's clear we just won't pay."

By 1988 the original debt strategy was a shambles. Debtors, banks, and creditor governments wanted to get off the carousel.

9

The "Good Name" Fallacy

A puzzled, somewhat skeptical Alice asked the Republican leadership some simple questions:

"Will not the printing and selling of more stocks and bonds, the building of new plants and the increase of efficiency produce more goods than we can buy?"

"No," shouted Humpty Dumpty. "The more we produce the more we can buy."

"What if we produce a surplus?"

"Oh, we can sell it to the foreign consumers."

"How can the foreigners pay for it?"

"Why, we will lend them the money."

"I see," said little Alice, "they will buy our surplus with our money. Of course, these foreigners will pay us back by selling us their goods?"

"Oh, not at all," said Humpty Dumpty. "We set up a high wall called the tariff."

"And," said Alice at last, "how will the foreigners pay off these loans?"

"That is easy," said Humpty Dumpty, "did you ever hear of a moratorium?"

And so at last, my friends, we have reached the heart of the magic formula of 1928.

—Franklin Delano Roosevelt, campaign speech,
Columbus, Ohio, 20 August 1932, in Herbert Feis,
Diplomacy of the Dollar: First Era 1912–1932 (1950)

THE WRONG LESSONS FROM THE 1930s

The most powerful argument deterring Latin American debtors from outright repudiation during the difficult 1980s was
that if they broke with the banks, they would risk repeating
the experience of the 1930s and 1940s. In those years, it was
argued, Latin countries had freely defaulted on debts contracted in the 1920s with the result that they were shut out of
the international financial markets for more than two decades.
Better to stick with the negotiating process and accept the
restructuring terms offered by the banks, however harsh. But
creditors and debtors learned the wrong lessons and, by per-
sisting in the fiction that debtors must ultimately pay in full
to protect their "good name," repeated the very worst aspects
of the earlier crisis.

Although the conditions surrounding the sovereign-debt
defaults of the early 1930s and the sovereign-debt crisis fifty
years later differ in important respects—most notably in the
depth of the world depression—there are many striking par-
allels. As investors began to show a more cautious attitude
toward foreign issues in 1928, debtors increased their reliance on short-term credit. By the time the stock market
crashed in October 1929, German banks, corporations, and
state enterprises had short-term debts (including acceptance
credits, interbank deposits, advances, overdrafts, and other
short-term accounts) totaling $3 billion. Austria was in a sim-
ilar fix. A sudden withdrawal of some of these lines of credit,
particularly by French banks reacting to political developments in Germany and Austria, helped precipitate the collapse of Kreditanstalt, Austria's largest bank. This was
followed by a rapid withdrawal of foreign credits from German banks.

Moreover, as credit flows dried up, economic activity and
trade sharply contracted. Between October 1929 and October
1930 manufacturing in the United States fell by 25 percent,

accompanied by rapid price deflation (which left real short-term interest rates at 15 percent). Commodity prices and trade volumes fell even more as a result of depressed demand and protectionism, and the export revenues of forty-one primary producing countries dropped by more than 50 percent.[1]

Brookings Institution economist Cleona Lewis argued in *America's Stake in International Investment* that although "the immediate cause of defaults on foreign bonds was the world depression . . . factors inherent in the terms and conditions of the loans themselves and in the peculiar political and economic situation of some of the countries would have made the maintenance of debt payments extremely difficult in a few years, even had there been no recession in world business."[2]

Lenders ignored the vulnerability of borrowers whose economies depended almost solely on one or two commodities (Chile on copper and nitrates then, Mexico on oil now) and "ignored the relationship between new issues and the amounts of foreign capital already invested in the borrowing country." W. W. Aldrich, president of the Chase National Bank, testified to a congressional committee that lenders had carefully examined the books of individual German borrowers but had never taken account of Germany's total foreign indebtedness. Lenders also did not consider the effect of other transfer payments, such as dividends to foreign companies, on a country's ability to service its debts. Chile's copper and nitrate exports, for example, in 1929 generated $240 million in revenues, but only $60 million returned to Chile; the rest was paid out to the foreign companies that owned the production facilities. Finally, of course, some issues involved outright fraud by the borrower, the biggest being that of Ivar Kreuger, the Swedish match king who extracted nearly a quarter of a billion dollars from American investors on the basis of juggled books. His bank underwriters neglected to insist that he submit his books for the customary audit by American accountants.

According to Lewis, debtors responded to the withdrawal of their credits much as they did in the 1980s. "With the volume of American lending greatly curtailed, and with other capital markets practically closed to them, the debtors had to rely principally on their export trade for meeting interest and amortization on earlier borrowing. Under existing price conditions this became more and more difficult, for the quantity of goods required to meet a given payment steadily increased as prices fell. In their efforts to obtain funds for various foreign payments required of them—including the cost of imports and foreign debt service—the debtors reduced their purchases of imports and attempted to force an expansion of exports by price reductions and other methods."[3]

A similar path was followed in the most recent crisis. MIT Professor Rudiger Dornbusch has estimated that trade surpluses financed three-quarters of the heavily indebted countries' interest on foreign debt in 1984 to 1985 and half the interest in 1986 to 1987. Most of these surpluses resulted not from higher export earnings but from a severe compression of imports. Import volumes of the heavily indebted countries fell an average of 11 percent per year in the period 1982 to 1985. On an expenditure basis, imports declined 6.2 percent per year in 1980 to 1987. Export volumes increased, but export earnings did not because commodity prices fell by 25 percent relative to the price of manufactured goods imported from the industrial countries. Protectionism, as in the 1930s, and domestic subsidies for agriculture in the industrial nations hampered the ability of debtors to export their way out of trouble.

There are other similarities between the two crises. Capital flight was a problem in the 1930s. U.S. Treasury Department statistics show a $4 billion net inflow of gold from abroad in the years 1934 to 1936 after Roosevelt had raised the price of gold. This inflow represented a severe depletion of other countries' reserves. Latin Americans, whose own countries were in default on U.S. and other loans, accumulated bank deposits in the United States and were in a net creditor position on short-term account vis-à-vis the United States; in the mid-1930s, as in the mid-1980s, the flow of capital reversed itself, and the heavily indebted countries became net providers of funds rather than takers.[4]

In the 1930s, as in the 1980s, countries did not repudiate their foreign debts; they just didn't pay. They negotiated rescheduling agreements, then couldn't meet the scaled-back payments and defaulted again. When Max Winkler published his *Foreign Bonds, An Autopsy* in 1933, foreign governments were in default on more than $20 billion in bonds, the equivalent of $120 billion in 1980 dollars. Interest arrears were more than $12.5 billion. Eighty-two percent of Latin America's dollar bonds were in default by the end of 1934. Forty percent of America's loans to Europe were in default.[5] Bondholders weren't the only losers. National City Bank had an amount equal to 50 percent of its capital at risk in the German and Chilean defaults alone.[6] Like other underwriters, it had often supported foreign borrowers with short-term bridge loans. Germany, for one, had more short-term debts to banks than it had long-term bonds outstanding.[7]

Central, state, and municipal governments declared themselves unable to pay, while private companies that were still solvent found themselves prevented by the proliferation of exchange controls from transferring payments to foreign creditors. Then, as now, sovereign loans traded at a discount in a secondary market, and some debtors took advantage of the discount. Chile, for example, bought back a third of its foreign debt for about fifteen cents on the dollar,[8] and in the 1980s, too, has been an active purchaser of its own debt.

THE SECRET ROLE OF THE DEPARTMENT OF STATE

It is instructive to examine the role of the U.S. government in this earlier protracted debt crisis. The U.S. government was much more directly involved from the beginning than it was willing to admit in public. Indeed, it went to considerable effort to hide the State Department's very active role in debt restructurings. During the 1932 election campaign Franklin Roosevelt attacked the Republicans for encouraging irresponsible foreign lending by Wall Street. The many private bondholders who in the 1930s appealed to the government to do something to recover their money were invariably told by the State Department that "this Government considers difficulties or controversies arising between American holders of foreign bonds and foreign governments to be primarily matters for negotiation and settlement between the foreign debtors and the American bondholders."[9]

In fact, quite the opposite was true: the government considered the debt question to be a vital matter of public policy. Private creditors' committees were created at the State Department's behest to give the appearance that negotiations were a strictly private affair—the International Committee of Bankers on Mexico in 1921 to negotiate a settlement of Mexico's pre-revolutionary debts, and the Foreign Bondholders Protective Council in 1933 to negotiate with the many other Latin debtors then in default.[10] One State Department document is particularly revealing of the department's extreme sensitivity about its own role in these matters. In 1941 a court sought government documents concerning the debt negotiations with Mexico. The State Department legal adviser objected to submitting the voluminous correspondence between Thomas W. Lamont, the Morgan banker who chaired the Committee of Bankers on Mexico, and senior State Department officials because the government's role would become public. "Even though the Committee presumably functions as an independent organization, the correspondence clearly indicates that 'effective control of the policy' of the Committee is 'to be maintained by the Department of State, and that is already understood and agreed to,' " wrote the legal adviser, quoting from a letter to Under Secretary of State Sumner Welles from the head of the Mexico committee.[11]

Mexico in 1914 had stopped paying on its prerevolutionary debts of about $500 million ($100 million owed to U.S. citizens), and in the 1920s the U.S. Department of State organized the International Committee of Bankers to ensure a U.S. lead in the negotiations and to keep the Europeans— who had the bulk of the claims—from setting the negotiating terms. Lamont, who had represented the U.S. Treasury at the Paris Peace Conference, chaired the committee and conducted the negotiations with the Mexican government on behalf of bondholders.

Lamont negotiated with Mexico for nearly two decades, always in close consultation with the State Department. Numerous restructuring agreements were reached and then breached by Mexico, a country in extreme political turmoil from the beginning of the revolution in 1910 until the 1930s and the presidency of Lázaro Cárdenas, who nationalized U.S. and all other foreign oil interests.

With each round of talks the creditors surrendered more of their claims—first interest arrears and eventually most of the principal. A 1930 restructuring agreement wrote off all interest arrears and tied future debt servicing to Mexico's ability to pay. (The long-running Mexican debt problem elicited many proposed solutions over the years. An organization of retired military officers in San Diego suggested to the State Department that the government should pay off Mexico's debts in return for Mexico ceding the United States Baja California. Mexican negotiators at one point suggested that bondholders be given the option of replacing their claims with perpetual notes paying three pesos per year [sixty cents] on every $100 of old debt. The Mexicans later suggested to the British government that it buy up the bonds in the secondary market where they were selling for $4 per $100. The Mexican government would then buy them back at a premium, giving the British government a tidy little profit on the deal. Whitehall was outraged and anxiously sought assurances from Washington that the U.S. government would not agree to any such scheme either.)

As noted, President Roosevelt had little sympathy for Wall Street, and recouping the investors' money gradually became less of a priority than protecting other U.S. commercial and political interests in the debtor countries. As the Depression dragged on, Washington became convinced that "the southern market was the key to the recovery of the entire export trade of the United States."[12] Umbrella trade agreements with Latin America were negotiated at Montevideo in 1933, and the Export-Import Bank was created in 1934 to finance foreign purchases of U.S. goods. Washington pressured bankers to renew their loans—not to finance debt repayment but to protect commerce.[13]

As war loomed, the U.S. government became even more anxious to improve political relations with Latin America and to tie those economies more closely to the United States. The Ex-Im Bank even took the politically risky step of making a substantial loan to Brazil in 1939 while that country was still in arrears on bonds held by private U.S. investors. Internal State Department memoranda indicate a preoccupation with getting the debt issue out of the way so that a more aggressive trade promotion program could be pursued.

Once World War II began, the State Department was prepared to take matters into its own hands, with the result that final debt settlements with key countries were reached that were highly favorable to the debtors. The final Mexican settlement in 1942, covering half the outstanding debt, required Mexico to repay $206 on every $1,000 of principal outstanding by 1968, with five years' grace. Interest arrears, which amounted to significantly more than principal, were forgiven. Subsequent interest payments were reduced from a rate of 4 to 6 percent to 0.75 to 1.25 percent, depending on the type of bond. A 1946 agreement covering most of the remaining debt had similar terms, with twenty-nine years to repay, in pesos at a guaranteed exchange rate of one peso to the dollar instead of the dollar gold equivalent called for in the original loan contracts. Ultimately, the agreements reached between 1942 and 1946 allowed Mexico to settle debts of more than $1.5 billion for a sum of $125 million. This included compensation of American oil companies' claims arising from the nationalization of the oil fields in 1938.[14]

Negotiations with other debtors were more problematic for the U.S. government. The bondholders' council chairman Francis White, a former assistant secretary of state for Latin America, apparently felt the government was giving investor interests short shrift and came to be regarded by the State Department as an obstacle to settlement. The State Department worried that Brazil was about to cut a separate deal with British and European creditors—and worse, that Brazil would succumb to Nazi Germany's ever more eager diplomatic advances. (Lenders were not linked through multinational syndications to the extent they are today and thus could be played off, one against another.)

A quick and favorable debt settlement was thought to be the best way to protect the United States' relationship with Brazil.[15] To get around White, the U.S. ambassador to Brazil began direct government-to-government negotiations on the private claims. In March 1940, after negotiations that deliberately excluded the bondholders' council, the parties announced a temporary four-year agreement negotiated by the U.S. ambassador in Rio that called for partial resumption of Brazilian debt servicing: "When it seemed to the Department [of State] that we had obtained as much as we could, we went to the Council and requested that if it could not approve the settlement, it at least not express objection. A week of terrific argument ensued with Francis White. This argument culmi- nated in a two-hour session in the Secretary's office, after which White reluctantly agreed that the Council would not attack the settlement."[16] Shortly thereafter, White was suc- ceeded by another former State Department official, Dana Munro. The final settlement, in November 1943, reduced Bra- zil's debt obligations by about 75 percent. Bondholders were given a year to register their acceptance of the new terms. Appeals to the State Department to force Brazil to live up to the original terms fell on deaf ears.

Under the agreement, interest arrears totaling $98 million were liquidated with a cash payment of $6 million, and future interest and principal payments were reduced sharply. A 6.5 percent Federal Republic of Brazil bond issued in 1926 with an original maturity of 1957, for example, had its coupon reduced to 3.375 percent and the maturity extended to 1979. Brazil serviced these bonds under the new terms, and inves- tors who had bought the bonds in the secondary market at $9 profited handsomely in the 1960s when the price climbed back up to the $100 face value and the Brazilian government redeemed the paper before the due date. Colombia and Pan- ama also negotiated reductions in the interest rate on their bonds, while Argentina, which had built up its foreign- exchange reserves with the surge of wartime exports, man- aged to buy back bonds with a face value of 25 million pounds sterling.[17]

Brazilian president Getulio Vargas in a speech in Belo Ho- rizonte called his country's 1943 debt settlement "useful to the Treasury but no less useful to the creditors who hurried, eagerly, to accept it by reason of the rule which is universal throughout the business world: 'Let the rings go provided the fingers stay.' "[18]

WASHINGTON BREAKS RANKS WITH THE BANKS

In fall 1988 James Baker's pre-election replacement at Treasury, Nicholas Brady, made a hard-line presentation to the annual meeting of the IMF-World Bank. Following the departing Reagan administration's party line, he gave no quarter to debtors, calling for more "adjustment" on their part and more lending by commercial banks. But a radically different debt policy was soon in the works. And the following March, before the Bretton Woods Committee conference in Washington, D.C., the U.S. government launched the "Brady Plan" for Third World debt. (Asked about the name, the president said cheerfully, "If it's a success, we'll rename it the 'Bush Plan.' ") Brady listed the shortcomings of what had been done so far:

> Despite the accomplishments to date, we must acknowledge that serious problems and impediments to a successful resolution of the debt crisis remain. . . . Growth has not been sufficient. Nor has the level of economic policy reform been adequate. Capital flight has drained resources from debtor nations' economies. . . . Neither investment nor domestic savings has shown much improvement. . . . Inflation has not been brought under control. Commercial bank lending has not always been timely. . . . Prosperity remains . . . for many, out of reach.[19]

And now Brady added a critical new item to the menu of terms for a bank-debtor settlement: "The path towards greater creditworthiness and a return to the markets for many debtor countries needs to involve debt reduction." Brady was putting the "good name" fallacy to rest. The road to righteousness no longer passed through full payment of all debts, no matter what. The emphasis was now on the recovery of economic viability for the debtor, even if that meant some debts would never be paid. A senior Treasury Department official later explained that the new policy signaled a recognition that "a long-term rise in debt is not a way out" and that "the debt is not worth 100 cents on the dollar." Proposing debt reduction, he added, was not going to kill prospects for new loans from banks because there weren't any. The process of closing the books on the debt debacle of the 1980s had finally begun.

In a speech in London some days later, Brady made a crucial addendum to the new policy. The World Bank and IMF, he said, might lend even if a country had no settlement with its banks and had fallen behind on interest payments to them. In other words, the multilateral agencies would no longer necessarily use their financial leverage to support the commercial banks' negotiating position. The common front of creditors was no more.

The shift in U.S. government policy—which had the support of other key creditor countries—was prompted by two considerations. First, it had finally become obvious to all that losses on Third World claims were inevitable. Second, it had dawned on government lenders that if the debt policy continued as before, most of the losses were going to end up on their books.

Losses were inevitable because the debt policies of the 1980s had left most debtors less rather than more creditworthy. Foreign indebtedness had increased sharply while economic capacity to service the debt had declined. In Latin America, for example, the external debt had increased by 20 percent while per capita output had declined by 10 percent since 1981.

Neither "adjustment through austerity" (1982 to 1985) nor "adjustment with growth" had solved the debt problem. The essence of the Baker Initiative, presented at the World Bank–IMF annual meeting in Seoul in 1985, was that if debtors would keep paying interest and would adopt economic policies along "Reaganomic" lines—privatization of state enterprises, an end to subsidies, opening the economies to foreign goods and investment, and so on—the creditor countries would lend them enough money to get out of recession. A former Treasury Department official reported that the proposal had been "pasted together quickly in breakfast meetings" with the secretary and Fed chairman Volcker as a response to Peru's rejection of the existing debt strategy.[20] Fidel Castro's campaign to rally the Latin American left around the debt issue may also have influenced Washington's thinking.

For Latin Americans there must have been a certain irony in the Baker proposals. His recommendation of a little more money for troubled debtors garnered most of the press attention. But the proposed reforms on which the money was to be conditioned went much further than the standard IMF nostrums of devaluation, reductions in the public-sector borrowing requirement and control over the money supply, and decontrol of wages and prices. This was not lost on the debtors. After all, putting the national patrimony on the block for sale to foreign interests was precisely what these countries had been trying to escape when they began large-scale borrowing from the banks in the 1970s.[21]

Few would argue with the need for growth and economic reform in the debtor countries. Many debtor governments have pursued abysmal policies (in some cases only marginally better than when the banks were lending them all that money). Too often they sabotaged their own best efforts at critical points in economic recovery in order to meet the political calendar. In 1985, for example, the Mexican government spent virtually its entire annual budget in the first six months of the year to stimulate the economy in advance of important regional elections. And in 1987 Brazil delayed a crucial easing of wage and price controls despite rising inflationary pressures because the ruling party feared the political consequences in the upcoming elections. Setting economic policies by the political calendar is not uncommon in the rich countries either; the difference is that creditor countries can afford to make these mistakes and poor debtor countries cannot.

The greatest miscalculation in the debt strategy since 1982 was its chilling effect on investment in the debtor countries. The current level of investment largely determines the future level of economic output. Since debts ultimately can be paid only with real goods and services, investment also largely determines future debt-servicing capacity. Gross investment in Latin America was $50 billion less in 1983 and 1984 than it had been in 1981. Overall, investment was 5 to 6 percent of GNP lower in the 1980s than it was in the 1970s. Developing countries need real economic growth of at least 4 to 6 percent per year to generate employment and raise the standard of living for rapidly growing populations. To achieve that level of growth, development economists estimate that they need an investment to GDP ratio of at least 20 percent and preferably 25 percent. During most of the 1980s investment ratios in the major debtor countries averaged 17 to 18 percent and in several countries declined to 12 to 15 percent. By comparison, the investment ratio for the fast-growing four "Asian Tigers" averaged 27 percent of GDP during the decade.

A number of factors tied to the debt problem contributed to the investment decline. Constantly shifting domestic economic policies and political uncertainty contributed to the general lack of confidence, but most damage was done by the steady pressure of the external debt. Debtor economies as a whole generated trade surpluses and hence foreign exchange. But the governments, which by the late 1980s owed most of the debt, had to generate the budgetary resources to purchase the foreign exchange for debt servicing. As was noted in chapter 6, in the absence of foreign loans to the government, they could do this only by borrowing or, worse, by printing money. Both drove domestic interest rates sky high.

With a real return of 30 percent or more on domestic government debt, why should a private investor who still is willing to keep money in the country invest in anything else? Foreign private direct investment also dried up in the middle of the crisis. "LDCs have the perfect 'poison pill defense,' " joked a senior Argentine debt negotiator in 1986. "No investor who looks at those debt ratios wants to buy a piece of the enterprise."

Debt servicing, foreign and domestic, absorbed a rising share of total government spending—60 percent of Mexico's federal budget in 1989, for example. Since the cadre of public employees is large and politically influential, and since transfer payments and direct and indirect subsidies were equally politically sensitive, requisite spending cuts fell mostly on capital projects. In 1981 Mexico's public-sector capital spending was equal to 12.9 percent of GDP, and interest expense on the public debt was 5 percent of GDP. By 1986 to 1987 capital spending was 5.5 percent of GDP and interest expense was 19.5 percent.[22] Even the vital oil sector was short-changed for investment capital during much of a decade. The same pattern was followed in other heavily indebted countries. The decision to put a floor under some public-sector wages—which dictates overall wage scales in these economies—added to the inflationary pressures already present and building as a natural consequence of the trade surpluses. The inflation then called forth more devaluations, and the spiral continued downward.

High real interest rates may yield some repatriation of capital for a time, but as noted in chapter 6, the money tends to go into highly liquid financial instruments that offer a good rate of return *and* an opportunity to get out if the situation suddenly deteriorates. "As long as we have to make these massive debt payments," said one Mexican official before there was a debt-reduction agreement, "the peso will be devalued, foreign exchange will continue to be in chronic short supply, and that makes the dollar the best investment around."

Over time, the absence of investment is catastrophic. Each

time a successful export effort generates domestic growth—
or the government stimulates domestic demand by boosting
wages—supply constraints quickly develop, domestic prices
rise, and exports are diverted once again to the domestic market. And the effort to grow out of the debt by exporting more
is undermined. The government is then forced to repeat the
cycle, with a new round of devaluations and austerity to free
up resources for debt servicing. This further discourages investment. In the absence of new flows from abroad, and with
continuing capital flight from home, debtor governments face
a choice of subjecting their people to a steadily declining
standard of living in order to meet their debt-servicing obligations, or of not paying and being judged an outlaw in the
eyes of the international financial community.

With new lending becoming a trickle and world interest
rates on the rise again in the late 1980s, debtors simply
stopped paying, as they had in the 1930s. Many smaller debtors stopped paying in the mid-1980s and were later joined by
large debtors. Argentina stopped servicing its bank debt in
November 1988, and Brazil declared its second moratorium
in May 1989, stating simply that, from now on, budget reform
and domestic growth would take precedence over debt servicing. Two years later Brazil still did not have an agreement
with its banks and was not paying. (The first moratorium had
been declared with depleted foreign-exchange reserves; the
second time around, Brazil moved while reserves were still
ample.) By late 1990 arrears on payments to banks were ap-
proaching $30 billion. Even the multilateral agencies that in
principle never reschedule were experiencing significant payment arrears. To come current for 1990 Brazil, for example,
would have had to pay out more than $16 billion, plus an-
other $3 billion in arrears to multilateral institutions.

Chile was the notable exception to this bleak picture. At
the beginning of the crisis, Chile had the highest interest-
payment burden relative to GNP of any large debtor. Several
factors account for the difference in outcome. Although the

government ended up with the private-sector foreign debt on its books, the sale of state enterprises in the late 1970s had relieved the budget of their heavy operating deficits and reduced the public-sector employment cadre. An authoritarian Pinochet regime was also in a stronger position to suppress wages and prices in the economy, all of which helped to hold down inflation and interest rates. Domestic government debt costs were lower than in high-inflation countries, and domestic investment recovered more quickly.

A sharp increase in copper prices in late 1987 helped external balances. And Chilean economic policies found favor with foreign creditors—particularly with the Reagan administration. Consequently, Chile received much more generous official financing than any other Latin American debtor, so that the net resource drain of debt servicing was far smaller. And in 1988 banks agreed to let Chile put off half its interest payments to the following year—after a referendum on the presidency. Pinochet ran a classic populist economic policy for the two years leading up to the referendum. Chile's money supply increased by 80 percent in 1988 and in 1989. Imports were 35 percent per annum. Pinochet lost anyway, but no other debtor got such generous treatment from its bankers. Finally, Chile pursued an aggressive debt-equity swap program that allowed equity investors to exchange Chilean foreign debt, purchased at a discount from the holders, for local currency at a highly favorable rate of exchange. This program resulted in a substantial reduction of Chile's external debt burden. In short, Chile handled some—but by no means all—of its economic problems better than other debtors, but it also had more outside support. As far as most debtors were concerned, the 1980s were a "lost decade." By the end of the decade, the question finally had to be faced, whether either growth or "adjustment" was possible without substantial debt relief.

THE DREAD "F" WORD GAINS RESPECTABILITY

The original debt strategy engineered by Volcker and de La-rosière and reinforced by James Baker's initiative, was that banks and government lenders would share the burden of keeping debtors afloat until IMF-designed economic reforms took hold and allowed these countries to begin growing again and begin repaying their debts. Meanwhile, by avoiding losses of their LDC loans, banks could buy time to build up reserves and capital and to grow out of *their* problems by expanding into, presumably, less risky markets. It finally dawned on Washington that the lending banks were buying that time at the expense of their own governments. Banks were getting out from under by shifting more and more of the risk onto official lenders. As Brady pointed out in his Bretton Woods speech, "Commercial bank exposure to the major debtors since 1985 has declined slightly, while the exposure of the international institutions has increased sharply. If this trend were to continue, it could lead to a situation in which the debt problem would be transferred largely to the international institutions, weakening their financial position."[23]

OECD data show that in 1981 commercial banks supplied 42 percent of total net credit flows (net of amortization) to all developing countries, while official development finance contributed 37 percent. By 1988 banks provided only about 6 percent of net debt flows, while official development finance was 88 percent of the total. The official share of outstanding claims on the highly indebted countries had gone from 22 percent in 1982 to 37 percent by 1988. Since banks had reduced their exposure only slightly, most of the official financing had been used to help debtors pay interest to the banks. World Bank data indicate that from 1982 to 1988, developing countries received $25 billion more from official creditors than they paid out to them. But they had paid to commercial banks $183 billion *more* in interest and amortization than they had received in new bank loans. The new Bush administration reasoned that if the new money under the "new money strategy" was all going to have to come from government sources and wasn't going to solve the problem, then the strategy had to be abandoned. And since debtors could not pay without additional financing, debt reduction—for commercial loans—was the only alternative.

The door to this policy shift had already been opened by the banks themselves. In late 1987 Mexico had worked out a plan with the help of Morgan Guaranty—to which it owed more than $1 billion—to offer its creditors an exchange of twenty-year bonds for bank debt of a higher face value. The new bonds would be collateralized with a special twenty-year U.S. government zero-coupon bond the Treasury Department had reluctantly agreed to issue. The bond exchange was received unenthusiastically in the banking community; most banks were not yet ready to concede the inevitability of debt reduction. But the critical precedent had been set. The bond exchange offer had forced banks to begin to put a real market value on their LDC loans.

Other banks gradually came around to Morgan's view that some sort of debt relief was probably inevitable. In the spring and summer of 1988 a panel that included senior officers of Morgan, Citi, Manny Hanny, Chemical, Security Pacific, and Dresdner Bank; Brazil's ambassador to the United States; and, informally, officials from the World Bank and IMF, met under the auspices of the United Nations Association of the United States to try to set the parameters of a new approach to the debt problem. The panel concluded that

voluntary debt service reduction should be pursued as a serious alternative or complement to more lending. . . .

Concerns have been raised that debt service reduction in any form would discourage future lending. On the contrary, most panel members believe: If debt service reduction is carried out cooperatively . . . and has the desired effect not only of reducing outstanding claims against the country but of aiding economic recovery, then "credit-worthiness" will come sooner rather than later.[24]

The *Financial Times* read—correctly—between the lines of the panel's final report and trumpeted on its front page, "Bankers propose debt forgiveness for Third World."[25] The headline created a furor in the international financial community, and some panel members panicked. Participating banks denied that "debt service reduction" meant debt forgiveness. Despite the impression that was later given—that this was somehow a rogue panel not reflecting the real views of its participants—the principals had attended almost every meeting and had vigorously debated virtually every word of the final recommendations. The principals included co-chair Rod Wagner, vice chairman of Morgan's credit committee, who kept Morgan's chairman and CEO Lewis Preston informed every step of the way; Bill Rhodes, Citibank's and the banking community's chief debt negotiator, who examined the final report and reviewed Citibank's mild dissent (it found the assessment of what had been achieved so far unduly critical but did not disagree with the recommendations) with CEO John Reed. And it was Tom Johnson, president of Chemical Bank (now president of Manny Hanny), one of the most vulnerable institutions, who first articulated the view that the old strategy was at a dead end and that "despite the losses entailed, debt-service reduction transactions can have considerable benefits for creditor banks as well [as for debtors]."

Although bankers were not ready to utter the dread "f" word, they simply could not escape the logic of their situation. Not only had the LDC problem not been solved, but the banks' debt problem had not been solved either. Banks had reduced their exposure relative to capital quite significantly, by issuing more stock and especially by adding to loan-loss reserves (which until 1990 counted as capital under U.S. regulatory standards). The capital exposure of nine large U.S. banks to Latin America had declined from 177 percent of capital in 1982 to 84 percent of capital at year end 1988. All other U.S. banks had reduced their exposure from 79 to 22 percent. Banks around the world had added to loan-loss reserves against future losses on LDC debt. German banks had reserves equal to 50 to 70 percent of loans; French banks had reserves of 35 to 50 percent; U.K. banks, 25 to 50 percent; Canadian banks, 35 percent. Only Japanese banks, for tax reasons, continued to have very low loan-loss reserves.

An active secondary market for trading and selling developing-country bank loans had grown rapidly. By 1990 the market was estimated to be trading at least $60 billion of LDC debt. Most loans traded at a deep discount. Argentine debt sold for thirteen cents on the dollar, Brazilian debt for twenty-three cents, Mexican debt for thirty-five cents to the dollar, and Chilean debt for sixty cents.[26] Debtor countries were probably the biggest purchasers. But there were also banks seeking to change the country mix of their portfolio, investors who wanted to use the claims for debt-equity conversion in the debtor country, and speculators attracted by the potential high yield if the debtor's fortunes should turn around. Many banks as well as investment houses acted as third-party agents for trades for a fee. (By 1990, debt trading, ironically, had become a major source of revenue for the big banks. The Latin American division was the most profitable part of the bank for Morgan that year, largely because of the activities of its LDC trading desk.) Despite the size of this active market, bank accountants allowed banks still holding these loans to persist in the fiction that the market was too "thin" to set a real market price. Thus banks could carry the loans not sold off at 100 cents on the dollar.

Investors were not fooled. Since 1983 Congress had required banks to disclose detailed information about their exposure. Investors tired of the debt saga. Banks carrying large exposures were viewed with increasing distaste. Big bank stocks lagged the run-up in the bull market to the crash of October 1987 and lagged the recovery of Fortune 500 stocks since. Regional banks, which shed their LDC loans and took their losses early, sold at far higher price/earnings ratios by the late 1980s than the money-center banks. And with smaller banks fleeing the whole business in droves, a few very large banks were left holding most of the risk exposure.

U.S. regulators had begun pressing the money-center banks to increase capital ratios since the debt crisis began (the definition of primary capital still included loan-loss reserves). And in 1987 American, British, Japanese, and other industrial country regulators presented a joint agreement to impose new and joint capital adequacy requirements on their banks, to be phased in from 1990 to 1992. More capital would be required for riskier assets, and only a small portion of loan-loss reserves could be counted as capital. Banks would have to have a solid core of 4 percent equity capital against assets. Bank analysts estimated that most large banks would have to either shed assets or issue new stock to meet the new requirements.

Raising more bank capital would be expensive, given investors' sour mood. If LDC loans were yielding ample returns, including tax benefits, the capital could be financed. But with interest arrears mounting and a growing portfolio of nonperforming LDC loans, the bank's other assets would have to carry the capital, making the cost to the institution prohibitive. As the decade wore on, the situation would only be made worse by banks' desperate efforts to cover lost LDC earnings with high-yield, high-risk leverage buy-out financing and aggressive real estate lending. By the end of the 1980s banks needed debt relief almost as much as the debtors.

STRUCTURING DEBT REDUCTION

The banks were not willing to take their losses and give up claims without something in return. As the U.S. Treasury began discussions on a debt-reduction plan, they made clear that two conditions had to be met before they would agree to negotiate debt relief for developing countries. First they wanted the debts remaining after debt reduction to be securitized and converted into marketable claims like bonds. Although loans were being traded and sold in the secondary market much like securities, this was not always strictly legal under the terms of the loan contract. Some loan contracts stipulated that the claim could not be transferred without prior approval of the debtor. And if a loan was part of a syndication, the seller was technically obligated to share any proceeds from the sale with all other members of the syndicate. Banks wanted these complications out of the way so they could sell off their portfolios anytime.

The second condition was that governments in the banks' home countries, or the multilateral institutions, should offer "enhancements" or collateral to back the reduced LDC debt *and* the interest on that debt. Banks would then have smaller but less risky LDC assets, and stockholders would presumably look more kindly on debt reduction and on the banks that continued to hold such loans. This second demand almost derailed the Brady Plan. The idea of government guarantees was unpalatable to Treasury since the main objective of the new plan was to get the U.S. government out of the commercial bank–LDC debt problem altogether. The banks, Treasury argued, were now strong enough to stand on their own and take a hit, if need be, without government assistance. Treasury Undersecretary for International Affairs David Mulford, principal architect of the plan, resisted the idea of guarantees and proposed to the Fed that it threaten the banks with harsh regulatory measures if they did not comply with debt reduction without official "enhancements." But the Fed refused to play along. Treasury finally yielded, in part.

European governments, particularly the British and the Germans, opposed any additional commitment of official resources. There was a strong feeling the governments had been bailing out the banks. Governments had already done enough lending to cover the banks and had rescheduled more than $90 billion in bilateral government loans and interest due from troubled debtors. Only strong French and Japanese finance ministry support for the Treasury proposal overcame their objections. "As we discussed the issue," said one participant in the intergovernmental discussions, "we finally concluded that the only way to end the protracted crisis was for governments to take some risks to catalyze debt reduction." The governments promised to make available $30 billion to $35 billion to collateralize debt-reduction transactions.

However, the method of collateralization in part defeats both the debt-reduction effort and the effort to put a cap on government risk. The IMF and World Bank collateralization will not take the form of outright guarantees for debt-reduction transactions—which would be cheapest for the debtor—but loans to the debtor to finance the purchase of collateral such as zero coupon bonds to back debt-reduction securities. Thus the debtor has to take on more official debt to buy reduction of its commercial debt. And government financing is still being diverted from meeting development needs to getting banks out of the mess they have gotten themselves into.

Despite the promise of official backing, many banks opposed the whole concept. Some British bankers, and Commerzbank's chairman Walter Seip, were adamantly opposed to negotiated debt reduction. Deutsche Bank, on the other hand, was supportive. Alfred Herrhausen, international spokesman and dominant board member (later killed in a terrorist bombing), spoke in favor of debt cancellations already in the fall of 1988 (somewhat to the consternation of his fellow board members).[27] Herrhausen's view was that Germans should look sympathetically on such a proposition.

Mexico, inevitably, became the test case—the first debtor to negotiate under the Brady Plan format what was cast as a "final" settlement of its obligations to foreign banks. The economic program of Carlos Salinas de Gortari, the young U.S.-trained economist and de la Madrid protégé who became president of Mexico in 1989, was music to U.S. ears. He proposed to privatize state enterprises, enlarge the role of foreign investment, drastically reduce trade barriers, and move quickly to integrate Mexico in the modern world economy. He even pledged to move toward real democratic government.

Secretary Brady took a direct role in the Mexican debt negotiations. When they appeared to be stalling, he urged that bank chairmen get directly involved. Bank of America's Clausen, Citibank's Reed, and a senior officer of Swiss Bank—to speak for non-U.S. banks—eventually came to Washington to iron out the final disagreements with Mexico's long-term debt negotiator Angel Gurria and the finance minister himself, Pedro Aspe, at Treasury. Gerald Corrigan, president of the New York Federal Reserve, presided. According to the *New York Times*, Volcker's successor as chairman of the board of governors, Alan Greenspan, attended but did not actively participate. Throughout his tenure at the Fed, Greenspan has seemed most reluctant to become actively involved in the debt issue.

These Washington meetings were the conclusive round of the Mexican talks, and an outline agreement was announced on July 22, 1989. Treasury sided with Mexico on the issue of "recapture," that is, the right of banks to raise interest rates on rescheduled debt if oil prices rise sharply sometime in the future and give Mexico a windfall. The banks got a recapture clause, but it can only be activated in 1996 and only in limited amounts per year. Another outstanding issue involved Treasury directly. IMF and World Bank funds to support the agreement would be disbursed over three years. But Mexico needed more cash immediately to purchase the zero-coupon U.S. Treasuries that were to secure the debt-reduction bonds it would issue to the banks. Treasury apparently came to the rescue by agreeing to sell the zero-coupon bonds to Mexico at somewhat less than market price. (Treasury officials deny the price was concessionary.) By the time Treasury intervened in the negotiations, however, the key portions of the agreement had already been settled—the amount of debt reduction Mexico would get and how much interest relief. Mexico got little of either.[28]

The Mexican agreement covered $48.5 billion in bank loans. It reduced the old bank debt (but not Mexico's total debt) by $7 billion and stretched maturities out thirty years. Creditor banks were given a choice of swapping their claims for new thirty-year "debt-reduction" bonds carrying a 35 percent lower face value than the swapped debt and paying LIBOR plus thirteen-sixteenths. Or they could choose a thirty-year "par value" bond paying a fixed 6.25 percent rate of interest. (Mexico pledged never to seek rescheduling of these terms nor to ask for new loans from the bondholders.) Or banks could stick to the old plan and lend the equivalent of 25 percent of exposure in new money over three years. The last was included at Citibank's insistence, and Citi was one of the few banks to choose that option. Banks swapped more than 90 percent of their total Mexican debt holdings for either principal or interest reduction bonds. (If Mexico fully recovers economic health, of course, Citibank's gamble will pay off: losses taken by the other banks will have helped make Citibank whole in Mexico.)

Although the deal gave Mexico cash-flow relief and some protection against a rise in interest rates, the net result was very little debt reduction. The Salinas government had to borrow $7 billion—$5.8 billion from official sources and $1.2 billion from banks—to fully collateralize the deal. Mexico was left with roughly as much debt as when debt reduction began—but on better terms. The government claims the package reduces Mexico's resource transfer to creditors from 6 percent of GNP per annum to 2 percent. But that projection, of course, includes a lot of variables, including growth.

The ultimate success of the package depends not only on the amount of debt-relief granted but on the credibility awarded to Salinas's long-range economic plans for his country. It appears, after one year, that Mexicans themselves and foreign investors believe that Mexico's debt problem is behind them at last and they can begin to plan and invest for the future. Salinas's steady barrage of new initiatives for the economy has sustained the sense of forward momentum. The prospect of a free trade agreement with the United States and Canada has stimulated direct investment from abroad. But Salinas still faces a horrendous domestic debt problem, and domestic interest rates have been slow to come down. His anti-inflation program based on a strong peso and open borders runs the risk of exacerbating a tight balance-of-payments situation. Mexico had a $5.2 billion current account deficit in 1990, and worsening trade figures early in the year suggest the gap may be even larger in 1991. Salinas can only hope that foreign direct investment and capital repatriation will continue to cover these deficits. Salinas accepted far less than he wanted in the debt negotiations in order to hold together his anti-inflation program and maintain the momentum of his reforms. Consequently, the debt reduction agreement leaves no margin for error.

Brady Plan settlements have been reached for other sovereign debtors with varying degrees of debt relief and many variations on a theme. By the end of 1990 Venezuela, Costa

Rica, Bolivia, and the Philippines had also settled with the banks under the Brady Plan. Nigeria settled with its banks in early 1991. Brazil was locked in difficult negotiations with the banks over its insistence on a much different and more generous deal than Mexico's and its refusal to pay interest arrears until the framework had been agreed. Argentina was still sorting itself out. Interest arrears for the two countries had reached 20 percent of their combined total debts of some $180 billion.

U.S. bank regulators have belatedly insisted that banks begin to write off substantial chunks of their loans to both countries—at long last using the ATRR provisions of the 1983 Lending Supervision Act as Congress intended. Foreign and U.S. banks have continued to increase loan-loss reserves. Lewis Preston, highly respected chairman and CEO of JP Morgan, as a final act before retiring took it upon himself to raise Morgan's loan-loss reserve against troubled Third World loans to 100 percent. (Preston became president of the World Bank in August 1991.) The contrast with Walter Wriston, who left the mess he had made to his successor to clean up, was much commented upon in the banking community. Other U.S. banks increased their reserves to well over 50 percent. Ironically, only Citibank insisted that its 38 percent reserve was adequate. Since these are general reserves that have to absorb mounting losses on other kinds of loans, too, further large write-offs of LDC loans could still take a sizeable bite out of bank capital.

Claims on non-OPEC LDCs reported by the Bank for International Settlement showed a decline of $40.5 billion in 1989 and the first half of 1990.[29] Some of this was the result of negotiated debt reduction, some of loan sales in the secondary market—where some $50 billion to $60 billion in LDC paper was being traded by 1990. Some of the decline reflected repayment of private-sector debt; some was balance-sheet revaluation by the banks. Including Mexico, a total of

$72 billion of debt had been renegotiated, with a net debt and interest reduction worth about $17 billion to the debtors.[30] The relief seems marginal relative to the remaining debt burden. Other countries, meanwhile, were buying up their own debt at deep discounts in the secondary market with the money they had saved by defaulting.

According to the Bank for International Settlements, banks in the major lending countries reached a peak exposure to developing countries in 1987, with $517 billion in loans outstanding (including OPEC). By the second quarter of 1990 the total had declined to $469 billion. The retreat is not limited to troubled debtors. These banks have reduced their lending to nonindustrial countries almost across the board, to Asia as well as to Africa and Latin America. Loans to Eastern Europe and the Soviet Union declined by $6.4 billion in the second quarter of 1990.

Foreign bank lending by American banks has declined most sharply. Between December 1986 and June 1990, U.S. bank claims on Latin America shrank 45 percent, from $79 billion to $45.3 billion. Claims on all developing countries fell from $100 billion to $69.7 billion. Loans to Eastern Europe and the Soviet Union are a minuscule $2.5 billion.[31]

With the likely conclusion of debt-reduction agreements between banks and Brazil and Argentina in 1991 or 1992, continued debt-equity and other debt conversions through the secondary market, and straight debt buy-backs by the debtors, banks will have reduced their exposure to levels that might make new lending to these countries at least a theoretical possibility in the not too distant future.

Some of the transactions that clear the banks' books also help clear the debtors' books of unpaid foreign obligations. Loans that have been sold by banks to third parties still constitute a future claim on the debtor, of course. And even loans that have been converted into local equity can be a claim on resources if the owner is a foreigner. Future payments will be made in the form of dividends to the foreign shareholder and can also cause a balance-of-payments strain. Nevertheless, for the first time since the crisis began, there is a sense in many of these countries that the worst of the debt problem is over.

THE PRICE OF A GOOD NAME

The lesson to be drawn from the history of sovereign lending is not that governments always pay but that sooner or later their creditors will settle for less than 100 cents on the dollar. It is, as Brazil's Lemgruber said, "just a question of how often we meet"—of how much time will pass and how much damage will be done to the debtors and to their creditors before that reality is faced.

Is is now obvious to everyone that lending more money to countries already overburdened with debt, for the sole purpose of enabling them to pay interest on the old debt, is no solution to their problem. An early negotiated debt moratorium reducing interest payments to a sustainable level after the first panic over Mexico's 1982 default had subsided would have done far less damage on all sides than the policy that was followed. Only the governments of the major industrial countries could have made that happen. Banks would certainly not volunteer and debtors were too weak to make them. Brazil's and Peru's experience with unilateral moratoria show that such actions may bring cash-flow relief for a time but have other costs. Unilateral measures that make a nation an outlaw in the eyes of the world community undermine domestic confidence, create uncertainty for the business community, and can lead to economic slowdown and capital flight as everyone hunkers down to await what happens next.

Negotiated debt relief early in the crisis would have been the optimum solution. Debtors would not have had to take on tens of billions in added debt and would not have suffered the sharp fall-off in investment that reduced future debt-servicing capability. People in the debtor countries would not have suffered the terrible decline in living standards they experienced in the 1980s. The outbreak of cholera in Peru that is spreading to other parts of the continent is one portent of the long-term health costs of the protracted crisis. Mexican officials estimate that real wages have declined by 50 percent since 1982. The wealthier classes meanwhile have become even richer by investing in high-yield domestic government debt.

The banks, too, would probably have been better off with a negotiated moratorium. Instead of adding more risky loans to their books, they could have halted, then reduced, their exposure. Regulators would not have been compelled to force immediate write-offs, any more than they did when Argentina and Brazil stopped paying. But banks should have been required to use any income on these troubled loans to retire principal. Instead, during the 1980s, American banks in particular were allowed to pay high dividends, sometimes taken out of capital, to convince investors there was nothing to worry about. A no-dividend policy would have hit bank stocks hard at the time, but it is debatable whether the market reaction would have been any more severe than the bitter retribution disillusioned investors wreaked on banks later, when they discovered there was in fact plenty to worry about. And the build-up of bank capital through retained earnings could have proceeded more rapidly.

Finally, an early moratorium would have prevented the anomaly of official development agencies financing payments to commercial creditors, and the current anomaly of their taking out more in interest and principal from some needy countries than the new money they are putting in. As President Bush's Enterprise for the Americas initiative, announced in 1990, implicity recognizes, the failure to force *commercial* debt reduction early on makes *official* debt reduction inevitable now.

10

The Recovery of International Lending

The goal of the highly indebted countries has not changed: as in the 1980s it is to return to sustained growth and external creditworthiness.
—The World Bank, 1990

I would like to leave you with one final thought. In the past several years the world banking community has been tarred with its own brush. The reputation of our industry has been damaged by a number of issues. . . . I believe it is crucial to the further growth and future well-being of international financial markets that banks reestablish their position as the best credits available.

Achieving this will almost certainly result in banks reassuming with new vigor their traditional role as intermediaries.
—Werner Blessing, Deutsche Bank

THE STRUGGLE TO REGAIN CREDITWORTHINESS

Cleona Lewis wrote in 1938, "In retrospect it is easily seen that the defaults of the 1930s are the painful aftermath of the excessive and ill-advised lending of the 1920s. It is also readily apparent that American lenders and foreign borrowers both played a part in bringing this period of large-scale American lending to its unhappy denouement."[1] After examining the evidence, one can only draw the same conclusion about the 1970s and 1980s. The recent debt crisis was not caused primarily by forces beyond the control of participants. It was largely a disaster of the participants' own making. Banks, borrowers, and the political establishment that oversees the modern international financial system share the blame. In October 1982, before a group of Japanese bankers, Wall Street's Henry Kaufman summed up the systemic failure:

> The roots of the monetary debasement are the liberal credit practices which neither the regulators nor the regulated have controlled adequately over the past 15 years. Financial deregulation, floating interest rates, and "spread banking" techniques have not turned out to be escape hatches from market and monetary disciplines as many market participants expected them to be. On the contrary, these new elixirs, having numbed caution, encouraged massive lending at higher and higher interest rates, imposed huge debt burdens on borrowers, and created marginal assets on bank balance sheets. The result is a riskier world for us all.[2]

It is too soon to say that recent Brady Plan agreements have finally closed the books on the debt problem—that debtors have achieved a supportable level of external obligations and banks a tolerable level of risk exposure. Certainly many countries are closer to that point than at any time in the last nine years. Recovery by the banks from the multiple disasters of the last two decades seems more distant. It is the market's judgment that large commercial banks are no longer the "best credits available." The leading investment rating agencies—Moody's, Standard & Poors, and IBCA, a European agency that specializes in large multinational banks—give only six large banks around the world a triple A rating. They are Union Bank of Switzerland, Crédit Suisse and Swiss Bank, Rabobank of the Netherlands, Blessing's own Deutsche Bank, and Barclays Bank in the United Kingdom. Among American banks, only JP Morgan is likely to join this elite group any time soon.[3]

In 1990, large U.S. banks saw their share prices fall by two-thirds. Japanese bank stocks were down 40 percent to 50 percent. Standard and Chartered of the United Kingdom lost 60 percent of its share price. Citicorp, the largest bank in the United States, saw its stock price drop more than 50 percent. Non-equity sources of capital have become prohibitively expensive for many banks. U.S. banks raised nearly $30 billion in the Eurobond and note market from 1985 to 1989. But by early 1990, Chase Manhattan was paying 13 percent on its two-year bonds and Chemical was paying 2.30 percent over LIBOR on its short-term floating-rate notes. In fall 1990, Citicorp suspended its issuance of subordinated debt because the market was asking it to pay from 2 percent to 3 percent more to investors than it could charge prime corporate borrowers for loans. The basic function of a financial intermediary is to raise funds for the end-user more cheaply than the user could raise them himself. The loss of credit standing means that many large banks appear to have lost this essential capacity.

The big banks' fall from grace is easily explained. As Federal Deposit Insurance Corporation chairman L. William Seidman said when the government had to take control of Bank of New England in January 1991, "They made loans that could not be collected."[4] The dry rot in bank balance sheets began in the LDC loan portfolio that had generated the bulk of big bank profits in the 1970s, then spread to the domestic side as banks tried to compensate by plunging into activities that turned sour even more quickly. Sharply rising real estate prices in Europe, the United States, and Japan stimulated enormous demand for real estate financing from eager developers. In 1989, one-third of all U.S. money-center bank loans were for real estate.[5] Easy money provided by banks—and the savings and loan industry—financed egregious overbuilding of commercial properties just when Congress took away special tax breaks for real estate investors, and the widespread introduction of personal computers into office life and a streamlining of corporate management structures assured a decline in demand for clerical and middle-management office space.

It became fashionable to say the bank of the future would be more "transaction oriented." "We have felt for some time that the medium-term syndicated credit market has passed its peak," said Michael Rose, division head for Bankers Trust in London, in 1985. "The trend now is to liquefy your book by selling off assets you would previously have held to maturity. Either banks will act as investment banks where only the fee touches your balance sheet, or we'll whistle loans through so fast they barely touch the sides."

Unhappily for the banks, many of these hasty loans have stuck to the walls—and have gone bad. Not just real estate. Though still mostly barred by the Glass-Steagall Act from direct securities underwriting, banks in the United States could participate in the corporate take-over craze of the 1980s—and its attendant fees—by providing "bridge loans" to corporate mergers and issuers of junk bonds until long-term financing could be arranged. Some of these bridges led nowhere, and the large banks have added to their already large stock of LDC losses with deepening red ink from Campeau Corporation's busted take-over of Federated Department Stores, Donald Trump's collapsing casino and real estate empire, and thousands of unsung smaller real estate loans. U.S. banks have been worst hit. But since the international banks all now play in each other's back yard, European and

Asian banks, too, have their share of Campeau's, Trump's, et al.'s bad paper.

"Globalization" became another financial catch-phrase of the 1980s. It meant being in the most expensive markets: at a minimum, New York, London, Tokyo, and probably Frankfurt. A wave of financial liberalization in Britain and Japan, followed later in continental Europe, opened the door for foreign institutions to hold seats on the local stock exchanges, own insurance companies, be primary dealers in host government debt issues, and engage in other financial activities previously restricted to domestic firms. Many British and U.S. banks, in particular, rushed in with a vengeance, acquiring expensive office space, purchasing stock brokerages, trying to incorporate trading and investment banking strata (at trading and investment banking compensation levels) within the commercial banking culture.[6] One exception, JP Morgan, hung back and was ridiculed as stodgy and behind the times.

The results merely compounded banks' woes. Overhead costs at the "global" institutions soared, and staff morale suffered through repeated management reorganizations as banks tried to arrange their disparate pieces into a coherent whole.[7] Worst of all, the anticipated huge returns from these new ventures never materialized. As part of the general bloodletting in the financial services that began in earnest in 1990, banks have sold—sometimes at a loss—the stock brokerages so expensively acquired just a few years ago, have quietly withdrawn from primary dealerships, and have fired whole trading departments. In late 1990, Security Pacific announced a general retreat from merchant banking and a staff reduction of more than 5,000 in that part of its operations. Peter Eby, vice chairman of its Canadian investment bank, commented: "Security Pacific had perhaps too big a strategy in trying to do both commercial and investment banking at the same time." "Nobody," he added, "has really made an integrated global securities business work."[8]

BANKS IN SEARCH OF A MISSION

The financial industry's recent travails mask a deeper problem. For the last twenty years, large American banks have
been institutions in search of a mission. They have lost their
role, probably permanently, as the principal financiers and
boardroom nannies to leading corporations in their home
market. Modern communications and computerization have
given corporate treasurers access to market information that
only bankers used to have. And with the institutionalization
of private savings—in pension funds, mutual funds, and
money-market funds—prime-rated corporations can access
money directly without the costly intermediation of a bank.
Instead of shrinking as prime corporate demand for their
services drained away into the commercial paper market, however, the large banks grew rapidly on the chassis of foreign and,
especially, developing-country loans. The Eurocurrency market
freed banks from dependence on domestic retail branches for
funds, and the massive liquidity that OPEC infused into the
system and subsequent growth of the international wholesale
banking market funded excessive and irresponsible lending. In
the absence of any requirement that expanding loans and deposits be supported by more investor capital, there was no need
to validate this strategy in the market.

The loss of corporate business is so far mostly a problem
for large U.S. banks. But as decontrol of domestic interest
rates raises the cost of funds for banks in Japan and other
countries, and as deregulation allows competing financial
mechanisms to develop, the U.S. money-center banks' foreign
competitors are likely to suffer a similar erosion of core corporate business. In Germany this already is beginning. Said
the senior officer of a major German bank in fall 1990, "We
aren't abandoning our corporate clients: they're walking away
from us." Even companies in which the bank has a major
ownership stake are beginning to look at alternative sources

of finance. Japan's long-term credit banks are beginning to see some slippage of their dominant position as "main bank" to large Japanese firms.

Lending to prime sovereigns has followed much the same pattern. Sweden securitized its sovereign loans in the early 1980s, long before there was a Brady Plan. It faced an uncomfortable bunching of maturities. To avoid a balance-of-payments squeeze and possibly the embarrassment of joining the long list of troubled sovereign debtors, the kingdom prepaid most of its syndicated bank loans by refinancing in the capital markets. With the support of its bankers, Sweden pioneered the jumbo ($1 billion) floating-rate note (FRN) issue, then moved into the Euronote market, which evolved into the Euro-commercial-paper market. Although no one had prepaid sovereign credits before, the banks went along. "They saw it's where the market is going, and they had ambitions to do more in the capital markets and saw Sweden as a vehicle," said Peter Engstrom, who engineered the maneuver for the Swedish debt office. "Many of the notes have in fact ended up on the banks' books. The banks earn less interest than on a standard bank loan, but the asset is in theory at least, more liquid." Denmark, Spain, the United Kingdom, the EC, and other governments regarded by the market as prime risks have since shifted their borrowing principally to the capital markets and away from syndicated bank credits.

In the United States, the erosion of the large banks' position—made worse by strong domestic competition from foreign, particularly Japanese, banks—has triggered demands in both bank and government circles that something be done to restore the "competitiveness" of American banks. The assumption behind the Treasury Department's proposed rewrite of U.S. banking loans is that if large commercial banks are free to compete in all areas of financial services, they will somehow be more competitive and thus attract the investment capital necessary to shore up the industry. The previous international debt crisis gave us Glass-Steagall; this one may give us repeal.

It is unlikely, however, that any amount of deregulation can save all the large banks. Certainly the argument gains little support from the banks' performance in deregulated overseas markets. Many of the services into which banks would be allowed to expand already suffer from over-capacity. The U.S. insurance industry is in deep trouble; the securities industry has suffered almost as severe failures and cut-backs as the banks in the last two years. While some commercial banks can offer economies of scale and other advantages in underwriting and other financial services, others that would try to do so would be losers. A simplification of this country's complex financial sector may well be warranted in its own right. But it will not solve the banks' problem. The first step to restoring the health of the banking industry in this country most probably is to eliminate outright a number of large banks.

Even then, the remaining large banks must answer the question, "Who needs us?" At least a partial answer may well be that they are needed by the very foreign customers the banks are now shunning: companies, and even governments, in countries outside the OECD area.

WHO WILL FINANCE THE RE-EMERGING ECONOMIES?

Governments are unlikely to provide all the capital the developing countries and Eastern Europe will need for economic recovery and integration with the developed world. Official lending agencies are in the same position as commercial lenders—taking more out of developing countries in interest and repayments than they are putting in in new loans. The 1990 World Development report warned of a "significant and unsustainable increase in reliance on official creditors."

The next round of debt restructuring will almost certainly have to involve official debt reduction.

Even when a country is not overburdened with debt, excessive reliance on official sources of finance can be troublesome. Official credits have provided temporary financial respite or long-term development assistance for the very poorest. It has not been, historically, a foundation on which an economy can build extensive financial links to the outside world on normal market terms. Indeed, there is a substantial body of evidence that extended reliance on official grants and loan programs can distort patterns of economic development.[9] It may particularly stunt the growth of the private sector. Results in Africa hardly inspire confidence in official financing. And indeed Latin America's own experience immediately after World War II illustrates that debt problems can occur with official flows as with private credit. Latin American leaders now look to Spain and Portugal in the Europe of 1992 as a development model, not to the aid-dependent Latin America of the 1950s and 1960s. Let official lenders use their resources to help meet the desperate social infrastructure needs of these countries and leave commercial lending to the banks and other financial intermediaries.

Many developing and former communist countries have put out the welcome mat for foreign direct investment, and some, like Chile, Mexico, and Czechoslovakia, are beginning to attract significant flows. But however strong their need for capital, none of these countries is likely to permit foreign companies to dominate completely key industrial sectors (any more than the United States is willing to let Japanese companies dominate the automobile or computer industries in this country). They will want local ownership control for economic reasons—profit repatriation can be a heavy drain on a country's balance of payments—and political reasons. Significant state ownership will probably also continue to be a fact of life in most cases, in part because domestic investors for privatization cannot always be found and the state will not want to sell everything to foreigners. Many of these ventures, including foreign multinationals, will need some outside financing in order to raise investment to a level that gives some hope of sustainable economic growth. Foreign banks have a role to play if they want it.

Unlike major corporations in the wealthy countries, enterprises in the emerging market economies of Eastern Europe or Latin America need financial nannies. Most of these economies are capital-short and lack the mechanisms for mobilizing savings for investment outside government channels. Such enterprises, including state companies weaning themselves from the government printing press, will need access to foreign financing and financial expertise. Most of them have neither the "name" nor the credit standing to access foreign credit directly. Most will need the "good name" of a bank to borrow, and would benefit from long-term relationships in the traditional banking sense.

There is a fundamental difference between a financial "transaction" such as a one-up underwriting, and a financial "relationship." A commercial bank used to make term loans which it held to maturity. It had to live with the consequences of its actions. If the clients got into trouble during that time, so did the bank. Consequently, a good banker was one who knew his client's business inside and out. The sense of a common fate is what made bank-client relationships special. In the 1970s, banks forgot or misjudged the long-term implications of their lending decisions. They mistakenly believed that clever financial manipulation could replace credit judgment. And the consequences were brought home to them by a vengeful reality. In the 1980s, they tried to escape them altogether by "securitizing" loans and selling them off before term—without showing much better results.

There are indications that some banks may be willing to return to "relationship" banking based on a long-term commitment to the client. After Citibank's financing of Campeau's Federated Department Stores take-over turned into a likely loss, a chastened John Reed told interviewers for the Harvard Business Review in late 1990: "If all you want to do is make money, you do what the Wall Street guys do: convince your customers to do things that generate big fees right away. That's not our business. It was not our best moment when we financed Campeau. . . . I would suggest that if your customer goes bankrupt within one year of a deal, then the deal was not good business for you. . . . A smart organization would have said we shouldn't do the deal—even while knowing that if we didn't, someone else would."[10]

Those familiar with Citibank's notoriously aggressive, elbows-out mode of operation may take Reed's new-found humility with a grain of salt. But if he takes his own words to heart, Citibank, at least, may have finally learned a lesson banks should have learned long ago: A deal is good only if it brings long-term benefits to the debtor as well as the creditor. (And the mere fact that another bank might be willing to step in is not by itself sufficient reason to lend.)

Reed's prescription for curing what ails his own bank, and presumably other U.S. banks, includes the usual shibboleths of cutting out management layers and clarifying the mission of each part of the bank. But he adds an interesting point about staffing a modern bank: "We know how to hire smart people and put them in an organization; that doesn't automatically produce a smart organization. . . . You can devalue the truly knowledgeable industry experts, the people to whom others look for advice, in favor of people with big, bold management jobs or who are great number crunchers. . . . Today we have to rebuild the bankers."[11]

A case can be made that it is Reed and his colleagues who should lead the way. Even if the future financing of developing countries and Eastern Europe involves a mix of bond underwriting and loans, a Deutsche Bank, a Morgan, or a

Citibank may be more qualified as an intermediary than a Salomon or a Shearson Lehman. The large banks have a reduced but still extensive network of offices and employees in these countries, and the length and depth of their involvement with a Chile or Mexico or Brazil, or even with Poland and Hungary, is far greater than any investment bank's. Commercial banks and debtor countries have been through purgatory together and now know each other inside out. During the debt restructurings, the banks have taken apart the countries' balance sheets and gone over the government books with a magnifying glass. The people on the debt-restructuring teams know far more about the strengths and weaknesses and vulnerabilities of the debtor economies than the lending officers and risk analysts knew in the 1970s. And the debtors have learned a lot about the strengths and weaknesses of the banks. For better or worse, the banks and the debtors have already forged a new relationship out of this miserable experience. Given the still large block of claims on the banks' books, this relationship will have to continue for some time. The debt conversion agreements have given the banks an equity stake in these countries: the better their performance, the more valuable are the sovereign bonds banks now hold in lieu of loans.

The regulatory framework in which a revival of cross-border bank lending outside the industrial countries would take place is very different from the 1970s in two crucial respects: First, the market-distorting hidden subsidy of the foreign tax credit has largely been eliminated. The market price of credit should therefore more accurately reflect risk and reward. That in turn should be a deterrent to the kind of egregious overlending and overborrowing of earlier decades.

Second, bank owners will have to put some of their own money on the table for every new loan. New capital requirements adopted in 1989 by all the major financial centers under the auspices of the Bank for International Settlements

(BIS) require banks to maintain a fixed ratio of invested capital to assets. After 1991, a bank must raise $4 of equity (or long-term subordinated debt) and another $4 of more loosely defined capital for every $100 of risk-weighted loans it makes. The market's good opinion of a bank and its customers is thus essential. A bank that must pay a higher premium for risk capital than it can charge its customers for loans will simply be unable to expand. Loans to government entities outside the OECD (or Saudi Arabia) carry a much higher risk-weighting than government loans within the OECD. As long as banks are capital-short, they will be reluctant to take on the added capital cost of lending to an LDC. On the other hand, loans to any corporation, even an IBM, carry the same risk-weighting as a loan to an LDC government or corporation. If the latter is deemed creditworthy and is willing to pay more than IBM for credit, it can be a more attractive customer for a bank. History has shown repeatedly that cross-border lending is inherently risky. But sound, well-capitalized banks will be able to lend, even to relatively riskier borrowers.

THE SEEDS OF RECOVERY

At the moment, few banks show any inclination to return to the site of their latest foreign loan debacle. There was no increase in lending by the BIS reporting banks outside the industrial countries in 1989 (while lending inside the area rose by more than $500 billion) and a substantial decline in outstanding loans in the first half of 1990. This may change, however, as debtors begin to work down their obligations— even at the banks' expense. The history of sovereign lending suggests that potential lenders care more about the relative level of outstanding indebtedness and economic outlook of a country than they do about its past payment performance. At the end of the day, even bank managers tend to be more concerned with prospective new business than about the losses their predecessors may have incurred. The attitude of the market can change quickly once there is a firm settlement of outstanding debts—even a settlement that is highly favorable to the debtor. Indeed, the more favorable the settlement to the debtor, the more attractive the debtor may seem to the next lender.

The first tender shoots of market recovery are already beginning to sprout. Some debtors have once again begun to attract direct foreign investment. According to a JP Morgan trader of LDC debt paper, Mexico in 1990 "became the darling" of portfolio investors willing to commit some risk capital. In early 1991, the investment firm Goldman Sachs set up a seven-man shop to follow "emerging markets," and Chile became the first Latin American country since 1982 to go to market with a straight, unadorned bond issue. Mexico soon followed. JP Morgan began to extend loans to Mexican corporations—but, said one officer, echoing James Green on the recovery of lending in the 1950s, "only on a collateralized basis." The net resource flows are still small relative to need after the economic devastation of the 1980s. Nevertheless, one can say that these countries are beginning to recover their creditworthiness.

The apparent finality of debt settlements with foreign banks gave the initial boost to confidence in the economic outlook for debtors with Brady Plan agreements. Governments in Venezuela, Mexico, and Chile have enhanced their standing by embracing many of the structural reforms creditors long have urged upon them—particularly cutting government spending, privatizing state enterprises, and opening their economies to foreign trade and investment.

The liberal economic model does not by itself guarantee long-term creditworthiness, however. A successful heavily-indebted country like South Korea has been no less state-interventionist or closed to foreign interests than many countries in Latin America. Certainly, South Korea's greater emphasis on exporting is a crucial factor. But in Korea, land reform (1940s) and an equitable education system have helped both rural and industrial productivity to rise and incomes to spread relatively evenly through the economy. The income distribution gap in Korea, unlike that of Latin America, has closed, not widened, in the last two decades. A more equitable distribution of the fruits of growth meant the government relied less on price subsidies and loss-making *parastatals* to deter social unrest. That, and an effective tax regime, kept the government from running a huge operating deficit. Foreign borrowing could thus be dedicated primarily to pay for capital goods imports and provide low cost loans for industrial investment.[12] (What Korea needs now is to add democratic political reforms to the social agenda.)

One reason for modest optimism about the future of a country like Chile is its government's announced commitment to address social issues. The Alwyn government says it will do what it and many other developing countries tragically failed to do during the years of easy credit and high growth—to systematically address and eradicate the deep social and political inequities that plague the society. Chile's Alwyn government has raised income and corporate taxes to finance increased social spending. Sixty-five percent of the 1991 budget is to be spent on health, housing, education, and other social programs. New labor laws will end the Pinochet era's repression of workers and allow for collective bargaining. President Salinas of Mexico, responding in part to strong election pressure from the left, has taken a similar line, though it remains to be seen if the ruling party structure will permit its realization. Brazil's President Collor, also strongly challenged by parties on the left, promises to follow the same path once inflation is under control. It remains to be seen if any of these governments has the strength or the will to tackle the highly-charged issue of land reform. But if social reforms are carried out in tandem with economic liberalization, the political risk of lending to these countries will be greatly diminished.

Many large banks have highly profitable local-currency banking operations in developing countries. Citibank's lucrative and multifaceted operation in Brazil is in many ways a prototype for the kind of full-service financial institution Citibank would like to be worldwide. In Brazil, the bank and its Crefisul Group have achieved the degree of penetration and diversification into everything from investment banking to insurance that, until recently, tight regulation barred in other countries, including the United States. It is far more likely to try to expand the Brazil operation than withdraw. And as developing countries join the deregulation trend, other banks may have an opportunity to follow.

With regard to Eastern Europe, banks are understandably wary of plunging in where the political situation remains highly volatile, where the rules of ownership and private enterprise are not fully articulated, and where relations with the West can suffer a sudden reversal. Western banks are clearly fearful that the next debt crisis will be the Soviet Union's. Japanese and European banks lent freely to the USSR until 1990. Even then its debt was deemed modest relative to national economic output and export capacity. But political upheaval and economic decentralization have disrupted Soviet foreign-exchange cash flow. Fortunately, the banks with large unguaranteed exposures in the USSR appear for the most part to be strong institutions, able to take large provisions against their loans without undue strain. Since Deutsche Bank announced in January 1991 that it was provisioning against Soviet loans and would make no more, other lenders are believed to have followed suit. Western governments are engaged in a complex debate about whether and how to aid the Soviet Union's unsteady move toward economic and political

reform. The policy considerations would be even more difficult if these governments had to worry about the effects a
Soviet payments crisis would have on their financial systems,
as with Mexico in 1982.

So far, only German, Austrian, and Finnish banks seem willing to take up the challenge in Eastern Europe. Even Western
multinationals trying to finance joint venture investments in
Eastern Europe are finding it difficult to get support from
Western banks, particularly U.S. banks. Colgate-Palmolive has
recently made a number of investments in Eastern Europe
and the Soviet Union. Colgate's experience has been that except for Citibank in Hungary (where it has a domestic bank),
U.S. banks are not interested in supporting these ventures.
"If you are an American company looking for financing now,
you just don't look to U.S. banks. You go to the West German
or Austrian banks," Edgar Field, Colgate-Palmolive Company
group vice president in charge of Eastern Europe, told a conference in October 1990.

If these early ventures succeed, however, even U.S. banks
may follow.

A quarter of a millennium ago, David Hume wrote that he
could not prove the sun would rise tomorrow morning but
he believed it would. No one can prove that the banks will
again at some time lend money to sovereign borrowers and
to enterprises in developing countries that can sing the right
siren song. But it will happen; from the Fuggers to Walt Wriston, borrowers far away have found bankers who insist on
believing them. The open question is whether the return to
such lending will occur while those who have learned lessons
from the last round, banks and borrowers alike, are still in a
position to use the experience so expensively gained.

Postscript

Troubled debtors, particularly in Latin America, are once again attracting foreign credit and investment. The combination of greater fiscal responsibility, privatization, deregulation of foreign investment, and high interest rates has brought back the banks and their customers. The Mexican Brady Plan debt restructuring has served as a model for other debtors. Argentina and Brazil have negotiated, although not yet closed, similar settlements with their creditors. Meanwhile, the markets behave as if the deals were already done. Banks to which Argentina still has large interest arrears have cheerfully underwritten bond issues for Argentine borrowers. Bank hiring for the international division is surging along with profits. The stock of troubled debt has become a source of profit as loans and "Brady bonds" are traded in a large and volatile market or used to fund complex third-party investments in the debtor country. As predicted, the commercial banks have used their long involvement in developing countries to hold eager investment banking competitors at bay: JP Morgan dominates business with Mexico; Citibank has converted dollar claims on Brazil into a growing and lucrative domestic retail banking business. Happy times are here again. Maybe.

It seems appropriate for this book to end as it began, on a note of caution. The debt burdens of many developing countries remain too large relative to their economic bases. Recovery in growth is still uneven, and no government has yet seriously tackled the enormous social inequities that characterize most of these societies. A surge in imports is making life better, but growing current account deficits are being financed with foreign capital—much of it very short term. International "private banking" is thriving, indicating that Latin Americans are still hedging their bets by keeping some of their money abroad. Indirect borrowing is going on. More than half the deposit liabilities of Argentina's domestic banks are U.S. dollars. Someone is running a huge exchange risk.

The judgment of large banking institutions is still suspect. With the United States in stubborn recession and Europe and Japan following, the big banks are once again looking to developing countries to provide the profits to support their capital and cover the multiple sins of bad real estate loans and busted mergers and acquisitions. And there probably is not enough good business to go around. Management structures may still be a source of problems. During the cost-cutting 1980s, banks shed experienced lending officers left and right. Small cadres of senior officers baptized in the debt crisis still head the international divisions, but the day-to-day credit judgment is being made by freshly recruited, young, eager-beaver MBAs and MAs with only the dimmest awareness of what went on in the 1970s and early 1980s. Peddling the very latest in financial engineering of swaps, options, and convoluted hedges, they may think they are invulnerable.

Bank regulators are trying to keep pace with the overseas activities of their charges. The IRS is trying to collect back taxes on Brazilian loans, but as the recent scandals involving BCCI and the Banco Nazionale Lavoro (BNL) demonstrate, there are still large holes in the regulatory net. The valuation of many overseas assets, one suspects, is suspect.

Most depressing of all, the international financial establishment does not seem to have internalized the lessons of the debt crisis. The August 1992 tenth anniversary brought forth a wave of self-congratulatory articles and statements from top IMF and central bank officials about how well they had managed the problem—as if the solution they finally, reluctantly, hit upon in 1989 had not been obvious and doable many years before. Even in late 1992, with the shattered remains of the Soviet Union slipping deeper into economic crisis, Western banks and governments inexplicably continue to insist that debt relief, in their case, is not in order.

Have any lessons been learned? One can only hope.

April 1993

Notes

CHAPTER 1

1. *American Banker*, 9 July 1987.
2. Based on BIS data from banks in the Group of Ten countries plus Luxembourg, Austria, Denmark, Finland, Ireland, Norway, Spain, Bahamas, Bahrain, Cayman Islands, Hong Kong, Netherlands Antilles, Singapore, and U.S. bank branches in Panama.
3. *International Banking and Financial Market Developments during the Fourth Quarter of 1989* (Basle: Bank for International Settlements, May 1990).
4. S. C. Gwynne, *Selling Money* (New York: Weidenfeld and Nicolson, 1986), 15.
5. Vincent P. Carosso, *The Morgans* (Cambridge, Mass.: Harvard University Press, 1987), 419.
6. The *1985 Annual Report of Citicorp* (New York: Citicorp, 1986) explains, "Whenever Citicorp lends, places or invests funds across a national border or in a currency that is 'foreign' to the borrower, it incurs a transfer and/or convertibility risk, commonly referred to as 'country risk.'" Banks use the term sovereign risk for such loans when the government is the borrower or guarantor.

7. Henry C. Wallich, "Perspective on the External Debt Situation" (Comments at the annual meeting of the American Economic Association, Dallas, 28 December 1984).
8. Foreign Bondholders Protective Council, *Annual Report of 1934* (New York: Foreign Bondholders Protective Council, 1935).

CHAPTER 2

1. The hearings were later released.
2. A full text of correspondence between the subcommittee and the banks can be found in "First Session on Multinational Banks and U.S. Foreign Policy, July 16, September 11 and 18, October 9 and 29, 1975," in *Multinational Corporations and Foreign Policy, pt. 15* (Hearings before the Subcommittee on Multinational Corporations of the Senate Committee on Foreign Relations, July-October 1975) 94th Congress, 1st Session, app. (hereafter referred to as MNC Subcommittee Hearings, pt. 15, July-October 1975).
3. A history of the Chase notes the bank had to seek waivers to the secrecy laws from customers at its Swiss subsidiary in order to comply with the Fed's examination requirements. John Donald Wilson, *The Chase: The Chase Manhattan Bank, N.A., 1945–1985* (Boston: Harvard Business School Press, 1987), 178.
4. MNC Subcommittee Hearings, pt. 15, July-Oct. 1975, 58.
5. Ibid., 27.
6. Ibid., 53.
7. Jahangir Amuzegar, "Oil Exporters' Economic Development in an Interdependent World" (IMF Occasional Paper 18, Washington, D.C., April 1983), 63.
8. Bank of England, *Quarterly Bulletin*, September 1982, 358.
9. Bank for International Settlements, *51st Annual Report* (Basle: BIS, June 1981).
10. MNC Subcommittee Hearings, pt. 15, July-October 1975, 2–3.

11. Ibid., 46.

12. Ibid., 65.

13. Ibid., 50.

14. Ibid., 55.

15. Ibid., 60.

16. "Federal Response to OPEC Country Investments in the United States," Hearings before the Subcommittee on the House Committee on Government Operations, 97th Congress, 1st Session (1981), pt. 1, 462–63.

17. MNC Hearings, pt. 15, 21. In addition to offering the Saudis confidentiality, the Treasury Department arranged for them to buy U.S. government paper by private auction rather than having to bid for the IOUs publicly, with all other investors. This facility was later offered to other central banks.

18. The categories were the six largest banks, second-largest six banks, and nine other banks. Since 1977 the Treasury Department has collected and published semiannual data (quarterly as of 1983) on the foreign loans of U.S. banks. This *Country Risk Lending Survey* also uses aggregations. The government still does not publish a single report on country-by-country data on the foreign liabilities of U.S. banks, although the numbers for certain countries can be derived by combining various sources.

19. Charles P. Kindleberger, *Manias, Panics, and Crashes* (New York: Basic Books, 1978), 15, 41.

20. Bank of England, *Quarterly Bulletin* (June 1981): 187.

21. Denis Healy, quoted in *Institutional Investor* (June 1987): 66. Cited by Jerome Levinson, "A Perspective on the Debt Crisis," *American University Journal of International Law and Policy* 4, no. 3 (Summer 1989): 501.

22. Standard Oil of New Jersey (Exxon), Standard Oil of California (Chevron), Mobil, Texaco, Gulf, British Petroleum, and Royal Dutch Shell.

23. The standard formula for dividing the spoils between the governments and the oil companies had been that the companies paid a 12.5 percent royalty on the official or "posted" price per barrel plus a 50 percent "income tax" on the re-

maining profits after costs—costs having been set by negotiation.

24. Martin Mayer, *The Money Bazaars* (New York: Dutton, 1984),
    237.

25. Amuzegar, "Oil Exporters' Economic Development," 94.

26. Measuring countries' balance of payments is an inexact
    science, and numbers of this class should be taken as ap-
    proximations. The 1981 to 1982 U.S. balance of payments,
    for example, showed a current account deficit of $7 bil-
    lion, but "errors and omissions" (the discrepancy between
    inflow and outgo that could not be accounted for) were
    $65.4 billion. The discrepancy on world accounts that year
    was $135.6 billion. Part of the discrepancy is apparently
    due to systematic underrecording of investment income
    by oil-exporting countries and others. See Bank of En-
    gland, *Quarterly Bulletin* (September 1982): 356, and Rich-
    ard P. Mattione, *OPEC's Investments and the International
    Financial System* (Washington, D.C.: Brookings Institution,
    1985), 6 n. 2.

27. Mattione, *OPEC's Investments and the International Financial
    System*, 23.

28. Steven Emerson, *The American House of Saud* (New York:
    Franklin Watts, 1985), 45.

29. Amuzegar, "Oil Exporters' Economic Development," 62, ta-
    ble 27.

30. Emerson, *The American House of Saud*, 55.

31. Ibid., 46–47.

32. "Foreign Military Sales, Foreign Military Construction Sales
    and Military Assistance Facts as of September 1981," U.S.
    Department of Defense Security Assistance Agency, Wash-
    ington, D.C.

33. William R. Cline, *International Debt and the Stability of the World
    Economy* (Washington D.C.: Institute for ,International Eco-
    nomics, 1983), 20.

34. Author's conversation with the South Korean government's
    chief economic planner, Kim Jae Ik, in 1979. Kim was later
    killed by an assassin's bomb in Burma.

35. Amuzegar, "Oil Exporters' Economic Development," 62, table 27.

36. Mattione, *OPEC's Investments and the International Financial System*, 147.

37. See R. M. Pecchioli, *The Internationalization of Banking* (Paris: OECD, 1983), 138, table 9. Note the large unknown category "Other," which may include loans to less developed countries (LDCs).

38. Mattione, *OPEC's Investments and the International Financial System*, 13.

39. Ibid., 60.

40. Author's interview with former head of Iran's central bank, Mohammed Yeganeh, New York, 6 June 1986.

41. Tom Redburn, "David Mulford: America's New Front-Line Commander," *The International Economy*, Washington, D.C. (March/April 1989).

42. *Wall Street Journal*, 13 March 1981.

43. Dan Dorfman, "Kuwait Oil Profits Buy $7 Billion Worth of U.S. Securities," *Washington Post*, 31 May 1981; Dan Dorfman, "Kuwait Puts Citibank on Investment Hot Seat," *Washington Post*, 7 June 1981. Cited in Mattione, *OPEC's Investments and the International Financial System*, 102. The *Wall Street Journal* reported on 15 September 1981 that Kuwait had shifted its portfolio to Morgan Stanley and Chemical apparently because of irritation over the leaks and a lackluster Citibank investment performance.

44. *Wall Street Journal*, 15 September 1981.

45. Emerson, *The American House of Saud*, 47.

46. Treasury Department Memorandum of November 1977, quoted in "Federal Response to OPEC Country Investments in the United States" (Hearings before a Subcommittee of the House Committee on Government Operations, 97th Congress, 1st session) (1981), 711.

47. Darrell Delamaide, *Debt Shock* (New York: Doubleday, 1984), 30.

48. The Eurocurrency market is a financial market in which

loans and deposits in dollars and other currencies take place outside the national regulatory and monetary restrictions of the country of issuance.

49. Wilson, *The Chase*, 242.
50. Pecchioli, *The Internationalization of Banking*, 35.

CHAPTER 3

1. Hanover merged with Manufacturers Trust in 1961.
2. George S. Moore, *The Banker's Life* (New York: Norton, 1987), 167.
3. Harold van B. Cleveland and Thomas F. Huertas, *Citibank 1812–1970* (Cambridge, Mass.: Harvard University Press, 1985), 261 n. 7.
4. Moore, *The Banker's Life*, 168.
5. Michael Dooley et al., "An Analysis of External Debt Positions of Eight Developing Countries through 1990" (International Finance Discussion Paper No. 227, August 1983, Federal Reserve Board, Washington, D.C.), app. table 2.
6. See, for example, William A. Darity, Jr., "Loan Pushing: Doctrine and Theory" (International Finance Discussion Paper No. 253, February 1985, Federal Reserve Board, Washington, D.C.), 13, table 2.
7. Eduardo Wiesner, "Latin American Debt: Lessons and Pending Issues" (Paper presented at the American Economic Association Annual Meeting, Dallas, 28 December 1984).
8. In September 1940 the U.S. Export-Import Bank extended a $20 million loan to Brazil over the loud protests of private U.S. holders of defaulted Brazilian bonds. The loan was to finance Brazil's first major steel complex, at Volta Redonda, and to block Germany, which had also offered to finance the complex. See Stanley E. Hilton, *Brazil and the Great Powers 1930–1939* (Austin: University of Texas Press, 1975), cited in Mancilio Marques Moreira, *The Brazilian Quandary* (New York: Twentieth Century Fund, 1986), 76.

9. Paul Einzig, *Foreign Dollar Loans in Europe* (London: Macmillan, 1965), 32.

10. Cleveland and Huertas, *Citibank 1812–1970*, 213–14.

11. Lester B. Pearson, chair, Commission on International Development, *Partners in Development* (New York: Praeger, 1969), 154–55.

12. Jerome Levinson and Juan de Onis, *The Alliance That Lost Its Way* (Chicago: Quadrangle Books, 1970), 12.

13. Pearson, *Partners in Development*, 384–85, table 20.

14. Sheldon Annis, "The Shifting Grouds of Poverty Lending at the World Bank" in *Between Two Worlds*, Richard E. Feinberg ed. (Washington, D.C.: Overseas Development Council, 1986), 89.

15. Pearson, *Partners in Development*, 394.

16. Richard S. Newfarmer and Willard F. Mueller, "Multinational Corporations in Brazil and Mexico: Structural Sources of Economic and Noneconomic Power" (Report to the Subcommittee on Multinational Corporations of the Senate Committee on Foreign Relations, 94th Congress, 1st Session, August 1975), 146, 148 (hereafter referred to as MNC Subcommittee Report, August 1975).

17. Levinson and de Onis, *The Alliance That Lost Its Way*, 21.

18. Albert Fishlow, "The State of Latin American Economics," in *Economic and Social Progress in Latin America* (Washington, D.C.: Inter-American Development Bank, 1985), 131–32.

19. MNC Subcommittee Report, August 1975, 10.

20. Report of the U.S. Tariff Commission to the U.S. Senate Committee on Finance, "Implications of Multinational Firms for World Trade and Investment and for U.S. Trade and Labor," cited in MNC Subcommittee Report, August 1975, 10.

21. Isaiah Frank, *Foreign Enterprise in Developing Countries* (Baltimore: Johns Hopkins University Press, 1980), 60.

22. Inter-American Development Bank, *Economic and Social Progress in Latin America: 1979 Report* (Washington, D.C.: IADB, 1980), 85.

23. Carlos Tello, *La Nacionalizacion de la banca en Mexico* (Mexico City: Siglo Veintiuno Editores, 1984), cuadro 7 & 8, 48–49.

24. London interbank offered rate (LIBOR) is the interest rate at which banks will place short-term funds with each other in the international money market. LIBOR usually serves as the base rate for international loans to nonbank borrowers.

25. Paulo Nogueira Batista, Jr., et al., *Ensaios sobre o setor externo da economia Brasileira* (Rio de Janeiro: Estudos Especiais Ibre No. 2, Instituto Brasileiro de Economia Editora da Fundaçao Getulio Vargas, 1981).

26. Monica Baer, *La Internacionalicion financiera en Brazil* (Mexico City: Instituto Para America Latina, 1983), 88.

27. Philip A. Wellons, *Borrowing by Developing Countries on the Euro-currency Market* (Paris: OECD, 1977), 105.

28. Data from Banco do Brazil and Morgan Guaranty Trust, *World Financial Markets*.

29. George J. Clark, executive vice president, Citibank N.A., before the Subcommittee on International Finance and Monetary Policy, Senate Committee on Banking, Housing and Urban Affairs, 98th Congress, 1st Session, 15 February 1983.

30. Marques Moreira, *The Brazilian Quandary*, 15.

31. Banco do Brazil, in Nogueira Batista et al., *Ensaios*, 5.

32. Marques Moreira, *The Brazilian Quandary*, 15.

33. Data on electrical sector from Diomedes Christodoulou and Roberto Hukai, "The Formation and Use of Capital in the Brazilian Electrical Sector" (Paper presented at the Fernand Braudel Institute of World Economics, São Paulo, August 1988).

34. MNC Subcommittee Report, August 1975, 150.

35. Bela Belassa et al., *Toward Renewed Economic Growth in Latin America* (Washington, D.C.: Institute for International Economics, 1986), 137.

36. Jeff Frieden, "Third World Indebted Industrialization: International Finance and State Capitalism in Mexico, Brazil, Algeria and South Korea," *International Organization* 35 (Summer 1981): 412–13.

37. Luis Rubio, "The Changing Role of the Private Sector," in *Mexico in Transition*, Susan Kaufman Purcell, ed. (New York: Council on Foreign Relations, 1988), 36.

38. Pedro-Pablo Kuczynski, *Latin American Debt* (Baltimore: Johns Hopkins University Press, 1987), 55.

39. Rosa Olivia Villa M., "Nacional Financiera: Banco de fometo del desarrollo economico de Mexico" (Mexico City: Nafinsa, 1976), cited in Frieden, "Third World Indebted Industrialization," 415.

40. "Las relaciones economicas con el exterior en 1979," *Commerciao Exterior* 30 (5 May 1980), cited in Frieden, "Third World Indebted Industrialization," 417.

41. Data from World Bank, noted in David Cox, *Latin American Debt: Facing Facts* (Oxford: Oxford International Institute, 1989), 7.

42. Argentina, Bolivia, Brazil, Chile, Colombia, Costa Rica, Ecuador, Guatemala, Mexico, Peru, Uruguay, Venezuela. Guy P. Pfeffermann and Andrea Madarassy, "Trends in Private Investment in Thirty Developing Countries" (Discussion Paper 6, International Finance Corporation, Washington, D.C., 1989), chart 1.

43. Peter Knight et al., "Brazil Financial Systems Review," *World Bank Country Study* (July 1984): 7.

44. The World Bank and other development banks usually require borrowers to commit a specific amount of local-currency "counterpart funds" to help finance a project and as a token of the government's commitment to the undertaking. It is ironic that Mexico should have been raising these funds in the international credit markets.

45. *World Bank World Development Report 1985* (New York: Oxford University Press for the World Bank, 1985), 49, fig. 4.3.

46. Michael Dooley et al., "An Analysis of External Debt Positions of Eight Developing Countries through 1990" (International Finance Discussion Paper 227, Federal Reserve Board, Washington, D.C., August 1983), app. table 2.

47. Inter-American Development Bank, *Economic and Social*

Progress in Latin America (Washington, D.C.: ADB, 1985), 411–13.
48. For U.S. banks the legal lending limit was 10 percent of capital until the limit was raised to 15 percent in 1983.
49. *Pemex Information Bulletin*, New York–Washington Office, April 1987.
50. Speech at Columbia University, 28 September 1990.
51. Bank for International Settlements, "International Banking Statistics 1973–83 (Basle: BIS, April 1984).
52. Clearing House International Payment System (CHIPS), based in Manhattan, clears virtually all international dollar payments. Daily clearings in 1990 were more than $1 trillion dollars.
53. BIS, "International Banking Statistics 1973–83."
54. Data on commercial bank claims on individual countries is gathered by the Bank for International Settlements. The BIS has broadened its data base several times during the 1980s to cover more banks and more offshore centers. The shift from series I to series II produced a $70 billion increase in reported bank claims on non-OPEC developing countries for 1982.

CHAPTER 4

1. Walter B. Wriston, *Risk and Other Four-Letter Words* (New York: Harper & Row, 1986), 155.
2. "International Debt," Hearings before the Subcommittee on International Finance and Monetary Policy, Senate Committee on Banking, Housing, and Urban Affairs (15 February 1983), 224.
3. "Risks in International Bank Lending" (New York: International Banking Study Group of the Group of Thirty, 1982), 7.
4. Bank for International Settlements, "International Banking and Financial Market Developments" (Basle: BIS, various issues).

5. George Moore, *The Banker's Life* (New York: Norton, 1987), 147.

6. Committee on Banking Regulations and Supervisory Practices, "Management of Banks' International Lending: Country Risk Analysis and Country Exposure Measurement and Control" (Basle: BIS, March 1982).

7. Moore explains, "We favored branches rather than acquisitions. When you buy a bank abroad you often find the owner has all his relatives working for him. The bookkeeping is not easy to understand; the auditors have trouble figuring out what you bought. There are often loans to the owner and his relatives. When your new partners come to New York, you have to take them out to the best restaurants and to the opera." Moore, *The Banker's Life*, 198.

8. I. D. Bond, "The Syndicated Credit Market" (Discussion Paper No. 22, Bank of England, March 1985), 55–56. Bond gives an extremely lucid explanation of the syndication process.

9. Since 1984 U.S. banks have had to amortize over the life of the loan all fees not directly attributable to loan management expenses.

10. Bond, "The Syndicated Credit Market," 55.

11. Bond found that fees averaged about 1 percent of the loan total.

12. "The Witteveen Facility and the OPEC Financial Surpluses," Hearings before the Subcommittee on Foreign Economic Policy, Senate Foreign Relations Committee (21 September 1977), 26.

13. Ibid., 28.

14. Ibid., Church 39, Solomon 30.

15. Quoted in Harold Lever and Christopher Huhne, *Debt and Danger: The World Financial Crisis* (Boston: Atlantic Monthly Press, 1985), 49.

CHAPTER 5

1. The allocation would be according to the distribution of domestic and foreign loans (not income) in a bank's portfolio. James R. Kraus, "Tax Ruling May Curb LDC Debt Writeoffs," *American Banker*, 2 May 1989, 1; Jim McTague and James R. Kraus, "Money Center Banks Most Affected by IRS Rule: Analysts," *American Banker*, 3 May 1989, 3.

2. Saloman Bros., "Tax Reform: It's Complex But Highly Manageable," *Bank Weekly*, 3 October 1986, fig. 2.

3. Ibid., fig. 4. The twelve do not include Bank of America, which had foreign tax credits of $142 million. Net pretax income is pretax income less the sum of current state and local taxes and 50 percent of tax-exempt income.

4. Bartlett Naylor, "Bid to Curtail Foreign Loan Tax Credit May Cool Lending to Indebted Nations," *American Banker*, 15 May 1986.

5. For a discussion of the evolution of these and other foreign tax-credit issues, see Charles I. Kingson, "The Coherence of International Taxation," *Columbia Law Review* 81 (October 1981): 1262–66.

6. The following formula is used to calculate the overall limitation on foreign tax credits against U.S. taxes: foreign source income divided by worldwide income times the total U.S. tax liability in dollars equals the maximum amount of foreign tax credits that may be claimed. This means that for a bank with total worldwide income of $800,000, of which $500,000 is foreign source, the maximum amount of U.S. tax the bank may offset with foreign tax credits is $500,000/$800,000 = .625 × (46% of $800,000) = $230,000.

7. The fungibility of expenses between foreign and domestic operations has been under IRS review since passage of the Tax Reform Act of 1986.

8. This formula is used for grossing up the interest rate: LIBOR + Spread/1 − Withholding tax = Grossed-up rate.

9. Bankers call these *net loans*.

10. "Citicorp's Reed Outlines Path on Third World Loans," *Wall Street Journal*, 28 May 1987.

11. Kingson, "Coherence of International Taxation," 1263–64.

12. William Clairborne, "Foreign Tax Credits of Banks," *Washington Post*, 30 November 1977.

13. These so-called income taxes (and much smaller royalties) paid by the foreign companies that actually produced and marketed the oil were the principal source of Saudi Arabia's soaring wealth until Aramco was nationalized in 1982.

14. As described in *Multinational Petroleum Companies and Foreign Policy* (Hearings before the Subcommittee on Multinational Corporations of the Senate Committee on Foreign Relations, 93rd Congress, 2nd Session, 30 January 1974), 3, the Treasury Department, in the summer of 1950, at the urging of the Department of State, agreed to a system in which the companies would increase their payments to the oil-producing governments, and the American government would permit them to reduce their U.S. tax payments correspondingly. The mechanism for accomplishing this objective was the establishment in the Persian Gulf of a posted price system. . . . This figure bears no necessary relationship to the actual market price of crude oil, but it is used as the base for calculation of so-called income taxes charged by the oil-producing governments to the oil companies. . . . Wall Street lawyers were sent to the Middle East to help these countries rewrite their laws to bring them within the purview of the tax-credit provisions of the U.S. Internal Revenue Code. The resulting "taxes" were credited directly against U.S. income tax due, rather than being treated as an ordinary business expense.

In 1980 the IRS issued new regulations that foreign taxes would not be creditable "if liability for the charge is clearly related to the availability of a credit for the charge against income tax liability to another country." If retained, this rule would have jeopardized not only the oil tax credits but the banks' withholding tax credits as well. But as Kingson explained, "Apparently, having American lawyers concoct a source tax with only residence impact would no longer work. . . . But theories must confront power, and the regulations end with witty self-mockery. Having constructed an elaborate and consistent idea of an income tax, they largely nullify it by allowing credit for charges with no source country significance as taxes in *lieu* of income taxes." Kingson, "Coherence of International Taxations," 1266. Banks and oil companies retained their valuable tax credits.

15. John J. Duffy, "Staggering Tax Bill Could Hit U.S. Banks in United Kingdom," *American Banker*, 22 December 1986; John J. Duffy, "British Tax Proposal Could Hit U.S. Banks," *American Banker*, 27 March 1987.

16. John P. Forde, "Onetime Gains Boost Earnings at Banks," *American Banker*, 28 October 1987, 2.

CHAPTER 6

1. Argentina, Brazil, Chile, Korea, Mexico, Peru, Philippines, Venezuela. From Michael P. Dooley, et al., "An Analysis of External Debt Positions of Eight Developing Countries through 1990" (International Finance Discussion Papers No. 227, August 1983), 3–4.

2. Manuel Pastor, Jr., "Capital Flight and the Latin American Debt Crisis" (Washington, D.C.: Economic Policy Institute, 1989). Pastor calculates: Capital flight = (Change in debt + Foreign direct investment) − (Current account deficit + Change in reserves).

3. James V. Houpt, "Performance and Characteristics of Edge Corporations" (Staff paper for the Board of Governors of the Federal Reserve System, Washington, D.C., January 1981), table 6.

Some banks also run regional Latin American offices out of Miami. Bank of America has its entire Latin America division except the Mexico desk in Miami. Mexico, in keeping with its importance to Bank of America and its proximity to California, is managed by the domestic division in San Francisco. Chase operates its regional office for the Andean countries and Colombia out of Miami; Bankers Trust has its regional headquarters for Venezuela, Ecuador, Colombia, and the Caribbean there.

4. John D. Wilson, *The Chase: The Chase Manhattan Bank, N.A., 1945–1985* (Boston: Harvard Business School Press, 1986), 225.

5. James S. Henry, "Where the Money Went," *New Republic*, 14 April 1986.

6. *New York Times*, 25 July 1985.

7. Gary Hector, "Nervous Money Keeps on Fleeing," *Fortune*, 23 December 1985.

8. See Richard Goode, *Government Finance in Developing Countries* (Washington, DC: Brookings Institution, 1984), 91. Numbers are for 1980.

9. Bank for International Settlements, "International Banking and Financial Market Developments" (Basle: BIS, November 1990), table 5b.

10. Benedicte Vibe Christensen, "Switzerland's Role as an International Financial Center" (Washington, D.C.: International Monetary Fund, Occasional Paper 45, July 1986). See tables 8 and 11.

11. *New York Times*, 4 February 1987.

12. George Moore, *A Banker's Life*, (New York: Norton, 1987).

13. Gunnar Myrdal used the term kleptocracy in his brilliant essay on official corruption and "the soft state," crediting a speech by Singapore minister of foreign affairs S. Rajaratnam. One excerpt from the minister's speech is the perfect epitaph for the Marcos regime: "A kleptocracy will steer itself, whether those in power want it or not, into more and more corruption and finally into economic and political chaos. This has been the life cycle of societies in Asia during the past two decades." See Gunnar Myrdal, *The Challenge of World Poverty* (New York: Pantheon Books, 1970), 228.

14. Mohsin S. Khan and Nadeem Ul Haque, "Foreign Borrowing and Capital Flight: A Formal Analysis," *IMF Staff Papers* (December 1985): table 1.

15. "The Use of Cash and Transaction Accounts by American Families," *Federal Reserve Bulletin* (February 1986): 104.

16. From a paper by José Maria Dagnino Pastore, professor at the Argentine Catholic University, "Progress and Prospects of the Argentine Adjustment Program" (Buenos Aires, 1983). Nicolas Ardito Barletta, Mario Blejer, and Luis Landau, eds., "Economic Liberalization and Stabilization Policies in Argentina, Chile, and Uruguay" (Washington, D.C.: World Bank, 1983), 41.

17. José Maria Dagnino Pastore, "Assessment of an Anti-inflationary Experiment: Argentina in 1979–81," in Barletta, Blejer, Landau, eds. "Economic Liberalization and Stabilization Policies," 33.

18. Pastor, "Capital Flight and the Latin American Debt Crisis."

19. Statement of James A. Baker III, Secretary of the Treasury of the United States, before the Joint Annual Meeting of the International Monetary Fund and the World Bank in Seoul, Korea, 8 October 1985.

20. Rudiger Dornbusch, "International Debt and Economic Stability," *Economic Review*, Federal Reserve Bank of Kansas City (January 1987).

21. Henry, "Where the Money Went."

22. Ibid.

23. Under the Financial Institutions Regulatory and Interest Rate Control Act of 1978 (Sections 1102 and 1103) U.S. banks may not give even U.S. government authorities access to customer records without the customer's authorization or a written subpoena. But the bank may notify authorities that it has information relevant to possible illegalities.

24. See John E. Hoffman, Jr., "The Bankers' Channel," in *American Hostages in Iran* (New Haven: Yale University Press, 1985), 235. Also Karin Lissakers, "Money and Manipulation," *Foreign Policy* (Fall 1981): 107.

25. Hoffman, *American Hostages*, 239.

26. See "International Drug Money Laundering: Issues and Options for Congress" (Report prepared for the Committee on Foreign Affairs, U.S. House of Representatives, by the Congressional Research Service, October 1990).

CHAPTER 7

1. A. Sack, *La Succession aux dettes publiques d'état* (1929), cited in M. H. Hoeflich, "Through a Glass Darkly: Reflections upon the History of the International Law of Public Debt in Connection with State Succession," *University of Illinois Law Review* 1 (1982): 39.
2. This form of revenue raising precedes well-defined national borders. "La Hacienda," Mexico's sprawling finance ministry, was built for Cortez to house the customs collectors of the tolls the Spaniards charged on all goods brought into the walled Mexico City.
3. E. Feichenfeld, *Public Debts and State Succession* (1931), quoted in Hoeflich, "Through a Glass Darkly," 55.
4. British Lord Chancellor in De Haber v. Queen of Portugal, [1851] 17 Q.B. 171, 207, quoted in Anatole Kaletsky, *The Costs of Default* (New York: Twentieth Century Fund, 1983), 22.
5. Max Winkler, *Foreign Bonds: An Autopsy* (Philadelphia: Roland Swain Co., 1933), 29.
6. Confidential memorandum sent by Blumenthal to the IMF in 1981.
7. Benjamin J. Cohen, *In Whose Interest? International Banking and American Foreign Policy* (New Haven: Yale University Press, 1986), 104.
8. Cleona Lewis, *America's Experience as a Creditor Nation* (Washington, D.C.: Brookings Institution, 1938), 341.
9. Jeffrey Frieden, "The Internationalization of United States Banking and the Transformation of U.S. Foreign Policy, 1890–1940" (Draft paper written at Columbia University, December 1980, cited with permission of the author), 17–18.
10. *New York Herald Tribune*, 26 September 1940, quoted in Willy Feurleing and Elizabeth Hannan, *Dollars in Latin America* (New York: Council on Foreign Relations, 1941), 28.
11. Carl P. Parrini, *Heir to Empire: United States Economic Diplomacy, 1916–1923* (Pittsburgh, 1969) 185–86; Herbert Hoover,

Memoirs, 3 vols. (New York, 1952,) vol. 2, 13–14; and Josepp Brandes, *Herbert Hoover and Economic Diplomacy: Department of Commerce Policy 1921–1928* (Pittsburgh, 1962) 153, quoted in Joan Hoff Wilson, *American Business and Foreign Policy, 1920–1933* (Lexington: University Press of Kentucky, 1971), 107–8.

12. Strong memorandum to Secretary of State Hughes, 14 April 1922, quoted in Wilson, *American Business and Foreign Policy*, 111.

13. Even so, the very limited role played by the government became the target of attack after the collapse of the sovereign bond market. Democrats blamed the Republican administration for appearing to condone the lending binge, and Franklin Delano Roosevelt promised in his 1932 campaign for the presidency that if he were elected "it will no longer be possible for international bankers or others to sell foreign securities to the investing public of America on the implied understanding that these securities have been passed on or approved by the State Department or any other agency of the Federal Government." Speech at Columbus, Ohio, 20 August 1932, quoted in Herbert Feis, *The Diplomacy of the Dollar* (Baltimore: Johns Hopkins Press, 1950), 14.

14. Cleona Lewis, *America's Stake in International Investment* (Washington, D.C.: Brookings Institution, 1938), 377.

15. Ibid., 380.

16. Cleveland, *Citibank 1812–1970*, 139–45.

17. Ibid., quoting National City Bank president Charles Mitchell, 136.

18. For an extensive description of the hearings, see Vincent P. Carosso, *Investment Banking in America* (Cambridge, Mass.: Harvard University Press, 1970), chapter 16.

19. Ibid., 330.

20. Hjalmar Schacht, *My First Seventy-six Years* (London: Allan Wingate, 1955), quoted in David Gisselquist, *The Political Economics of International Bank Lending* (New York: Praeger, 1981), 1.

21. Paul Einzig, *Foreign Dollar Loans in Europe* (London: Macmillan, 1965), 33.

22. Benjamin Cohen, *In Whose Interest* (New Haven: Yale University Press, 1986), 196–97.

23. See affidavit by Anthony Solomon, president of the Federal Reserve Bank of New York, 14 February 1984, in Banque Companfina v. Banco de Guatemala, 84 Cir. 1061 (S.D.N.Y. 1984), cited in Kaletsky, *The Costs of Default*, n. 23.

24. Kaletsky, *The Costs of Default*.

25. Ibid., 28.

26. See Mark Hulbert, *Interlock* (New York: Richardson and Snyder, 1982), 109–11.

27. For a fuller discussion of the Iran asset freeze, see Karin Lissakers, "Money and Manipulation," *Foreign Policy* (Fall 1981). Also see Council on Foreign Relations, *American Hostages in Iran* (New Haven: Yale University Press, 1985), and House Committee on Banking, Finance and Urban Affairs, *Iran: The Financial Aspects of the Hostage Agreement*, July 1981.

28. John Marcom, Jr., "U.K. Court Says U.S. Bank Owes Money to Libya," *Wall Street Journal*, 3 September 1987.

29. See Walter Wriston, "Banking against Disaster," *New York Times*, 14 September 1982.

30. Winkler, *Foreign Bonds*, 19.

31. Although as already noted in chapter 4 many, if not most, of the loans to banks were on-lent by the local banks to the government.

32. John Evans, "British Court Warns Lenders Not to Rely on Letters of Comfort," *American Banker*, 6 June 1989, 7. The case was brought by Kleinwort Benson Ltd. against the Malaysian Mining Company and grew out of the collapse of the tin market in 1985.

CHAPTER 8

1. U.S. banking regulations permit banks to report scheduled interest payments as received, even if the payments are late. But once a loan is more than ninety days overdue, it must be reported as *nonperforming*, and interest can be credited only as actually received. Nonperformance requires no other action by the bank if the arrearages are reasonably expected to be temporary. But mounting nonperforming loans may adversely affect a bank's standing with customers and investors and may eventually lead to supervisory intervention.

2. Walter B. Wriston, *Risk and Other Four-Letter Words* (New York: Harper & Row, 1986), 176.

3. See William R. Cline, *International Debt and the Stability of the World Economic System* (Washington, D.C.: Institute for International Economics, 1983).

4. William R. Cline, "A Quick Fix That Would Be Harmful," *New York Times*, 9 August 1987.

5. George J. Clark, executive vice president, Citibank N.A., Statement before the Senate Committee on Banking, Housing and Urban Affairs, 15 February 1983, 98th Congress, 1st Session, 198.

6. Joseph Kraft, *The Mexican Rescue* (New York: Group of Thirty, 1984).

7. As the size of rescue packages expanded to cover more than one year, a growing number of banks refused to participate, and the banks that stayed in were asked to put up a bigger share of new money. The 1986 multiyear rescheduling for Mexico asked banks to lend an amount equal to 12.9 percent of their original exposure.

8. Mario Enrique Simonsen, who was finance minister of Brazil during the years of heaviest foreign borrowing, joined the board of Citibank after he lost his government post.

9. Alan Riding, "Brazil Seeks to Mend Rift with Lenders," *New York Times*, 15 February 1988.

10. Kraft, *The Mexican Rescue*, 16.

11. James Sterngold, "Volcker Gets Princeton Chair and Post at

Investment Bank," *New York Times*, 3 March 1988, quoted in Walker Todd, "A Brief History of International Lending from a Regional Banker's Perspective," *George Mason University Law Review* 11:4 (Summer 1989): 2.

12. *American Banker*, 15 April 1987.

13. And this understates the hidden reserve because it includes only firms like Mercedes-Benz in which the bank has a controlling interest. Including minority holdings would add considerably to the hidden reserve. The information was provided by DB spokesperson Werner Blessing in a briefing to New York stock analysts in June 1987.

14. For a detailed comparison of the many complex tax, accounting, and regulatory differences affecting the international debt problem, see Jonathan Hay and Michel H. Bouchet, "The Tax, Accounting, and Regulatory Treatment of Sovereign Debt," *World Bank*, September 1989.

15. David Lascelles, "What It Costs to Forgive and Forget," *Financial Times*, 22 January 1988.

16. Data from the United Nations Economic Commission for Latin America and the Caribbean, *Latin Finance*, October 1988.

CHAPTER 9

1. Richard Portes and Barry Eichengreen, *Debt and Default in the 1930's: Causes and Consequences* (London: Center for Economic Policy Research, 1985), 15–16.

2. Cleona Lewis, *America's Stake in International Investment* (Washington, D.C.: Brookings Institution, 1938), 483.

3. Ibid., p. 389.

4. U.S. Treasury Department, "Statistics of Capital Movements between the United States and Foreign Countries," Report No. 5 (1938), cited in Lewis, *America's Stake in International Investment*, 494.

5. Foreign Bondholders Protective Council, *Annual Report for*

1934 (New York, 1934), cited in Jeffrey A. Frieden, *Banking on the World* (New York: Harper & Row, 1989).

6. Harold van B. Cleveland and Thomas F. Huertas, *Citibank 1812–1970* (Cambridge, Mass: Harvard University Press, 1985), 168.

7. David Gisselquist, *The Political Economics of International Bank Lending* (New York: Praeger, 1981), 33.

8. Willy Feuerlein and Elisabeth Hannan, *Dollars in Latin America* (New York: Council on Foreign Relations, 1941), 27.

9. National Archives. See, for example, numerous State Department responses to irate bondholders about Brazil in Diplomatic Folder, various years, decimal file 832.51.

10. Letter of 12 September 1941 from Thomas W. Lamont, chairman of the committee, to Under Secretary Sumner Wells. National Archives, Diplomatic Folder 1941, decimal file 812.51/2528.

11. National Archives, Diplomatic Folder 1941, decimal file 812.51/2489.

12. Joan Hoff Wilson, *American Business and Foreign Policy 1920–1933* (Lexington: University Press of Kentucky, 1971), 182.

13. Ibid., 181.

14. See Angus Maddison, *Two Crises: Latin America and Asia 1929–38 and 1973–83* (Paris: OECD, 1985).

15. National Archives, Diplomatic Folder 1940, decimal file 832.51/1867.

16. Staff memo to Under Secretary of State Sumner Welles, 28 March 1940, decimal file 832.51/1831. Public notice of the settlement terms gave bondholders a certain period in which to register their acceptance with an agent of the debtor government. An investor who failed to register ran the risk of being left out of the payments altogether.

17. Maddison, *Two Crises*, 27; Cleona Lewis, *Debtor and Creditor Countries: 1938, 1944* (Washington, D.C.: Brookings Institution, 1945), 33. Details on Brazilian bonds provided by Professor Rudiger Dornbusch of MIT.

18. Dispatch no. 2518 of 23 August 1945 from the American Embassy in Rio de Janeiro, to the Department of State, Na-

tional Archives, Diplomatic Folder 1945, decimal file 832.51/ 1945–49.

19. Remarks by Secretary of the Treasury Nicholas F. Brady to the Brookings Institution and the Bretton Woods Committee Conference on Third World Debt, Washington, D.C., 10 March 1989.

20. Robin Broad, "How About a Real Solution to Third World Debt?" *New York Times*, 28 September 1987.

21. Not everyone thought Baker's repackaging revolutionary. According to a participant, when German bankers met a few days later to decide how they should respond, most of the meeting was taken up with a discussion of whether to refer to Baker's proposal as a plan or an initiative. They settled on the latter as less definitive and therefore less binding on their institutions.

22. Helmut Reisen, "Public Debt, North and South," in Ishrat Husain and Ishac Diwan, eds., *Dealing with the Debt Crisis* (Washington, D.C.: World Bank, 1989), 120, table 6-6.

23. World Bank, *Quarterly Review* (Washington, D.C., June 1989), 3.

24. Economic Policy Council of UNA-USA, *Third World Debt: A Reexamination of Long-term Management*, Report of the Third World Debt Panel, New York, 7 September 1988, 39.

25. *Financial Times*, 8 September 1988.

26. "Indicative Prices for Less Developed Country Bank Loans, (New York: Salomon Bros., 4 January 1989).

27. Alfred Herrhausen, "Zeit Ist Geld," *Die Zeit*, 16 September 1988.

28. See Peter T. Kilborn, "How the Mexican Debt Pact was Achieved," *New York Times*, 31 July 1989.

29. Exchange-rate adjusted. See Bank for International Settlements, *International Banking and Financial Market Developments* (Basle: BIS, November 1990), 8.

30. *BIS Annual Report*, Basle, June 1990, 157.

31. Bank for International Settlements, *International Banking and Financial Market Development* (Basle: BIS, February 1991), table 5A.

CHAPTER 10

1. Cleona Lewis, *America's Stake in International Investment* (Washington, D.C.: Brookings Institution, 1938), 483.
2. A talk by Henry Kaufman, managing director of Salomon Bros., in Tokyo, Japan, 19 October 1982.
3. Deborah Hargreaves, "Japanese Banks Lose Top IBCA Rating," *Financial Times*, 5 November 1991.
4. Stephen Labaton, "U.S. Is Taking Over a Group of Banks to Head Off a Run," *New York Times*, 7 January, 1991.
5. Gerald Corrigan, Testimony before the U.S. Senate Committee on Banking, Housing and Urban Affairs, 3 May 1990, appendix VI, chart 15. The money center banks in this chart are Bank of America, Bank of New York/Irving Bank, Bankers Trust, Chase Manhattan, Chemical Bank, Citibank, Manufacturers Hanover, JP Morgan, and Security Pacific.
6. Glass-Steagall restrictions regarding the separation of commercial and investment banking do not fully apply to U.S. banks' overseas activities.
7. Average annual growth of non-interest expense at the money-center bank holding companies averaged more than than 16 percent from 1980 to 1987, then improved sharply from 1988 to 1989. Corrigan testimony, chart 21.
8. Alan Friedman, "Security Pacific Sounds Retreat," *Financial Times*, 12 December 1990.
9. See, for example, the discussion on official aid and poverty in the World Development Report 1990 (Washington, D.C.: The World Bank, 1990).
10. Noel Tichy and Ram Charan, "Citicorp Faces the World: An Interview with John Reed," *Harvard Business Review* (November-December 1990): 140–41.
11. Ibid., 140.
12. See, for example, Bijan B. Aghevli and Jorge Marques-Ruarte, "A Case of Successful Adjustment: Korea's Experience during 1980–84" (Washington, D.C.: International Monetary Fund, Occasional Paper 39, August 1984), 2–3.

Index